ROMAN ARABIA

The Wādī Ramm, looking south
(Photograph by the author)

ROMAN ARABIA

G. W. BOWERSOCK

HARVARD UNIVERSITY PRESS
CAMBRIDGE, MASSACHUSETTS
LONDON, ENGLAND

Printed in the United States of America
Fourth printing, 1996

First Harvard University Press paperback edition, 1994

Library of Congress Cataloguing in Publication Data
Bowersock, G. W. (Glen Warren), 1936–
Roman Arabia.

Bibliography: p.
Includes index.
1. Nabataeans—History. 2. Arabia, Roman—History.
3. Rome—History—Empire, 30 B.C.–476 A.D. I. Title.
DS154.22.B68 1983 939 82-23274
ISBN 0-674-77755-7 (cloth)
ISBN 0-674-77756-5 (pbk.)

MANIBUS
MATRIS

CONTENTS

ILLUSTRATIONS

PREFACE

THE GESTATION of this volume has been preternaturally long. When I began work on Roman Arabia some fourteen years ago, there seemed to be relatively little interest in the subject. I was aware that the material, both archaeological and textual, was as rich as it was challenging; and I knew that it would take time to master the necessary languages and acquire a sufficient familiarity with the land about which I was writing. To my surprise and undisguised pleasure, a preliminary report on the status of studies on the Arabian province, which I published in the *Journal of Roman Studies* in 1971, evoked considerable response and set several young scholars on the path of research and excavation in the Hashemite Kingdom of Jordan. The group of ancient historians interested in the Roman administration of the Arabian province has grown steadily. I have made many friends and learned much from the new wave of scholarship in this area. This book has gained from the recent work, and it is my hope that it will provide assistance to those who will be pursuing Arabian projects within the context of Roman history in the years ahead.

I have occupied myself principally with the Roman presence in the Nabataean kingdom and the Roman province which was subsequently created out of that kingdom. I have concluded these investigations with the reign of Constantine and the fragmentation of the original Arabian province. The story of Rome and the Arabs, of course, continues through the Byzantine age. But it was not so much the bulk of post-Constantinian evidence that deterred me from extending my work into late antiquity. It was rather my awareness of the important volumes on this subject that Irfan Shahîd of Dumbarton Oaks and Georgetown University has already written. His first volume, on Byzantium and the Arabs in the fourth century, should be available very soon; and I want to express my gratitude to Professor Shahîd for his generosity in showing me substantial portions of his work well in advance of publication. I have profited from conversation with him no less than from his writings.

I have also to thank, with equal warmth, the several scholars of the new generation of Arabian specialists who have been kind enough to keep in touch with me and to show me their work in progress. S. Thomas Parker, whose dissertation on the Arabian *limes* should soon be in print, is now leading an important excavation of the legionary camp at Lejjūn in Jordan. He has thoughtfully kept me apprised of his work at each stage. D. L. Kennedy, whose splendid volume of archaeological reports on the northeast frontier in Jordan has just appeared, has also been generous in sharing his research with me and keeping me posted on his activities (which now include the preparation of a valuable photographic archive). Maurice Sartre, whose thesis on Bostra and studies of Roman Arabia are of commanding quality, has supplied me faithfully with his work and afforded me the welcome hospitality of his home. David Graf, of the University of Michigan, has done remarkably perceptive studies of Roman Arabia and hopes soon to be engaged in an excavation project at Ḥumaima. He has unfailingly shared the important results of his surveys in Jordan with me, as well as his reflections on published evidence for the Arabian province. Henry MacAdam, now at the American University of Beirut, was kind enough to supply me with a copy of his valuable dissertation on the Roman province of Arabia almost as soon as it was completed in 1979. I look forward to the completion of his book on village and tribal organization in Roman Arabia: this is an area that still needs intensive study. A. C. Killick of the British School at ʿAmmān has recently undertaken the excavation of the legionary camp at Udhruḥ, and I am most grateful to him for sending me a text of his first preliminary report on the excavation.

I owe thanks as well to other colleagues and friends who have assisted me in various ways. D. R. Harris was a superb host and guide during my first visit to Jordan many years ago. I still see the major sites in that glorious country with the enthusiasm that he and I shared together. Michael Speidel at Honolulu has supplied me with offprints of his work, on both Arabia and other topics, and I have never failed to profit from them. John Eadie at the University of Michigan has done much in recent years to encourage frontier studies in the Near East, and I want to express my gratitude to him not only for his friendly interest in my work but for the encouragement he has given to students to work in this area. One of them, Steven Sidebotham, has lately sent me his dissertation on the Red Sea; he, too, deserves my thanks.

The close contacts and friendly exchange of research and ideas in the community of scholars interested in Roman Arabia have been an inspiration and, I am confident, will lead to work that is ever more profound and fruitful. The progress of my own work has been dramatically enhanced by my move to the Institute for Advanced Study in Princeton, where I have not only had the most extraordinary facilities for research but also the benefit of contact with a wide range of knowledgeable and stimulating scholars. In preparing the manuscript for publication, I have had the services of a truly remarkable secretary, N. A. S. Levine, whose knowledge of classical languages and ancient history can only be matched by her prodigious skills at the typewriter and the computer terminal. David Packard, Marian McAllister, Sarah George, and Nancy Moore have made it possible for this book to be typeset through the Ibycus system at the Institute.

David Graf, Christopher Jones, and Henry MacAdam were all kind enough to read through the complete manuscript and to provide valuable comments, corrections, and supplements. I am deeply indebted to them. For the courteous provision of photographs for publication I have to thank Paolo Costa, Alison Frantz, Mahmud Ghul, David Graf, David Kennedy, William Metcalf, Robert Reinhold, George Rinhart, and James Sauer. V. R. Boscarino drew the maps and plans.

In the spelling of Arabic words, I have endeavored to give, within reason, a transliteration which would allow the reader who knows Arabic to return the words to their original script. But I confess that I have not pursued this objective pedantically in the case of the most familiar names. I can only endorse the notorious remarks of T. E. Lawrence to a copyeditor who sought consistency in the names that appear in *Seven Pillars of Wisdom*. Finally, I hope I may use from time to time the much abused term "orientalist" without prejudice in referring to scholars of pre-Islamic Arab antiquities. I trust that the political considerations which make the word so charged now in Islamic circles have no relevance to pre-Islamic studies.

This volume could not have been completed without the good will and cooperation of friends in many Near Eastern countries. I should like to take this opportunity to thank Adnan Bounni in Damascus and Adnan Hadidi in ʿAmmān for the very special encouragement they have provided. I hope that they will find some satisfaction in this attempt to recover an important segment of the pre-Islamic Arab past. I hope as well that my colleagues and friends in Roman history will understand why I thought this long neglected area of the Roman Empire deserved so much of my time.

G. W. B.

The Institute for Advanced Study
Princeton, November 1982

ABBREVIATIONS

AAES	*American Archaeological Expedition to Syria, Part III*
AASOR	*Annual of the American Schools of Oriental Research*
ADAJ	*Annual of the Department of Antiquities of Jordan*
AE	*L'année épigraphique*
AJA	*American Journal of Archaeology*
AJP	*American Journal of Philology*
ANRW	*Aufstieg und Niedergang der römischen Welt*
AntCl	*L'antiquité classique*
ArchExplor	D. L. Kennedy, *Archaeological Explorations on the Roman Frontier in North-East Jordan*, BAR International Series 134 (1982)
ASOR News	*American Schools of Oriental Research Newsletter*
AthMitt	*Mitteilungen des deutschen archäologischen Instituts, Athenische Abteilung*
BAR	*British Archaeological Reports*
BASOR	*Bulletin of the American Schools of Oriental Research*
BiblArch	*The Biblical Archaeologist*
BCH	*Bulletin de correspondance hellénique*
BGU	*Berliner griechische Urkunden*
BMC	*Catalogue of Coins in the British Museum*
BSOAS	*Bulletin of the School of Oriental and African Studies*
Bull. épig.	*Bulletin épigraphique*
BZ	*Byzantinische Zeitschrift*
CIG	*Corpus Inscriptionum Graecarum*
CIL	*Corpus Inscriptionum Latinarum*
CIS	*Corpus Inscriptionum Semiticarum*
CNRS	*Centre national de la recherche scientifique*
CP	*Classical Philology*
CQ	*Classical Quarterly*
CR	*Classical Review*
CRAI	*Comptes-rendus de l'Académie des Inscriptions et Belles-lettres*
FGH	F. Jacoby, *Die Fragmente der griechischen Historiker*
FHG	C. Müller, *Fragmenta Historicorum Graecorum*
GGA	*Göttingische Gelehrte Anzeigen*
GRBS	*Greek, Roman, and Byzantine Studies*
HA	*Historia Augusta*
HSCP	*Harvard Studies in Classical Philology*
IEJ	*Israel Exploration Journal*

IG	*Inscriptiones Graecae*
IGLS	*Inscriptions grecques et latines de la Syrie*
IGR	*Inscriptiones Graecae ad Res Romanas Pertinentes*
ILS	*Inscriptiones Latinae Selectae*
JAOS	*Journal of the American Oriental Society*
JBL	*Journal of Biblical Literature*
JHS	*Journal of Hellenic Studies*
JÖAI	*Jahreshefte des österreichischen archäologischen Instituts*
JRS	*Journal of Roman Studies*
JSS	*Journal of Semitic Studies*
JTS	*Journal of Theological Studies*
NC	*Numismatic Chronicle*
MAMA	*Monumenta Asiae Minoris Antiqua*
OGIS	*Orientis Graeci Inscriptiones Selectae*
PAES	*Publications of the Princeton University Archaeological Expeditions to Syria*
ParPass	*La parola del passato*
PEQ	*Palestine Exploration Quarterly*
PG	*Patrologia Graeca*
PIR	*Prosopographia Imperii Romani*
ProcPhilSoc	*Proceedings of the American Philosophical Society*
PSI	*Papiri della Società Italiana*
QDAP	*Quarterly of the Department of Antiquities of Palestine*
RA	*Revue archéologique*
RB	*Revue biblique*
RE	Pauly-Wissowa-Kroll, *Real-Encyclopädie*
REA	*Revue des études anciennes*
REG	*Revue des études grecques*
REL	*Revue des études latines*
RES	*Répertoire d'épigraphie sémitique*
RhM	*Rheinisches Museum*
RIDA	*Revue internationale des droits de l'antiquité*
SDB	*Supplément au Dictionnaire de la Bible*, 7 (1966) unless otherwise noted
SEG	*Supplementum Epigraphicum Graecum*
SIG	*Sylloge Inscriptionum Graecarum*
SNG	*Sylloge Nummorum Graecorum*
TAPA	*Transactions of the American Philological Association*
ZDMG	*Zeitschrift der deutschen morgenländischen Gesellschaft*
ZDPV	*Zeitschrift des Deutschen Palästina-Vereins*
ZPE	*Zeitschrift für Papyrologie und Epigraphik*

ROMAN ARABIA

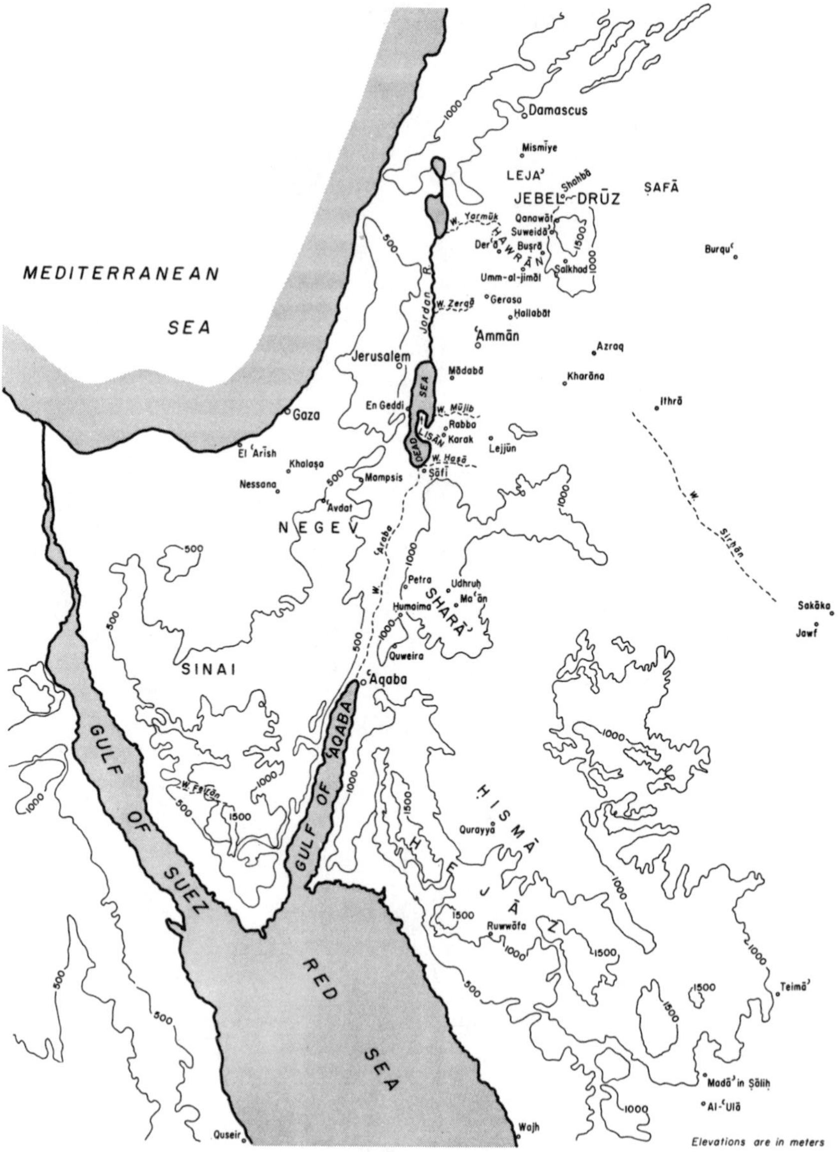

MEDITERRANEAN SEA
Damascus
Mismīye
LEJA'
Shahbā
JEBEL DRŪZ
ṢAFĀ
W. Yarmūk
Qanawāt
Suweidā
HAWRĀN
Der'ā
Buṣrā
Burqu'
Ṣalkhad
Umm-al-jimāl
Jordan R.
W. Zergā
Gerasa
Hallabāt
'Ammān
Azraq
Jerusalem
Mādabā
Kharāna
Ithrā
En Geddi
DEAD SEA
W. Mūjib
LISĀN
Rabba
Karak
Lejjūn
W. Hasā
Ṣāfī
Gaza
El 'Arīsh
Khalaṣa
Nessana
Mampsis
Avdat
NEGEV
W. Sirhān
W. 'Araba
Petra
Udhruh
Ma'ān
SHARĀ'
Humaima
Quweira
Sakāka
Jawf
SINAI
'Aqaba
GULF OF AQABA
GULF OF SUEZ
W. Feirān
HISMĀ
HEJĀZ
Qurayyā
Ruwwāfa
RED SEA
Teimā'
Madā'in Ṣāliḥ
Al-'Ulā
Wajh
Quseir
Elevations are in meters

I

THE REGION

ARABIA is a vague word. It obviously means the territory of Arabs; but since the Arab population, including nomads, has been traditionally spread across much of the Near East, the name for their homeland has been commensurately ambiguous. The ancients encountered Arabs from the northern reaches of Mesopotamia to the southern shores of the great peninsula that lies between the Red Sea and the Persian Gulf. Some were nomadic and lived in tents; others were sedentary and enjoyed a prosperity derived from successful commerce. The territory of the Arabs included the wastes of the Syrian desert and the agricultural zones of Transjordan. It included the mountains of the Ḥejāz and the inland corridors of the peninsula. Although the heartland of the Arab nations was what is known today as Saudi Arabia, the Romans gave the name Arabia to a province of their empire which lay south and east of Palestine, in the corner of the Mediterranean world between Syria and Egypt. It comprehended the present Negev, southern Syria, all of Jordan, and northwest Saudi Arabia.

When the emperor Trajan established the province by annexation in the early second century A.D., a little less than half of the imperial frontiers looked out upon the desert. Rome was a Mediterranean power, and the Mediterranean world was bordered at its southern and eastern extremities by desert—that huge, continuous geological phenomenon that embraces the Sahara, the Sinai, Negev, Saudi Arabia, and the great desert of Syria. With the acquisition of Egypt on the east coast of North Africa under Augustus and of Mauretania on the west under Claudius, the entire coast from the Pillars of Hercules to the edge of the Sinai had become a part of the Roman Empire. On the eastern shores of the Mediterranean, Pompey had already annexed Greater Syria (including all of modern Lebanon, as well as Antioch and its environs). Accordingly, when Augustus added to his realm the former kingdom of Judaea as a province under equestrian procurators, there remained in the circuit of imperial provinces along the desert's edge only the space extending across the Sinai from Egypt into and encompassing the Negev, together with the entire territory of Transjordan, from the Syrian Ḥawrān to the Gulf of ʿAqaba. It was this substantial tract that Trajan annexed in A.D. 106 under the name of the province of Arabia. This was Roman Arabia as distinct from the land of incense and perfume in the south of the peninsula,which was known as the kingdom of Saba, or, to the Romans, Arabia Felix.[1]

The importance of Roman Arabia for an imperial power in the Mediterranean cannot be overestimated. This often inhospitable region controls access to the Mediterranean, at ports such as Gaza and Rhinocolura (el ʿArīsh), from the interior of the peninsula as well as from the Gulf of ʿAqaba. It provides the southern flank for coastal Syria and Judaea. It dominates the route from Damascus to ʿAqaba. Furthermore, it is essential for communications across the Jordan Valley between the urban centers in Judaea and those of Transjordan, which, in turn, furnish links with the nomadic culture beyond. The strategic importance of the area was as great as life in it was difficult. With the exception of certain urban centers in northern Transjordan that had easy access to the Jordan Valley and to the cities west of it, most of Roman Arabia presented a thoroughly unfamiliar aspect to the Romans.

A province of such peculiar shape, situated athwart a multiplicity of Near Eastern countries that have not been traditionally stable, has made the exploration of ancient remains a task that is at once challenging and dangerous. Many intrepid explorers of the nineteenth and twentieth centuries laid the foundations for a solid history of Roman involvement in this region, including the administration of it as a province; but in general Roman historians have tended to give scant attention to this important area.

[1] On the kingdom of Arabia Felix, see J. Pirenne, *Le royaume sud-arabe de Qatabān et sa datation* (1961), and H. von Wissmann, "Die Geschichte des Sabäerreichs und der Feldzug des Aelius Gallus," *ANRW* II.7.1 (1976), 308–554.

When Wood published his account of the visit to Palmyra which he and Dawkins made in 1751, he justified their investigation by alluding to the neglect of the great Syrian sites in historical writing of the time: "It seems very remarkable, that Baalbek and Palmyra, perhaps the two most surprising remains of ancient magnificence which are now left, should be so much neglected in history."[2] The work of Dawkins and Wood in Syria soon encouraged fruitful research on Palmyrene culture and led eventually to the decipherment of the Palmyrene language. But even in the eighteenth century no one realized that there were still more perplexing remains of ancient magnificence to the south. No European had, at that time, ever set foot in Petra.

This is the celebrated city, "half as old as time,"[3] indisputably the most impressive ancient site in the whole of Roman Arabia and certainly among the greatest spectacles of the ancient Near East. When the Swiss explorer Johann Ludwig Burckhardt penetrated the fastnesses of Petra in 1812, he opened up a new era not only in western exploration of the Levant but also in western understanding of the history of the region.[4] It soon became apparent that much had survived from Roman and pre-Roman antiquity in the area of the province. Detailed reports from the more scholarly travelers provided a firm basis for historical reconstruction. The French explorer Léon de Laborde made a thorough study of Petra as early as 1828.[5] By the middle of the century J. C. Wetzstein complemented the studies of Laborde in the south with equally thorough examinations of the more northerly regions of Roman Arabia.[6] The epigraphist W. H. Waddington undertook a collection of the inscriptions of Syria, including the

[2] R. Wood, *The Ruins of Palmyra* (1753), p. 1.

[3] Dean John William Burgon's Newdigate Prize poem on Petra contains this famous phrase. It also describes the city as "rose-red." When the Dean visited Petra long after he composed his verses on it, he had to acknowledge that rose-red is scarcely the best description of its color. Cf. I. Browning, *Petra* (1973), p. 118. A peach would make a better comparison.

[4] J. L. Burckhardt, *Travels in Syria and the Holy Land* (1822).

[5] L. de Laborde, *Voyage de l'Arabie Pétrée* (1830).

[6] J. G. Wetzstein, *Reisebericht über Hauran und die Trachonen* (1860). Laborde himself had surveyed the most northerly Arabian cities (Qanawāt, Suweidā', Buṣrā) in 1827: *Voyage de la Syrie* (1837).

more northerly sectors of Arabia;[7] the south was again reviewed in detail by that eccentric and indefatigable British traveler Charles Doughty.[8] Meanwhile Petra was beginning to attract more than adventurers and scholars. Edward Lear went there in 1858 to make drawings of the amazing city,[9] while Francis Frith was able to provide the first photographs that anyone had seen of the remains.[10] By the end of the century the classical historian Domaszewski and the orientalist Brünnow had begun their series of explorations of Transjordan which were to culminate in the magisterial three-volume publication *Die Provincia Arabia.*[11] The subject had come of age.

Intimate acquaintance with the terrain was a prerequisite for understanding Roman contact with the Arabs of the province. Antiquity left no narrative history for western scholars to rely upon as a substitute for discovery and autopsy. There was no Arab Polybius, no Arab Josephus. It was essential, therefore, to build the history from scattered references in ancient authors, in conjunction with the surviving monuments and inscriptions, viewed within the context of the land itself. In the twentieth century more scholars returned in search of new evidence and greater familiarity with the terrain. French orientalists, such as Dussaud, Jaussen, Savignac, and Dunand,[12] were able to make massive contributions to our knowledge of the more remote and unexplored territories. Their example, together with that of Brünnow and Domaszewski, has provided the immediate impetus

[7] Waddington, *IGLS* (1870).

[8] C. M. Doughty, *Travels in Arabia Deserta*, 2 vols. (1888).

[9] Lear's account of his visit to Petra is well worth reading: "A Leaf from the Journals of a Landscape Painter," *Macmillan's Magazine* 75 (April 1897) 410–30. For the pictures see P. Hofer, *Edward Lear as a Landscape Draughtsman* (1967), plates 57 and 109.

[10] See the photograph, reproduced here as plate 5 by courtesy of the owner, George Rinhart.

[11] R. E. Brünnow and A. von Domaszewski, *Die Provincia Arabia*, 3 vols. (1904–1909).

[12] See esp. R. Dussaud and F. Macler, "Rapport sur une mission scientifique dans les régions désertiques de la Syrie moyenne," *Nouvelles archives des missions scientifiques et littéraires* 10 (1902), 411–744. Still indispensable is A. Jaussen and R. Savignac, *Mission archéologique en Arabie* I (1909) and II (1914). For M. Dunand, note "Rapport sur une mission archéologique au Djebel Druze," *Syria* 7 (1926), 326–35, and "La voie romaine du Ledja," *Mém. Acad. des Inscr. et Belles-Lettres* 13.2 (1930), 521–57.

for those who have renewed the historical exploration of Transjordan in recent years.

Probably no province of the Roman Empire had so great a diversity of geographical and climatic features as Arabia. This was due in part to the extraordinary shape of the province in the southeast corner of the Mediterranean. On the west the province confronted the sea. Sinai is a wasteland but a crucial one, as the history of modern times has made plain, in that it links Egypt and North Africa generally to the lands on both sides of the Jordan Valley—what may be traditionally called Palestine and Transjordan. Roman Arabia also included the tract of coast with Gaza as its principal port, as well as the Negev desert in the interior, constituting the natural extension of the Sinai and the Sahara. Accordingly, although Petra and many of the other principal cities of the region were located across the River Jordan on the plateau to the east of the Dead Sea, there was direct overland access to the Mediterranean as well as to Egypt.

The Negev itself is a singularly waterless and cruel area; but with techniques of irrigation that were well known to the ancients, it can be made fertile in parts and suitable for habitation.[13] It can provide way-stations to the coast as well as, for example, halts on the pilgrimage route to the great monastery of St. Catherine in the Sinai.[14] The ancient sites at Nessana, Shivta, Khalaṣa, ʿAvdat, and Mampsis are only the most conspicuous of the settlements that prove the Negev to have been a considerably more populous area in antiquity than might have been imagined.

The most pronounced geographical feature of the entire Levant is the long depression of the Jordan Valley that runs north to south in a line parallel to the Mediterranean coast. This is the depression across which the elevations of the Lebanon and the Anti-Lebanon confront each other, and it is the depression which incorporates the Sea of Galilee and the Dead Sea. The Jordan

[13] See, with careful attention to ancient methods, M. Evenari, et al., *The Negev: The Challenge of a Desert* (1971; rev. ed., 1982).

[14] P. Mayerson, "The Desert of Southern Palestine According to Byzantine Sources," *ProcPhilSoc* 107.2 (1963), 160–72; "The Clysma-Phara-Haila Road on the Peutinger Table," *Coins, Culture, and History in the Ancient World: Studies in Honor of Bluma Trell* (1981), pp. 167–76; "The Pilgrim Routes to Mount Sinai and the Armenians," *IEJ* 32 (1982), 44–57.

Valley lies below sea level, as does the Dead Sea itself. The whole configuration represents an underwater landscape in remote prehistoric times. South of the Dead Sea the depression continues to the Gulf of ʿAqaba in the form of a broad and steamy river bed known as the Wādī ʿAraba. Because of the heat in the ʿAraba, traffic north from ʿAqaba would rarely ascend the actual wadi but move instead to one side or the other of it. From the east it was naturally necessary to make a crossing in order to continue on across the Negev to the coast. Or one could continue in a northerly direction to Damascus. For a considerable period in antiquity the principal crossing of the ʿAraba was west of Petra, the main halt before turning toward Gaza.

The area of Transjordan, to the east of the Dead Sea, should be considered as composed of two major sections, of which the more northerly is the larger. Eastward from the Jordan Valley rises the Jordanian plateau, in height between 2,500 and 5,000 feet above sea level. This plateau is cut by a series of wadis running from east to west, representing drainage systems into the valley. The most northerly is the Wādī Yarmūk, which has traditionally separated Syria from its southern neighbors. Farther south comes the transverse cut of the Wādī Zerqā, north of ʿAmmān. South of the Zerqā, the plateau extends across the area of Biblical Moab, itself cut by the deep transverse depression of the Wādī Mūjib. Further south the Moab area is terminated by the Wādī Ḥaṣā, which forms the northern frontier of biblical Edom. The next transverse depression to the south is nothing less than the end of the plateau itself, which descends steeply below the modern town of Maʿān to a flat desert of hard mud with jagged extrusions of sandstone. The whole of the Jordanian plateau, with its transverse wadis—Yarmūk, Zerqā, Mūjib, Ḥaṣā—constitutes the larger and more northerly component of the landscape.

The principal rock of the plateau is limestone. This makes a striking contrast to the extensive lava fields which lie immediately to the north in southern Syria. It is worth emphasizing that to the north and east of the Yarmūk is a territory of former volcanic activity that has left its traces everywhere. The principal rock here is basalt; and the most important elevation in the area, the Jebel Drūz, is a volcanic mountain. To the northwest of the Jebel Drūz is the forbidding territory of the Leja', popular in all periods with brigands and terrorists. (The word Leja' itself means a "hiding place" or "refuge.") The Leja' is a plateau formed from lava.

In antiquity, as in the present, there was an inevitable symbiosis between the inhabitants of the Jordanian plateau and the residents of the lava fields to the north. A major reason for the constant interchange is the route that heads southeast from the lava fields to the great interior depression in the desert known as the Wādī Sirḥān. This long depression with major oases at its northern and southern ends has long been a favorite route between the interior of Saudi Arabia and southern Syria. Since the Wādī Sirḥān runs into southern Syria close to the point of juncture with the urbanized sections of the Jordanian plateau, the northern region became an important center for traffic from both the southern coast and the southern interior, as well as by way of the Wādī Yarmūk, which provided a means of access to the other side of the Jordan Valley.

The western part of the Jordanian plateau, overlooking the Jordan Valley and the Dead Sea, has traditionally been the most favored area for settlement. There is sufficient rainfall for cultivation of crops, and the cities in this area, which are situated near the major highway connecting the Gulf of ʿAqaba with Damascus, have reasonable prospects for commercial development. It was no accident that three of the greatest cities of Roman Arabia—Gerasa, Philadelphia, and Petra—were all located in the western section of the plateau.[15] The only city of comparable magnitude to lie outside this area was Bostra, and it dominated the crucial crossroads of the north, where the lava country, the Jordanian plateau, and the Wādī Sirḥān converge. Already in the southern part of the plateau, in the area of Petra and Maʿān, the local rock has changed from limestone to a mixture of granite and sandstone. The appearance of the terrain is correspondingly altered. The new textures account for the brilliant coloration of the rock at Petra, which has been perhaps the most celebrated glory of that city.

[15] Cf. Amm. Marc. 14.8.13: *Haec (sc. Arabia) quoque civitates habet inter oppida quaedam ingentes, Bostram et Gerasam atque Filadelfiam.* By Ammianus' day Petra had lost much of its former importance. For a detailed account of the region in modern times: David J. Burdon, *Handbook of the Geology of Jordan* (1959).

The southern part of the plateau is also the highest, ascending over 5,000 feet and then dropping abruptly into the plain of the Ḥismā below. The high elevation is known locally as the Sharā' and appears to have provided the name of the most widely worshipped of the local Arabian deities in antiquity, Dushara (Dousares)—Lord of the Sharā'.[16] The drop from the Sharā' into the Ḥismā is among the most memorable geographical sights in the Near East. Viewed from above at the way-station of Naqb Ashtār, the Ḥismā landscape looks as if it belongs to another planet. Bleak and barren, the dried mud flats and sand stretch out into the distance punctuated by craggy peaks of sandstone. Uninviting as it is, this country has to be traversed to gain access to the Gulf of ʿAqaba and the sea route to the Indian Ocean. In antiquity, as in the present, the route through the Ḥismā to and from ʿAqaba was infinitely preferable to a passage along the depression of the Wādī ʿAraba which, though convenient, was unendurably hot. At least when the sun goes down on the sand and the mud flats of the Ḥismā, the familiar cold wind of the desert comes up and allows the traveler some hours of good sleep.

The geographical links between the Saudi Arabian peninsula, stretching from ʿAqaba to the southeast, and the settled regions of Transjordan and southern Syria must always be kept in mind. The Wādī Sirḥān is an illustration of the symbiosis of the regions. Similarly there were close links between the Ḥismā and the interior coast of the peninsula, behind the mountains which immediately confront the sea. For those who did not take ship at ʿAqaba, it was possible to veer somewhat to the southeast when coming through the Ḥismā from the north, and to descend into the interior of the Ḥejāz (the northwest corner of Saudi Arabia) on a route which is familiar to Islamic travelers as the pilgrimage road. The Ḥejāz has traditionally formed a part of the complex of territories, comprising the Sinai, Negev, and Transjordan, which we have identified as Roman Arabia. The ancient bond between this

[16] For Dushara, cf. D. Sourdel, *Les cultes du Hauran à l'époque romaine* (1952), pp. 59–68, and J. Teixidor, *The Pagan God* (1977), p. 83. Dushara means "the one belonging to" (*du*) Sharā'. The name of the plateau, Sharā', evokes the Arabic root (*šr'*), meaning "to sell" or "to buy." The commerce of the inhabitants may have given the area its name. The god (Dousares in Greek) appears in Christian times in the syncretistic St. Zeus Dousares: J. T. Milik in C.-M. Bennett, *ADAJ* 24 (1980), 211.

corner of the peninsula and the lands to the north and west has become clear only in the last fifty years or so; but it cannot now be doubted, as we shall see.

This region of the peninsula has, in fact, been of inestimable importance in the history of Arabs from the beginning. Everyone knows that the origins of Muḥammad were here, but it is less well known that the Arabs who moved northward into Petra and established the kingdom to which the present remains give glowing testimony may also have had their origins in the Ḥejāz.[17] The movements of Bedouin tribes and the exigencies of landscape through which they move are fundamental to an understanding of the history of the region.[18] Any outside power wishing to be involved in this area would ignore such considerations at its peril. Pragmatic as always, the Romans were, as will be noted, quick to appreciate the constraints of geography on the people they proposed to control.

If sedentary life was possible on the western plateau of Transjordan as well as in the northern Negev (with the help of irrigation), there were still vast tracts that could only be left open to nomads—who were no less familiar in antiquity than in the present. They were distinguished, then as now, by living in tents as they moved from place to place. Theirs was the familiar pattern of human migration, or transhumance. It consisted of the seasonal passage of cohesive small units or tribes to a cooler terrain in hot weather and a warmer one in cold. Nomads are by no means gypsies or simple wanderers. Their movements are regulated and rational.[19] The pasturage which they seek for the sheep

[17] For Nabataean origins in the Arabian peninsula, see P. C. Hammond, *The Nabataeans—Their History, Culture, and Archaeology* (1973), p. 11. Recently, however, at the first conference on the history and archaeology of Jordan, held at Oxford in March 1980, J. T. Milik argued for the Persian Gulf area as the original home of the Nabataeans. E. C. Broome and F. V. Winnett have expressed a preference for the territory south of Jawf. (Information courteously supplied by David Graf.)

[18] Cf. M. Awad, "Nomadism in the Arab Lands of the Middle East," *The Problems of the Arid Zones*, UNESCO public. (1962). See also the excellent volume, *When Nomads Settle* (1980), ed. Philip C. Salzman, to which David Graf has drawn my attention.

[19] Stephen Humphreys has referred me to an illuminating study of Sudanese nomads: Talal Asad, "Seasonal Movements of the Kababish Arabs of Northern Kordofan [Sudan]," in *Peoples and Cultures of the Middle East*, ed. Louise E. Sweet, I (1970), 346-62.

and the goats that move with them is, as far as they are concerned, theirs when they want it. Squatters who move in when they are away will be expected to move out when they return. In the Syrian desert and steppe, this classic pattern predominates. Coupled with the seasonal migration of nomads is a tendency from time to time to move into entirely new areas, over which they may roam with better prospects of pasturage and water. Desert life is strenuous and aggressive; tribes are numerous. It is therefore natural enough to find the rhythm of seasonal transhumance in counterpoint with tribal migration from one region to another. The history of the pre-Islamic Arabs is a long story of tribal movements. Many Arabs, including those who ruled in Petra, came out of the Arabian peninsula, either under pressure from hostile tribes or perhaps in a restless search for a better life elsewhere.

There is always ample opportunity for conflict between the settled communities in agricultural zones and the Bedouin in the desert, but generally it is remarkable how resilient the society of the Near East has been in accommodating the rhythmic intrusions of the Bedouin and the ambition of the settlers to secure the desert. Brigands in the Leja' could be thought more threatening than the Bedouin coming in during the hot weather to the Jordanian steppe. It is important to recall that while one Bedouin tribe might war with another, and while one settled nation might send an army against another, there is virtually no evidence that the Bedouin ever systematically harassed or attacked the settled communities or that the settled communities ever launched a vendetta against the Bedouin.[20] There is no reason to think that the Bedouin code of honor was any different in antiquity from what it is now. The Bedouin are as natural in the desert as its oases and its flowers. It was not until they became sedentary or else were brought together in large confederations under politically minded leaders that they posed any major problem to those who would rule in the areas they traversed.

Despite the improbable shape that the Roman province of Arabia has on a map, the geography of the region gave it a natural coherence. That coherence was determined essentially by the

[20] Cf. B. Isaac, "Bandits in Judaea and Arabia," *HSCP*, forthcoming.

sweep of desert across the Sinai through the Negev and up into Syria on the one hand, and by the north-south link between Syria and the Gulf of ʿAqaba on the other. This was an area which, quite visibly, linked west to east and north to south. Although a home to the Bedouin, it had a potential for substantial economic growth through commerce and for a satisfactory sedentary life in the cities of the plateau. It was inevitable that a vigorous and determined people would assume the domination of this vital corner of the Mediterranean world. The Romans were not the first to do this. They took over what they called Arabia from another people who had developed the region with astonishing skill. These were the descendants of nomadic Arabs who had established themselves in Petra as their capital and had become known to the world as the Nabaṭaeans.

II

THE COMING OF THE NABATAEANS

IN THE REIGN of Caesar Augustus, towards the end of the first century B.C., the extensive territory of what was to become Roman Arabia comprised the Arab kingdom of the Nabataeans. At that pivotal time in the fortunes of Rome, these Arabs had achieved both a high culture and a powerful monopoly of the traffic in perfume and spices. What was known about them and the gradual course of their occupation of land in the southeast corner of the Mediterranean can be judged from two accounts written by contemporaries of Augustus. One, by the Sicilian historian Diodorus, who wrote a universal history in Greek when Augustus was still a boy, depicts the Nabataeans as enterprising nomads.[1] The other account, in Strabo's *Geography*, from at least several decades later,[2] provides a vastly different picture. For Strabo the Nabataeans are a settled people.

Although so close to one another chronologically, Diodorus and Strabo worked largely from different sources, and it is for this reason that they provide such strikingly discrepant evidence. In composing his narrative of the turbulent years following the death of Alexander the Great, Diodorus appears to have made generous use of the eyewitness history by Hieronymus of Cardia.[3] In that work he found not only what has proven to be the earliest historical reference to the Nabataeans, but also a detailed description of their way of life at that time. Strabo, by contrast, although acquainted with remarks about the Nabataeans in the later Hellenistic writer Agatharchides of Cnidus, was fortunate enough to have a contemporary report of these people from a personal

[1] Diodorus treats the Nabataeans extensively in 2.48–49 and 19.94–100. He identifies them as Ἄραβες οὓς ὀνομάζουσι Ναβαταίους, *νεμόμενοι χώραν τὴν μὲν ἔρημον, τὴν δὲ ἄνυδρον* (2.48).

[2] Strabo 16.4.21–26, C 779–84.

[3] Diod. 19.100.1: *Ἱερώνυμον τὸν τὰς ἱστορίας συγγράψαντα*. For a new study of this writer, see Jane Hornblower, *Hieronymus of Cardia* (1982), esp. pp. 44–50 on the Nabataeans.

acquaintance who had visited their capital at Petra.[4] It happens therefore that in two writers, Diodorus and Strabo, who could have met one another at Rome, we have records of the Nabataeans that reflect their history in the late fourth century B.C. and in the late first century B.C. respectively. We can see not only what they were but what they became.

In the year 312 B.C., according to Diodorus, Antigonus the One-Eyed, a former general of Alexander and among his most ambitious successors, decided that a natural complement to his conquests of Syria and Phoenicia would be the extension of his power into "the land of the Arabs who are called Nabataeans."[5] According to Diodorus, Antigonus dispatched one of his officers, Athenaeus, with 4,000 infantry and 600 cavalry under order to surprise the barbarians, as they were called, and to steal their cattle. Athenaeus had been advised that these Arabs gathered annually for a national festival, during which their possessions, together with their elders, women, and children, were deposited on a certain rock (*ἐπί τινος πέτρας*).[6] This rock is described as exceptionally strong, though unwalled—a description which suits admirably the site of Petra. Athenaeus waited for the time of the festival and then marched to the rock (*πέτρα*) with his army, from the western side of the Jordan. Reaching the rock in the middle of the night, he surprised the Arabs who were there, killed some, and imprisoned others, and in addition he managed to collect a substantial amount of frankincense, myrrh, and silver. Departing before dawn, he and his troops hurried back to the west in the sure expectation of hot pursuit by the Nabataeans.

But the forces of Athenaeus soon grew weary, as well as careless, and they made camp as soon as they thought they were out of danger. The Nabataeans, however, once they had learned of the Greek assault, lost no time in setting after Athenaeus' men. They fell upon them as they lay in their camp and destroyed virtually all the infantry and much of the cavalry. Returning to their rock,

[4] On Agatharchides, cf. Strabo 16.4.20, C 779. For Strabo's contemporary witness: 16.4.21, C 779 (*γενόμενος γοῦν παρὰ τοῖς Πετραίοις* Ἀθηνόδωρος, *ἀνὴρ φιλόσοφος καὶ ἡμῖν ἑταῖρος*).

[5] Diod. 19.94.1: *ἐπὶ τὴν χώραν τῶν* Ἀράβων *τῶν καλουμένων* Ναβαταίων.

[6] Diod. 19.95.1.

they wrote to Antigonus "in Syrian letters" to accuse Athenaeus.[7] Antigonus replied with statesmanlike mendacity, declaring that Athenaeus had acted contrary to his instructions. The king thus attempted by this explanation to take the Nabataeans off their guard against any subsequent attack. Although pleased with Antigonus' response, the Nabataeans nonetheless took care to place watchmen on various hills in their territory. When Antigonus had satisfied himself that they regarded him as their friend, he ordered his son Demetrius, known to the Greek world by his epithet the Besieger, to march into the country of the Arabs and avenge the defeat of Athenaeus. But the Nabataean watchmen were vigilant and communicated news of the Greek invasion by a series of fire signals; no sooner were the Greeks on their way than the Nabataeans installed a garrison to protect Petra. At the same time they cunningly divided their cattle into separate flocks, of which some were driven out into the desert while others were sent into remote places where the Greeks would be unlikely to penetrate. Demetrius was thus unable to take the Nabataean rock.

The Arabs sent him a message with some plain truths: it made no sense for the Greeks to make war against a people without water, wine, or grain, for the Arabs did not live like the Greeks and had no desire to be their slaves. After conferring with representatives of the Nabataeans, Demetrius finally agreed to withdraw, taking some hostages and gifts.[8]

The episodes of Athenaeus and Demetrius represent the entry of the Nabataeans into recorded history. It is impossible to say how long these Arabs had been in the regions where the Greek commanders found them. There is no secure basis for identifying them with the Nebaioth of the Old Testament or with peoples of similar name in Assyrian documents. Their history seems to be irrevocably dark before the year 312 B.C. Nevertheless, Diodorus' account, anchored in the contemporary testimony of Alexander's officer Hieronymus of Cardia, provides a vivid picture of Nabataean life toward the end of the fourth century. The military narrative shows, among other things, that the Nabataeans were already literate to some extent, in that there were at least scribes

[7] Diod. 19.96.1: *ἐπιστολὴν γράψαντες Συρίοις γράμμασι.*
[8] Diod. 19.98.1.

capable of writing "in Syrian letters," presumably a form of Aramaic. Since inscriptions and papyri from later centuries show that the Nabataeans regularly communicated in a dialect of Aramaic with their own distinctive script,[9] it would not be unreasonable to assume that this is what Diodorus and, through him, Hieronymus are referring to. Furthermore, the Nabataeans of the late fourth century were a pastoral people capable of removing their flocks into the desert. They assembled as a nation only once a year and maintained a great rock without walls as their stronghold during the occasions of this national gathering. From all this one would readily draw the conclusion that the people were largely nomadic. Fortunately, Diodorus leaves us in no doubt about this matter by excerpting from his source an ample description of the Nabataeans' way of life.

As they reminded Demetrius, their life was in the open, in a rough country without much water, where it was not easy to plant or to build. Their custom, strictly observed, was to have no houses at all, because they believed that those who did could easily be subjugated by others.[10] Some of the Nabataeans raised camels and others sheep. Overall they had acquired exceptional wealth, "for not a few of them were accustomed to bring down to the sea frankincense and myrrh and the most valuable kinds of spices which they procured from those who convey them from what is called Arabia Felix."[11] This means that the spice and perfume trade from southern Arabia and the East through the middlemen of the southwest corner of the Arabian peninsula depended upon the Nabataeans for the conveyance of goods to the Mediterranean by an overland route. In view of the location of the Nabataeans in the early days of Antigonus, there can be little doubt that this route passed northward into Transjordan and then to the west across the ʿAraba to Gaza and Rhinocolura.[12]

[9] The most comprehensive treatment of Nabataean language and script remains J. Cantineau, *Le nabatéen* I (1930), II (1932), although the forthcoming fascicle of *CIS* II by J. Starcky and J. T. Milik will take pride of place when it appears. For the incompatibility of *nbṭ* with the Old Testament *nbyt*, see Starcky *SDB* 900–3, and F. V. Winnett and W. L. Reed, *Ancient Records from North Arabia* (1970), p. 99.

[10] Diod. 19.94.4.

[11] Diod. 19.94.5 (ἐκ τῆς Εὐδαίμονος καλουμένης ᾿Αραβίας). Cf. N. Groom, *Frankincense and Myrrh* (1981).

[12] See A. Negev, "The Date of the Petra-Gaza Road," *PEQ* 98 (1966), 89–98.

Diodorus' report of the customs of the Nabataeans emphasizes in general, as well as in the particular case of the invasions of Athenaeus and Demetrius, their love of independence. Their ability to retreat to the desert and to survive there depended upon their skill in creating underground reservoirs that were imperceptible to strangers. From the exceptional skill which the Nabataeans displayed in creating irrigation systems in later phases of their history, this report is entirely credible.[13]

The Nabataeans did more than raise camels and sheep and convey, at vast profit, the spices and perfumes of the East. They were also apparently engaged in marketing asphalt from the Dead Sea. This enterprise can be inferred from an abortive undertaking by Demetrius after his unsuccessful assault on the Nabataean stronghold. When he attempted himself to harvest the asphalt from the Dead Sea, presumably to gain some kind of profit from his ill-starred operations in the region, "he put his men into boats which were immediately attacked by 6,000 Arabs."[14] Most of Demetrius' men perished in a rain of arrows.

The Nabataeans, as they appear in the pages of Diodorus, were an uncommonly energetic and successful nomadic people. Yet the portrait of them by Strabo, writing only a few decades after Diodorus' account but reflecting changes in circumstances over some three hundred years, is arrestingly different. Although the Nabataeans are seen in Strabo to occupy the same territory of Transjordan, they have become a completely sedentary people. They are so much given to the acquisition of possessions, says Strabo, that they impose fines on anyone who has diminished his, as well as give honor to those who increase them.[15] They are subjects of a king who lives in magnificent style; and their houses,

---

Observe Strabo 16.4.24, C 781: εἰς Πέτραν, ἐντεῦθεν δ' εἰς Ῥινοκόλουρα; and Pliny, *NH* 6.144: *Nabataei oppidum incolunt Petram. . . Huc convenit utrumque bivium, eorum qui ex Syria Palmyram petiere et eorum qui a Gaza venerunt.*

[13] Note the underground Nabataean reservoirs at Umm al-jimāl in the north (G. Lankester Harding, *The Antiquities of Jordan* [1967], p. 149) and Ḥumaima in the south (D. Graf, *Damaszener Mitteilungen*, forthcoming).

[14] Diod. 2.48. Note 2.48.6: λίμην τε μεγάλη φέρουσα πολλὴν ἄσφαλτον, ἐξ ἧς λαμβάνουσιν οὐκ ὀλίγας προσόδους. See P. Hammond, "The Nabataean Bitumen Industry at the Dead Sea," *BiblArch* 22 (1959), 40–48.

[15] Strabo 16.4.26, C 783.

built of stone, are extraordinarily luxurious.[16] Their principal city is the rock-bound city of Petra, which has a system of government that was much admired by Strabo's friend and informant. The city is an international place where Romans and other foreigners can be frequently seen. In fact, the law courts of Petra are said to be largely filled with foreigners, since the Nabataeans are such a peaceable people that they rarely engage in litigation.[17] Water, it appears, has been successfully exploited by irrigation, for Strabo declares that most of the Nabataeans' territory is well supplied with fruits and that even inside Petra there are gardens. The Nabataeans are still evidently engaged in trade, since Strabo comments on the abundance of imports from other places.[18] Clearly, between the late fourth century and the late first the Nabataean way of life had changed dramatically.

It is a difficult matter to trace the course of this alteration. There are no texts which describe the history of the Nabataeans during the long period of change—only those disparate and fragmentary scraps of evidence from which ancient history must so often be written. Yet there is just enough to be reasonably certain about the spread of Nabataean culture in the Hellenistic age. The operations of Antigonus guarantee the presence of the Nabataeans in Transjordan by the end of the fourth century. By the mid-third century they can be traced to the north in the area of the Ḥawrān, which was eventually to become as important a part of the Nabataean kingdom as Petra was in the south. Papyri in the archive of Zeno provide proof of the presence of Nabataeans in the north by 259 B.C. The Ḥawrān is named explicitly (Αὔρανα), as are the Nabataeans themselves.[19] Another text from the same archive refers to a person called Ῥάββηλος (Rabbel), a characteristically Nabataean name that

[16] A. Negev, in *PEQ* 114 (1982), 119–20, has recently asserted that the Nabataeans lived in tents until after A.D. 70. This opinion is indefensible in the light of Strabo's testimony.

[17] Strabo 16.4.21, C 779.

[18] Strabo 16.4.26, C 784.

[19] G. Vitelli, *Papiri greci e latini* IV (1917), no. 406, col. I, l. 17, εἰς Αὔρανα, and ll. 21–22, τοὺς Ναβαταίους (the papyrus has ἀναβαταιους, an error strikingly evocative of the error in the text of the *Periplus of the Red Sea* 19, where ἀναβαταιως stands for Ναβαταίων in the phrase εἰς Πέτραν πρὸς Μαλίχαν βασιλέα Ναβαταίων).

appears in the Nabataean king lists.[20] Despite recent suggestions that there is no evidence for Nabataean penetration of the Ḥawrān in the third century, the Zeno papyri put this fact beyond all doubt and establish these Arabs in one of the principal areas of their subsequent splendor.[21]

At the same time the Nabataeans had probably also moved across the ʿAraba to the west into the desert tracts of the Negev, where again they were to flourish in later centuries. The earliest Nabataean inscription comes from the site of Elusa in the Negev. Although the document is now lost, it is known from a photograph that shows letter forms of a very early date. The text reads: "This is the place which Nuthairu made for the life of Aretas, king of the Nabataeans."[22] If the inscription is as early as the most authoritative scholars believe, namely the first half of the second century B.C., then we have here a reference to the initial phase of the institution of Nabataean kingship.

An early ruler of the Arabs by the name of Aretas appears in the history of the Maccabees at about the same time. In 168 the former high priest Jason, while in flight from his people, appeared before a certain tyrant Aretas (ὁ τῶν ᾿Αράβων τύραννος).[23] It is possible that this Aretas is identical with the king commemorated on the Elusa inscription; and although the Aretas at Elusa could possibly indicate a still earlier king of that name, it is conventional to designate the ruler in the Books of the Maccabees as Aretas I. It would certainly not be legitimate to deduce

[20] C. C. Edgar, *Zenon Papyri* I (1925), no. 59004, ll. 27–29, dated to 259 B.C.: τοῖς παρὰ ῾Ραββήλου. A. Negev, "The Nabataeans and Provincia Arabia," *ANRW* II.8 (1977), 530, misinterprets this text because he is unaware of the references in n. 19 above.

[21] Cf. F. E. Peters, "The Nabataeans in the Hauran," *JAOS* 97 (1977), 263–77, where the situation is accurately described. For a denial of an early Nabataean presence in the Ḥawrān see Negev (above, n. 20).

[22] The text, with a drawing of the letters, may be conveniently found in J. Cantineau, *Le nabatéen* II (1932), p. 44, and in Negev (above, n. 20), 545-46, with a photograph of a squeeze: *znh ʾtrʾ / zy ʿbd / ntyrw / ʿl ḥywhy / zy ḥ[r]tt / mlk / nbṭw*. On the date, see F. M. Cross, *JBL* 74 (1955), 160, n. 25.

[23] 2 Macc. 5.8: ἐγκληθεὶς πρὸς ᾿Αρέταν τὸν τῶν ᾿Αράβων τύραννον. For ἐγκληθείς instead of the manuscript reading ἐγκλεισθείς, see Chr. Habicht, *2. Makkabäerbuch: Jüdische Schriften aus hellenistisch-römischer Zeit* I (1976), p. 255, n. 8. Negev (above, n. 20), 522, reproduces the manuscript text without any intimation of a problem.

from such evidence as Maccabees that, at the time of Jason's appearance before Aretas, the ruler of the Nabataeans had not yet assumed the title of king. There would be no inconsistency in a designation of *τύραννος* in the Books of the Maccabees and the title of king on an inscription.

In the year 163 the Maccabee brothers Judas and Jonathan went into the wilderness for three days and encountered the Nabataeans. It is reported that they treated the brothers peacefully and indicated to them the fortunes of those Jews residing in the land of Galaad.[24] The location of this meeting between the Maccabee brothers and the Nabataeans was almost certainly the Ḥawrān, where the Nabataeans had already been settled for at least a century. This is the only possible conclusion from the combination of three days' march and information about Jews in Galaaditis in northern Transjordan.[25]

It has long seemed as if the peaceable meeting between the Maccabees and the Nabataeans in the Ḥawrān as related in the first Book of the Maccabees was somehow belied by a parallel account in the second Book.[26] In this other narrative the brothers are said to have been the victims of a surprise attack, launched by Arabs who are described simply as pastoral nomads living in tents. Despite the open contradiction between these two accounts, scholars have been inclined to identify the marauding Arabs of the second Book of the Maccabees with the Nabataeans in the first Book.[27] Yet the Nabataeans were said to have approached the Maccabees in peace (*εἰρηνικῶς*), and the Arabs in the second Book who proved so vicious are nowhere described as Nabataeans. Although it is impossible to say how far the process of Nabataean sedentarization had proceeded in 163, it would seem more reasonable to assume that the raiders were distinct from the peaceful Nabataeans, who must have been at least in the process

[24] 1 Macc. 5.25–26.

[25] Negev (above, n. 20), 522, criticizes J. Starcky in *SDB* 905 for inferring "for no obvious reason" that the meeting took place in the Ḥawrān. The reason was so obvious that Starcky had neglected to enunciate it. For Galaaditis, see M. Avi-Yonah, *The Holy Land* (1966), p. 40.

[26] 2 Macc. 12.10–12.

[27] So Starcky, *SDB* 905; Habicht (above, n. 23), p. 262, n. 10; Negev (above, n. 20), 532.

of settling in the Ḥawrān after their first appearance there, nearly a hundred years before. The environs of the Ḥawrān have been and remain today favored haunts of brigands.[28] The Nabataeans themselves had to cope with the marauders who inhabited the lava plateau of the Leja' and the mountainous terrain of the Jebel Drūz.

A segregation of the raiding Arabs in the second Book of the Maccabees from the peaceful Nabataeans in the first is recommended further by the good relations which are seen to exist between Jonathan and the Nabataeans, named explicitly, some three years later. Again there is an attack of Arabs on the Maccabaean caravan, this time in the vicinity of Mādabā, but it is quite clear that the marauders were not Nabataeans. They are identified as the tribe of Amrai.[29] The interpretation of the evidence in the Books of the Maccabees illustrates the danger of assuming that any reference to Arabs in areas known to have been settled by the Nabataeans must automatically refer to them. On the contrary, there were many Arab tribes which continued to be nomadic and accordingly moved in and out of the emerging Nabataean kingdom. Besides there were certain groups of Arabs that made a living from brigandage. The Nabataeans were obliged to cope with these people just as invading armies had to do, and eventually the Romans as well.[30]

The only clearly documented case of pillaging on the part of the Nabataeans themselves involves, oddly enough, action on the high seas. Diodorus reports, presumably on the authority of Agatharchides of Cnidus, an undated and undatable phase in the growth of the Nabataean economy during which the Nabataeans took to piracy on the Red Sea. Diodorus reports that, after a certain period of success in their enterprise, the Nabataeans "were caught on the high seas by some quadriremes and punished as they deserved."[31] Strabo, too, seems to make reference to this

[28] Cf. Waddington, *IGLS*, no. 2329 [*OGIS* 424], with his commentary invoking Josephus, *AJ* 14.15.5, 15.10.1, and 16.9.1.

[29] 1 Macc. 9.35–42, identifying the Arabs as υἱοὶ Ἰαμβρι, i.e. *beni Amraï* (Starcky, *SDB* 905). See now the comprehensive treatment by J. T. Milik, "La tribu des Bani ʿAmrat en Jordanie de l'époque grecque et romaine," *ADAJ* 24 (1980), 41–48.

[30] See B. Isaac, "Bandits in Judaea and Arabia," *HSCP*, forthcoming.

[31] Diod. 3.43.5.

moment in Nabataean history when he writes: "These Nabataeans formerly lived a peaceful life, but later by means of rafts took to plundering the vessels of people sailing from Egypt. But they paid the penalty when a fleet went over and ravaged their country."[32]

The emergence of Nabataean piracy was probably due to concern over the new seaborne commerce that the Egyptians were developing as a result of the discovery of the monsoons.[33] Ships laden with perfume and spices could proceed directly to the ports of Egypt in the appropriate seasons, and from there the goods could be conveyed to the Mediterranean. The Nabataeans must have soon realized that the new traffic by sea would mean a gradual decline in the overland commerce which had been the basis of their prosperity and their sedentarization. Any fears they may have had were well grounded, for by the mid-first century A.D. the overland traffic through Petra had largely dried up.[34] The piracy of the Nabataeans should be viewed therefore in the context of the growing commerce between the spice and perfume centers of the East and the Egyptian ports on the west coast of the Red Sea. It is apparent from the accounts in both Diodorus and Strabo that the navy of the Ptolemies managed to suppress the Nabataeans' effort to stop the Egyptian inroad into Arab trade. But the encounter between Nabataeans and Ptolemies provides an intriguing glimpse into the competition between these two great powers in the second century B.C.

[32] Strabo 16.4.8, C 777.

[33] The principal evidence for the ancients' awareness of the monsoons is *Periplus of the Red Sea* 57 and Pliny, *NH* 6.100 and 104. Both authors refer to a wind named Hippalus; the *Periplus* affirms that this was the name of the κυβερνήτης who discovered the monsoon. It was probably exploited in the late Hellenistic period: A. Dihle, "Das Datum des Periplus des Roten Meeres," *Umstrittene Daten* (1965), p. 25. Pliny's anecdote in *NH* 6.84 on the freedman Annius Plocamus, whose ship was blown off course to Ceylon in the time of Claudius, has nothing to do with the discovery of the monsoon, as Dihle rightly emphasizes (p. 27, n. 24). Jehan Desanges believes that Eudoxus of Cyzicus was chosen by Ptolemy VIII to serve on an expedition which marked the beginning of Greek use of the monsoon for sea travel: *Recherches sur l'activité des méditerranéens aux confins de l'Afrique* (1978), p. 158.

[34] A. Negev (above, n. 12). R. Cohen has recently called into question the terminal date for the use of the Petra-Gaza road: *Eighth Archaeological Conference in Israel* (1981); see also R. Cohen, "New Light on the Petra-Gaza Road," *BiblArch* 45.3 (1982), 240–47.

The importance of the Nabataean kingdom alongside that of the Ptolemies toward the end of the second century B.C. can be documented in several sources. A much neglected passage in one of the inscriptions from Priene in Asia Minor lauds a local ambassador named Moschion in 129 B.C. for his diplomatic efforts in various parts of the Mediterranean world, including embassies to Alexandria and to Petra in Arabia.[35] We are not told the purpose of Moschion's embassies, nor is it clear exactly what he might have accomplished on behalf of Priene, but it is significant that he found it necessary to visit Petra as well as Alexandria at this crucial time. For in 129 B.C. the last of the Attalid kings had not long been dead, and the province of Asia, of which Priene was a part, had only recently been added to the Roman Empire.

Toward the year 100 B.C., according to a report in the *Jewish Antiquities* of Josephus, the inhabitants of Gaza, while under siege by Alexander Jannaeus, expected to be rescued by a certain Aretas, king of the Arabs.[36] Although their hopes were disappointed, the people of Gaza probably had good reason to expect the intervention of Aretas, not only because the Nabataeans were installed in the Negev, but precisely because Gaza was one of the principal ports through which the merchandise conveyed by the Nabataeans moved onto the ships of the Mediterranean. This Aretas at the end of the second century, who is conventionally styled Aretas II, must have been an energetic expansionist.[37] He appears to have been the first of the Nabataean kings to strike coins, and in so doing he followed closely on the example of Alexander Jannaeus and the Hasmonaeans.

It was only with the decline of the Seleucids and the Ptolemies that the various smaller states of the Near East became bold enough to mint their own autonomous coins.[38] The pieces which E. S. G. Robinson ascribed in 1936 to Aretas II in an important and generally accepted argument bear neither inscriptions nor any other identifying mark of the Nabataeans.[39] But they survive

[35] *Inschriften v. Priene*, no. 108, l. 168: τῆς Ἀραβίας εἰς Πέτραν.

[36] Josephus, *AJ* 13.360: Ἀρέτας ὁ Ἀράβων βασιλεὺς ἐπίδοξος ὤν.

[37] The Aretas of 2 Macc. 5.8 is called Aretas I.

[38] See Y. Meshorer, *Nabataean Coins*, Qedem 3, Monographs of the Institute of Archaeology, Jerusalem (1975), p. 9: Tyre began minting in 126/5 B.C. and Ashkelon in 104 B.C.

[39] E. S. G. Robinson, "Coins from Petra," *Num. Chron.* 16 (1936), 288–91.

in abundance and have been found notably in both Gaza and Petra. The obverse is a head with a crested helmet, and on the reverse is a figure of Victory with an object in her left hand and a wreath in her right. On certain of the coins a mysterious letter (either Λ or A) has been discerned, and it is possible that this letter represents the name Aretas. These early coins have always turned up in contexts of other Nabataean coinage. Only recently a hoard of 800 bronze coins of the Nabataean kings included a substantial number of this early, otherwise unidentified issue. The new hoard has even delivered two specimens which offer in place of the Λ or A the Hebrew letter ח, which would represent Aretas' Aramaic name חרתת (Ḥāritat).[40]

The episode at Gaza is the first indication of a collision between the Jewish house of the Hasmonaeans and the kings of the Nabataeans. Aretas, as we have seen, was an important figure in the region and may plausibly be identified with the mysterious Arab king Herotimus in Justin's *Epitome* of Pompeius Trogus.[41] This king is said to have presided over a race of Arabs who had been peaceable hitherto (one is reminded of the Nabataeans in the Books of the Maccabees), but who now were threatening both Egypt and Syria with armies. It is customary and entirely reasonable to identify King Herotimus with Aretas II. Herotimus represents a possible Greek equivalent of the king's Aramaic name (Ḥāritat),[42] and his distinction as an expansionist is adequately borne out by what we know about him.

Soon after the fall of Gaza at the hands of Alexander Jannaeus, Aretas appears to have been succeeded by a new Nabataean king, Obodas I,[43] who continued the warfare between the Nabataeans

[40] Meshorer (above, n. 38), pp. 10–11.

[41] Justin 39.5. According to this source, Herotimus could rely upon 700 sons, *quos ex paelicibus susceperat*.

[42] So also J. Starcky, *SDB* 905.

[43] Near the entrance to the Sīq at Petra is a *triclinium* in the rock, where an inscription in an early Nabataean script dedicates the space to Dushara and Obodas. The text was first published by G. Dalman, *Neue Petra-Forschung* (1912), as no. 90. It is no. 1432 in *RES* and no. 2 in Cantineau (above, n. 22), p. 2. The language in ll. 3–4 is *ldwšr' 'lh mnbtw 'l ḥyy 'bdt mlk nbṭw br ḥrtt mlk nbṭw šnt 1*: "to Dushara, the god of Manbatu, for the life of 'Obodat, king of the Nabataeans, son of Ḥāritat, king of the Nabataeans, year 1." Starcky, *SDB* 906, and Negev (above, n. 20), 536, reasonably identify this Ḥāritat (Aretas) with Aretas II. The 'Obodat (Obodas) is thus Obodas I. Negev's view, however, that this is the earliest evidence for the Nabataeans at Petra is quite untenable.

and the Hasmonaeans. In the year 93 or thereabouts, Alexander came into conflict with Obodas in a battle somewhere in the northern part of the Nabataean kingdom, at the city of Garada near the Golan.[44] Obodas was victorious in this encounter, and the Jewish leader almost lost his life. Not long afterwards Josephus reveals that Alexander was obliged to give up such conquests as he had made in Transjordan because of the pressures on him elsewhere. He is said to have surrendered to the king of the Arabs some territory he had conquered in Moab and Galaaditis and the strongholds there, "in order that he might not aid the Jews in the war against him."[45]

This is the first of several indications in the last century of the Roman Republic that the king of the Nabataeans saw substantial political opportunities in the internal divisions of the Jews at Jerusalem. By supporting one or another of the rival factions, he could maintain a constant instability in Judaea that would permit the strengthening of his own realm. Obodas' acquisition of Alexander's territories in Transjordan appears to have aided him in strengthening his resources at home. The growth of the Nabataean kingdom could well have become a source of concern to the increasingly enfeebled Seleucid regime in Syria to the north.

In 88/7 Antiochus XII, the new Seleucid king, launched two separate campaigns against the Arabs.[46] In the second of these he was decisively defeated by the forces of Obodas and himself killed. This great Nabataean victory, which Josephus locates in the vicinity of the village of Cana, cannot be dated with precision, but there is good reason for placing it in 87.[47] Obodas himself

[44] Josephus, *AJ* 13.375: *κατὰ Γαράδα κώμην τῆς Γαλααδίτιδος*. Niese saw fit to emend both proper names in this phrase, without justification or good sense. Garada is unknown, but Galaaditis (in the north of Transjordan) is not.

[45] Josephus, *AJ* 13.382.

[46] Josephus, *AJ* 13.387–91; *BJ* 1.99–102 (the chapter numbers are unfortunately reversed in the references provided by Starcky, *SDB* 906). Steph. Byz., *s.v.* Μωθώ (citing Uranius, *FGH* II.C.675, F 25), has nothing to do with these events: see Milik in Starcky, *SDB* 904, and G. W. Bowersock, *JRS* 61 (1971), 226.

[47] See M. Sartre, "Rome et les Nabatéens à la fin de la République," *REA* 81 (1979), 40, with note 30. Starcky, *SDB* 906, must be correct in arguing that the Arab king in Josephus' narrative of the battle of Cana is Obodas I. Milik, cited by Starcky, believes that the deified Obodas mentioned in Steph. Byz., *s.v.* Ὄβοδα, is Obodas I: Stephanus quoted Uranius (*FGH* II.C.675, F 24) as noting in his fourth book of

died soon after the battle, possibly as a direct result of it. He was succeeded by the king known today as Aretas III, who lost no time in continuing the now well established expansionist policy of the Nabataeans. In response to an appeal from the citizens of Damascus, who found themselves threatened by the rugged and predatory Ituraeans of the Anti-Lebanon, the forces of Aretas moved into the Syrian capital.[48] For some fifteen years, the city of Damascus was ruled by an official of the Nabataean government, and Aretas caused an impressive series of Nabataean coins to be minted at Damascus in commemoration of the new acquisition.[49]

By 82 Aretas felt strong enough to launch an offensive of his own against Alexander Jannaeus, and he invaded Palestine. He was able to defeat Alexander and dictate terms to the Jewish king.[50] But Alexander in turn went back to Transjordan and successfully stripped Aretas of at least a dozen villages, as well as the ports he had succeeded in opening up on the Mediterranean as a result of his earlier successes.[51] Upon Alexander's death, Aretas, who would have learned from his father Obodas the advantages of meddling in the internal dissension of the Jews, was able to deflect Alexandra, the widow of the Hasmonaean leader, from further hostilities by offering refuge to those Jews of her court who hated the Pharisees and could exploit an alliance with the Nabataeans to force Alexandra to act against their enemies.[52]

At Damascus Aretas clearly saw himself as the successor of the Seleucid kings. The coins minted there were evidently intended for circulation in that city. They continue the minting of the Seleucids, and their legends are in Greek rather than Nabataean Aramaic. They are, however, the first coins minted by the Nabataeans with the name and image of their king. In addition, Aretas has the epithet "philhellene," proclaiming his aspirations as a

---

᾿Αραβικά that Oboda was a place of the Nabataeans, *ὅπου ᾿Οβόδης ὁ βασιλεύς, ὃν θεοποιοῦσι, τέθαπται.* For epigraphic evidence of the cult of a Zeus Obodas at Oboda (ʿAvdat), see *IEJ* 17 17 (1967), 55, and below, pp. 62–63, n. 14. On the date of Uranius, J. M. I. West, *HSCP* 78 (1974), 282–84.

[48] Josephus, *AJ* 13.392; *BJ* 1.103.

[49] Meshorer (above, n. 38), pp. 12–16. The coins extend from 84 to 72 B.C.

[50] Josephus, *AJ* 13.392. The battle took place east of Lydda.

[51] Josephus, *AJ* 13.393–97; *BJ* 1.104–5.

[52] Josephus, *AJ* 13.414; *BJ* 1.111.

supporter of Greek traditions.[53] The issue continued down to the year 72, after which the city was captured by Tigranes, king of Armenia and a new claimant to the succession of the Seleucids.

Tigranes took over the coinage at Damascus from Aretas and thereby took upon himself the mantle of the Seleucids. Tigranes' coins last until 69, when he appears to have left Syria upon learning that Lucullus had invaded his own kingdom at home.[54] At this time the Nabataeans seem to have made no attempt to repossess Damascus. The city fell victim once again to the ravages of the Ituraeans, led on this occasion by a certain Ptolemaeus, son of Mennaeus. Alexandra, the widow of Alexander Jannaeus, tried to make capital of this crisis in much the same way as Aretas had done in a comparable situation in 87.[55] But the expedition which she sent to protect Damascus failed in its objective. The city was left in a kind of power vacuum between the departure of Tigranes and the arrival of the armies of Pompey the Great. In the year 69 the Damascenes issued coins in their own name and apparently proclaimed thereby their fragile and short-lived autonomy.[56]

In 67 Alexander Jannaeus' widow died. The consequences were momentous for the Near East. A sibling rivalry between her elder son Hyrcanus II and her younger son Aristobulus was fought out in a battle at Jericho. Hyrcanus was compelled to give up both the throne and the high priesthood in favor of his younger brother, and at the urging of an Idumaean by the name of Antipater he took refuge in Petra with Aretas III.[57] Once again the Nabataean king must have seen opportunities for his own people

[53] See the catalogue in Meshorer (above, n. 38), pp. 86–87, nos. 5–8: *βασιλέως* Ἀρέτου *φιλέλληνος*. All the coins are bronze, except for no. 5 in silver.

[54] Josephus, *AJ* 13.419–21; *BJ* 1.116. Meshorer (above, n. 38), pp. 14–15; Sartre (above, n. 47), 41.

[55] Josephus, *AJ* 13.418; *BJ* 1.115. It had been threats from Ptolemy, son of Mennaeus, that had caused the Damascenes to invite Aretas in the eighties: cf. Josephus, *AJ* 13.392. The exact date of the expedition dispatched by Alexandra is difficult to fix. The context in Josephus suggests 69 B.C. after Tigranes' withdrawal from Damascus but before his evacuation of Syria as a whole. Sartre (above, n. 47), 41, suggests the possibility of dating this episode to the period in 72 B.C. between the departure of Aretas and the arrival of Tigranes. He would, on this hypothesis, explain the Nabataean withdrawal as due to an Ituraean rather than Armenian menace.

[56] Starcky, *SDB* 909, approved by Sartre (above, n. 47), 41.

[57] Josephus, *AJ* 14.14–17; *BJ* 1.117–25. Note the references to Petra as *τὰ βασίλεια. . .τῷ* Ἀρέτᾳ (*AJ* 14.16) and as *βασίλειον. . .τῆς* Ἀραβίας (*BJ* 1.125).

in the dissensions of the Jews. The Idumaean Antipater had married a Nabataean woman of high station and was thus closely bound to the Nabataean court.[58] Antipater and Hyrcanus between them persuaded Aretas of the value of intervention and promised restitution of the dozen towns in Transjordan that Alexander Jannaeus had won from Aretas some fifteen years earlier.[59] Aretas' decision to intervene was but another illustration of a consistent foreign policy that had first been formulated by his grandfather Aretas II. But this time it was to bring the Nabataean people into direct contact with the legions of Rome.

[58] Josephus, *BJ* 1.181: *τούτῳ* (i.e., *'Αντιπάτρῳ*) *γήμαντι γυναῖκα τῶν ἐπισήμων ἐξ 'Αραβίας Κύπρον τοὔνομα*. . .

[59] Josephus, *AJ* 14.18.

III

POMPEY AND HIS SUCCESSORS

JUST AS ANTIPATER was successfully forging the fateful alliance between Aretas, the king of the Nabataeans, and the exiled Hasmonaean Hyrcanus, the legates of Pompey were arriving in Syria to bring an end to the chaos that had followed upon the dissolution of the Seleucid dynasty. The absence of a strong central authority had led to the emergence of numerous princelings and bandit chieftains, who were dividing up the country among themselves when it was not being terrorized by the invading forces of Armenians.[1] Aretas had himself once taken over Damascus, at the request of its citizens during a season of destructive tribal incursions, and not even he had been willing to return to the region when Tigranes pulled out after only two years in the city. The armies of Tigranes remained elsewhere in Syria as late as 65, the year in which Aretas contracted to lead a military expedition to Jerusalem to displace Hyrcanus' brother Aristobulus.[2] At about the same time, Q. Caecilius Metellus Nepos and L. Lollius, both legates of Pompey, moved into Syria and took possession of Damascus.[3] Under these circumstances the Romans arrived in Syria in the guise of liberators, and they soon managed to put a stop to the social and political disintegration of the former Seleucid territories.

Metellus and Lollius were followed by another of Pompey's officers, M. Aemilius Scaurus. Finding the situation in Damascus

[1] See A. R. Bellinger, "The Early Coinage of Roman Syria," *Studies in Roman Economic and Social History in Honor of A. C. Johnson* (1951), pp. 58–67, esp. pp. 58–60, for a survey of the situation. M. Sartre, "Rome et les Nabatéens à la fin de la République," *REA* 81 (1979), 42, n. 40, seems to have misunderstood Bellinger's reference to Aretas "driven off. . .by Scaurus" ("Aretas III, battu par Scaurus"). Sartre thinks Bellinger may have had in mind a defeat of Aretas after a second Nabataean occupation of Damascus in 65 B.C., but Bellinger's text shows clearly that he is simply referring to the removal of Aretas from the siege of Jerusalem.

[2] Josephus, *AJ* 14.20; *BJ* 1.126.

[3] Josephus, *AJ* 14.29; *BJ* 1.127. Probably in 65 B.C.: T. R. S. Broughton, *The Magistrates of the Roman Republic* II (1952), p. 164. Sartre (above, n. 1), 42, still allows the possibility of 66 B.C.

already under control, Scaurus moved on directly to Judaea, where representatives of the warring factions in Jerusalem came promptly to solicit his support.[4] In view of the alliance of Aretas and Hyrcanus, the fortunes of Arabia and Judaea happened to be intermingled at this moment. It was not unreasonable for Pompey and his officers to concern themselves with the affairs of both Jews and Arabs, inasmuch as the stability of Syria, which Pompey had every intention of securing, could scarcely be dissociated from the situation farther south. After weighing up the merits of the cases presented by Aristobulus and Hyrcanus, as well as the magnitude of the bribes they offered, Scaurus resolved to put Rome on the side of Aristobulus.[5] While Pompey's officer cannot easily be absolved of the charge of cupidity, he was undoubtedly moved by the present success of Aristobulus at Jerusalem in comparison with the desperate condition of the exiled Hyrcanus. Furthermore Scaurus recognized an important fact about the Nabataeans: they were unwarlike and not likely to provide serious opposition to Roman support of the Jewish incumbent.[6]

Scaurus promptly instructed the Arab king to lead away the Nabataean army which he had brought to Jerusalem or risk becoming an enemy of the Roman people.[7] This meant, in plain language, that if he did not give up his support of Hyrcanus and return to Petra, he could expect an invasion of Pompey's army in the near future. Aretas unquestioningly obliged and left Judaea, while Scaurus, taking with him Aristobulus' bribe, returned to Damascus. In the meantime Aristobulus himself took the occasion of Aretas' retreat and Scaurus' departure to lead his own army in pursuit of the Arabs, whom he defeated in a major battle at Papyron. He is said to have killed 6,000 of the enemy.[8]

It was at this point that Pompey himself arrived in Damascus and undertook the organization of Syria as a new province of Rome. The year was 64 B.C.[9] The annexation of Syria to the

[4] Josephus, *AJ* 14.29–31. For Scaurus, see Broughton (above, n. 3), p. 163.

[5] Josephus, *AJ* 14.30–31; *BJ* 1.128.

[6] On the unwarlike disposition of the Nabataeans: Josephus, *AJ* 14.31 (in the context of Scaurus' decision); Diod. 2.54.3; Strabo 16.4.23, C 780.

[7] Josephus, *AJ* 14.32. Cf. *BJ* 1.128, ἀπειλῶν Ῥωμαίους καὶ Πομπήϊον εἰ μὴ λύσειαν τὴν πολιορκίαν.

[8] Josephus, *AJ* 14.33; *BJ* 1.130.

[9] See Broughton (above, n. 3), pp. 163–64.

Roman Empire was due in large part to the power vacuum created by the virtual disappearance of the Seleucid royal house. Petty princes and bandit chieftains were struggling with Tigranes of Armenia for possession of the heartland of the Seleucid empire, much as animals over a carcass. Once Pompey had succeeded in ejecting the Armenian king, he was obliged to devote himself to the internal aspirants for power. In the early spring of 63, he made a tour of western Syria, where he visited Apamea, Ituraea, Tripolis, and the Leja'. He had one local tyrant beheaded and extracted a substantial fortune in reparations from another.[10]

In conjunction with the creation of the new Roman province, Pompey recognized the autonomy of a group of Hellenized Syrian cities of the interior known as the Decapolis. These were among the principal settlements of so-called Coele Syria.[11] Over several centuries they continued to celebrate their debt to Pompey by dating their events according to an era beginning with the year in which he recognized their independence. By no means all the cities of the Decapolis lay within the boundaries of the province of Syria.[12] It appears as if Pompey intended to ensure the stability of the region by securing in one way or another all the governments extending from the northernmost part of the Seleucid empire to the Red Sea.

It had been a traditional part of Roman republican foreign policy, as it was to be of the policy of the early emperors, to leave the more remote or inaccessible parts of the empire in the hands of

[10] Josephus, *AJ* 14.38–40. Dionysius of Tripolis was beheaded. Ptolemaeus, the son of Mennaeus, the bandit chieftain of the Leja' who had terrorized Damascus several times, paid for his crimes with 1,000 talents.

[11] For recent discussions of problems in the history of the Decapolis, see H. Bietenhard, "Die Dekapolis von Pompeius bis Traian," *ZDPV* 79 (1963), 24–58, as well as *ANRW* II.8 (1977), 220–61; S. T. Parker, "The Decapolis Reviewed," *JBL* 94 (1975), 437–41; B. Isaac, "The Decapolis in Syria, a Neglected Inscription," *ZPE* 44 (1981), 67–74; and, for the coins, A. Spijkerman, *The Coins of the Decapolis and Provincia Arabia* (1978).

[12] Several cities were in the heart of Nabataean territory, notably Canatha, Gerasa, and Philadelphia. As its coins attest, the last-named steadfastly considered itself a part of Coele Syria under the Empire, and Ptolemy's *Geography* (5.15) confirms this assignment. Isaac (above, n. 11) shows that by the late first century A.D. the Decapolis was supervised by an equestrian official serving under the legate of Syria.

friendly client kings.[13] This arrangement permitted the Roman government to rely, where appropriate, on experienced native resources without an outlay of funds and men. At certain moments, either from the weakness of a local dynasty, from disaffection, or from a need for more direct administrative intervention, the Romans periodically annexed the territory of what had once been a client kingdom or principality. When Pompey was in Syria, he must obviously have addressed the problem of the southern frontier of the new province. If he was able to secure it to some degree by guaranteeing the allegiance and autonomy of several cities of the Decapolis, he had also to be sure of the efficiency and good will of the monarchs in Judaea and the kingdom of the Nabataeans. Scaurus' negotiations at Jerusalem in 65 could not have been altogether reassuring to Pompey, and it is not surprising to find him contemplating a reassessment of the situation after his tour of the Syrian countryside in 63.

Much as the rival factions in Judaea had appealed to Pompey's officers in earlier years, Hyrcanus and Aristobulus made impassioned representations to Pompey himself.[14] In addition the Pharisees, at odds with both sons of Alexander Jannaeus, argued for a complete overthrow of the Hasmonaean dynasty at Jerusalem.[15] Pompey decided to defer his decision concerning Judaea, while he inspected the situation among the Nabataeans.[16] It has been almost universally assumed that he resolved at this point to launch an invasion of Nabataea, either with a view to incorporating the kingdom into the Roman Empire or simply to draw off some part of its wealth.[17] And yet the Jewish historian Josephus, to whom we are indebted for the meager information

[13] See the excellent study by Mario Pani, *Rome e i Re d'Oriente da Augusto a Tiberio* (1972).

[14] Josephus, *AJ* 14.41–45.

[15] Josephus, *AJ* 14.41.

[16] Josephus, *AJ* 14.46: *ἐλθὼν δ' εἰς τὴν χώραν αὐτῶν ἔλεγεν διατάξειν ἕκαστα, ἐπειδὰν τὰ τῶν* Ναβαταίων *πρῶτον ἴδῃ.*

[17] Cf. J. Starcky, *SDB* 909 ("Il décide de marcher contre les Nabatéens, sans doute pour les incorporer à la nouvelle province"); Sartre (above, n. 1), 43 ("l'expédition de Pompée contre le Nabatène"). I joined the consensus in *JRS* 61 (1971), 223 ("Aretas III against whom Pompey intended to launch a campaign at the time of the incorporation of the province of Syria"). Sartre lays emphasis on the attractions of Nabataean wealth.

about Pompey's intentions that we have, says only that he proposed to examine the situation in Nabataea. There is no word of an invasion. Josephus does subsequently mention that Pompey was proceeding in the company of troops,[18] but that is scarcely surprising for the commander-in-chief of Roman operations in the East.

Pompey's proposed visit to the kingdom of the Nabataeans in 63 has to be considered in the context of his visit to the various cities and territories of Syria earlier the same year. The visit was designed to guarantee the stability of the region in whatever way seemed appropriate—by making arrangements with the local rulers, inflicting appropriate punishments on those who resisted, and, if necessary, taking military action. The notion that Pompey planned a direct invasion of the Nabataeans has no basis in the text of Josephus, nor in probability. As it turned out, Pompey was deflected from his inspection of Transjordan because of the unwillingness of Aristobulus to wait for a Roman decision on the crisis in Jerusalem. Angered by Aristobulus' impatience, Pompey turned aside from Transjordan and moved directly into Judaea. His army took possession of Jerusalem, and Pompey himself entrusted the care of the city to his legate Piso.[19] The result of Aristobulus' imprudent conduct was that the Romans now gave their support to Hyrcanus, just two years after Scaurus had operated against him.

This was the last phase of Pompey's personal effort to organize the East. He returned to Rome in early 62, leaving Syria in the hands of none other than Aemilius Scaurus.[20] The principal piece of unfinished business was, of course, the settlement of the Nabataean territory. Whether Pompey intended to annex the kingdom or simply to win the good will of its king is not at all clear, and it was probably not clear to Pompey himself. On the other hand, once he had decided to give up the support of Aristobulus in favor of Hyrcanus, he had in effect taken the part of the Nabataeans

[18] Josephus, *AJ* 14.48: *τὴν ἐπὶ τοὺς* Ναβαταίους *ἀναλαβὼν στρατίαν*. . . This force was, as Josephus goes on to say, substantially supplemented with troops from Syria when Pompey decided to launch a real campaign—against Aristobulus.

[19] Josephus, *AJ* 14.48–52; *BJ* 1.141–43. The legate was M. Pupius Piso Frugi Calpurnianus: Broughton (above, n. 3), p. 171.

[20] Josephus, *AJ* 14.79.

and to that extent created a unified front on both sides of the Jordan Valley. In 62, however, Scaurus undertook a military expedition against the Nabataeans, although we have no evidence for his reasons.[21] He might have alleged almost any kind of border trouble, and he would certainly have seen the Arabs as one of the few people Pompey had not already dealt with in some way. Scaurus' army did actually not do any fighting. The expedition was called off when the Nabataean king agreed to provide 300 talents of silver.[22] Although Pompey's planned inspection of Nabataea was probably part of some larger scheme for administering the Near East after the annexation of Syria, there is every reason to suspect that Scaurus moved into the kingdom of the Nabataeans principally to avail himself of the wealth of its rulers, in conjunction with their humane disinclination to fight.[23] From the diplomatic perspective in 62, Rome had nothing to fear in Nabataea and no need to invade the kingdom.

From what has been observed already, it should be obvious that Roman intervention in the affairs of the Arabs cannot be ascribed to the same motivation or a single cause. It is more important to emphasize this point when the ancient text actually makes reference to Arabs who may not actually be Nabataeans. In his summary account of Syrian history, Appian declares that the successors of Scaurus, Marcius Philippus and Lentulus Marcellinus, spent their time in repelling neighboring Arabs who were causing trouble (*τοὺς γείτονας ἐνοχλοῦντας* Ἄραβας).[24] These vexatious Arabs, with whom the second and third governors of Syria were so much occupied, have been traditionally identified with the Nabataeans. But their behavior is inconsistent with the character of the Nabataeans in this period. Furthermore, as neighbors of the Syrian province, these Arabs may be most plausibly located in the rough area of the Leja' and northern Ḥawrān, precisely in a region that was notorious for brigandage. Here was the home of marauding Arab tribes who retreated into caves and hidden

[21] Josephus, *AJ* 14.80: *Σκαύρου δ' ἐπὶ* Πέτραν *τῆς* Ἀραβίας *στρατεύσαντος*. On Antipater's provisioning of Scaurus' troops during this episode without alienating his old friend Aretas, see the judicious remarks of Sartre (above, n. 1), 44, n. 53.

[22] Josephus, *AJ* 14.81.

[23] In this vein the reflections of Sartre on Scaurus' motivation (above, n. 1).

[24] Appian, *Syr.* 51.

places and threatened not only Romans and Jews but other Arabs as well.[25] The activities of Philippus and Marcellinus should be firmly separated from operations, attempted or contemplated, in the Nabataean kingdom.

In fact, during the years of these Syrian proconsuls, from 61 to 58,[26] we have no information in any literary source about the state of the Nabataean kingdom. There is some reason to believe from numismatic evidence that Aretas III, who had shown himself an expansionist and a discreet diplomat, may have died at this time. The portrait of an aged monarch identified as Obodas is noticeably different from the portrait of the only other king of that name who is known to have minted coins.[27] Accordingly, it may be that an otherwise unattested Nabataean king, whom certain scholars have pleased to call Obodas II, should be located between 62 and 56, or some part of that interval. The depredations to which Philippus and Marcellinus were obliged to respond could conceivably have been encouraged by a change in the rule of Nabataea, especially if the new monarch was of an advanced age.

During this period of obscurity in Nabataean history, M. Aemilius Scaurus, now back in Rome, took the occasion of his aedileship in the year 58 to issue a coinage in commemoration of his not altogether reputable expedition against the Arabs in 62.[28] The Scaurus coins depict King Aretas on his knees beside a camel and offering a branch in submission to the Roman commander. So grotesque a misrepresentation of Scaurus' exploits has long

[25] See pp. 6–7 on the Leja' and surrounding parts.

[26] Broughton (above, n. 3), pp. 180 and 185 (Philippus in 61 and 60 B.C.), pp. 190 and 197 (Marcellinus in 59 and 58 B.C.).

[27] Y. Meshorer, *Nabataean Coins*, Qedem 3, Monographs of the Institute of Archaeology, Jerusalem (1975), pp. 16–20. Meshorer, p. 16, connects the inscription in Dalman, *Neue Petra-Forschungen* (1912), no. 90, with this hypothetical Obodas. But the Obodas, son of Aretas, in that text is best identified with Obodas I: see above, p. 23, n. 43. Meshorer's claim that Obodas the god (*'bdt 'lh'*) in, e.g., *CIS* II, 354 (J. Cantineau, *Le nabatéen* II [1932], p. 6, no. 4), is the alleged king from 62 B.C. is equally weak since the first Obodas is the best candidate for this deification: again see above, p. 23, n. 43. There is thus no evidence apart from the coins for the existence of an Obodas king in the late sixties. Four specimens are registered in Meshorer's catalogue, pp. 87–88. Starcky, *SDB* 909, recognizes no Obodas in succession to Aretas III.

[28] M. H. Crawford, *Roman Republican Coinage* (1974) I, p. 446, no. 422. On denarius type 1b the words *Rex Aretas* identify the kneeling figure.

been recognized for the pomposity that it was, but it is perhaps more important to consider why he would have thought it worthwhile to make a claim of conquest over the Arabs. Only a few years earlier in a grandiose and magniloquent display of inscriptions borne in triumphal procession, Pompey had reported the names of all the various nations that he had conquered in the East, and among them was Arabia.[29] This was the first time in Roman history that any commander had produced so exotic and remote a realm among his conquests. Scaurus may have seen an opportunity to capitalize on his commander's boast and to pander to a new Roman curiosity about the Arabs by depicting their king and the most conspicuous animal of the desert on a commemorative coin. Scaurus' self-advertising may have contributed to his reputation for cupidity. In 54 B.C. he was prosecuted for extortion during his praetorian governorship of Sardinia.[30]

The new glamour of an Arab conquest back at Rome and the wealth which this people was known to possess probably induced another governor of Syria, A. Gabinius, in the year 55 to undertake yet another expedition against the Nabataeans. All that can be said of this campaign is that Gabinius proceeded against "the city of the Nabataeans," which is presumably Petra, and that he was victorious in a battle.[31] If it is right to recognize a King Obodas II in the years immediately after 62, there will have been still another king on the throne, Malichus, just a few years or less before Gabinius' expedition. The change of ruler may have again suggested instability or insecurity to the outlying nations, including the Roman governor in Syria. But easy victory and easy booty would have had their attractions, whether there had been two new kings or one within a decade. That Gabinius profited from his expedition can scarcely be doubted.[32] It becomes increasingly

[29] Plut., *Pomp.* 45.2. Cf. Pliny's report (*NH* 7.97) of Pompey's dedication of the shrine of Minerva at Rome from the spoils of his wars: *terris a Maeotio ad rubrum mare subactis.*

[30] Asconius, p. 22 (Stangl): *neque satis abstinenter se gessisse existimatus est et valde arroganter.* Cicero spoke for the defense (*ad Att.* IV.15.9, 16.6; and *QF* II.15.3).

[31] Josephus, *AJ* 14.103; *BJ* 1.178.

[32] Cf. Von der Mühll in *RE* 7.1, col. 428: "Der Streifzug, den er darauf gegen die Nabatäer unternahm, sollte wohl nur Beute bringen." For the date of accession of the king who was ruling in 55, see n. 35 below.

probable that as Arabia became better known to the Romans, it offered an increasingly tempting target for avaricious generals.

And yet the beginning of Roman contact with the Nabataeans under Pompey had, it should be emphasized, a quite different objective, namely the securing of the southern flank of the new province of Syria. When Pompey returned home in 62, he must have expected that Rome would be able to depend upon client kings in both Judaea and Arabia, for without them Syria would have been constantly threatened by disturbances to the south and would have lacked any means of overland communication to the Red Sea, not to mention the overland passage to Egypt. In Egypt, too, the once formidable power of the Ptolemaic dynasty had declined into a client kingship during the days of Pompey. The great commander had, therefore, the prospect of Roman influence all the way from the mountains of the Armenian kingdom to the Roman province of Cyrenaica on the North African coast.

The new Roman awareness of the Arabs, as revealed in the inscriptions of Pompey and the coinage of Scaurus, as well as in the prosecutions of both Scaurus and Gabinius, requires no further emphasis. A passage in the letters of Cicero to his brother Quintus has sometimes been adduced as an illustration of the emerging notoriety of the Nabataean king. In February of the year 54, the Senate contemplated renewing the right to wear the *toga praetexta* which had been granted to King Antiochus I of Commagene some ten years before. In opposing the renewal, Cicero, in our older texts of the letters, appeared to be saying that it would be foolish to permit such a grant to a Commagenean when the Romans were unwilling to allow it to a man from Bostra.[33] This person from Bostra was judged to be the king of the Nabataeans, and it has been argued that the appropriate translation for *Busrenus* (or, by emendation, *Bostrensis*) would be "the man from Bostra"—evidently the king—rather than "a man from Bostra." All such discussion now seems beside the point since a careful consideration of the textual tradition, as well as the context of

[33] Cic., *QF* II.10.3: *Vos autem homines nobiles, qui †Busrenum† praetextatum non ferebatis, Commagenum feretis? Busrenum* is the reading of C (marginal reading in an edition of 1528). V (fifteenth century) has *Burrenum*, defended by Shackleton Bailey in his commentary (1980), pp. 192–93.

the letter, has established beyond reasonable doubt that the man from Bostra is a phantom. Cicero never wrote the word but was making quite a different point in his letter.[34] Since Petra was undoubtedly the seat of the Nabataean kings in his day (and is indeed said by Josephus to have been the place where the king had his palace), it is odd that anyone could have believed that Cicero would have referred to the king of the Nabataeans as the man of Bostra. Bostra became the capital of the Roman province well over a hundred years later, and the Nabataean kings seem to have established themselves there, as well as in Petra, in the decades before the annexation. But in the late republic this was history that had not yet happened.

The king who came to power in Nabataea in the years immediately before the invasion of Gabinius in 55 was the first to bear the royal name of Malichus, a name which itself means "king" in the Semitic languages.[35] Malichus had the heavy responsibility of leading his people during the turbulent days of the civil war and the triumvirate at Rome. Amid the constantly shifting fortunes of the rival commanders, it was not easy for a client of the Romans to determine to which Roman leader he should give his allegiance and for how long. A clever victor, such as Octavian after the defeat of Antony, was able to recognize that a client who had remained faithful to an enemy until the end might, in fact, be a more reliable ally, once he had transferred his allegiance to the victor, than another who had switched loyalties prematurely. Over the years of his reign, Malichus had to confront a choice between Caesar and Pompey, between Caesar's murderers and Antony, between Antony and Octavian, and throughout all this

[34] Following H. I. MacAdam in his doctoral dissertation, Sartre (above, n. 1) abandoned on p. 53 in an afterword the argument concerning a man from Bostra on p. 47. MacAdam rightly expelled Bostra from the passage; he and N. J. Munday propose the reading *Osrenum* in a paper to appear in *CP* 78 (1983).

[35] The date of the accession of Malichus (or Malchus, *mlkw* or *mnkw* in Nabataean) is unclear. It has to be inferred from the numismatic evidence for 28 regnal years. Since his successor, another Obodas (conventionally II but, for Meshorer, III) acceded to the throne in 30 B.C. or a little later, Malichus' first year should be about 58 or 57 B.C., certainly 56 at the latest: so Starcky, *SDB* 909. But Meshorer, who knows no coin later than the twenty-eighth year, opts nonetheless for an accession in 60 B.C., after a short reign of the hypothetical Obodas whom he intercalates between Aretas III and Malichus I: (above, n. 27), pp. 20–28.

period between the claimants to the throne in Jerusalem. This was a heady exercise in diplomacy which he carried out with no little success.[36]

Antipater, the experienced Jewish diplomat with a Nabataean bride, had done much in previous decades to support the cause of Hyrcanus in the quarrels of the Hasmonaeans, and he continued to provide an important link between the courts of Judaea and Arabia when Pompey and Caesar turned against each other. It was Antipater who won the support of the Nabataeans for Caesar's cause in 47, when he persuaded Malichus to send cavalry to Alexandria against Pompey.[37] Upon the defeat and death of Pompey in Egypt the Jewish and Arab contingents must have felt that they had chosen well, but they had once again to make a difficult choice.

The group that struck down Caesar on the Ides of March in 44 fled to the East after the assassination and endeavored to build up support against Antony in that quarter. One of Caesar's former generals, however, decided to invoke the aid of an outside power—the Parthians—against the tyrannicides. The introduction of Parthian armies under the Roman Labienus, surnamed Parthicus, into the Roman sphere of influence in the eastern Mediterranean created havoc and confusion.[38] The clients of Rome were now confronted with an even more complex choice. Antony was far away in Italy and working in concert with a relatively unknown young man who had emerged as the heir of Caesar. Although assuming the name of Caesar from his adoptive parent, he is distinguished by modern historians as Octavian. For a king in the Near East, this new Caesar was a nonentity. On the other hand, closer to home there were Romans endeavoring to fleece the provinces in support of the specious liberty they thought they had achieved in removing Caesar the dictator; and there were other Romans and supporters of Rome who saw the salvation of the old order in the subversion of the alien power of the Parthians.

[36] See G. W. Bowersock, *Augustus and the Greek World* (1965), p. 57; Sartre (above, n. 1), 47–48.

[37] Josephus, *AJ* 14.128, mentions forces ἐξ Ἀραβίας, but the *Bell. Alex.* 1.1 is more precise: *equites ab rege Nabataeorum Malcho*.

[38] Cassius Dio 48.26.3–5.

In the year 40 the Parthian forces reached Jerusalem. By that time old Antipater was dead, the victim of poison three years earlier, and his son Herodes, better known as Herod the Great, was about to embark upon his momentous career as king of the Jews.[39] He was serving as an official in the court of his father's protégé Hyrcanus. With the arrival of the Parthians in the city, Herod thought it prudent to withdraw. Displaying a boldness and self-interest that characterized his entire career, he turned first to Malichus, from whom he demanded not only protection but the restoration of the territories that had been conceded to the Arabs by Antipater.[40] Not surprisingly, Malichus showed no interest in this proposition, whereupon Herod turned westward, first to Alexandria and then all the way to Rome itself. By making a dramatic appearance in the Senate and thereby showing his commitment to a Roman government that had only just achieved the temporary stability of the Triumvirate, Herod was able to secure from the Romans an official designation as king in Judaea.[41]

As a result of turning Herod away because of his excessive demands, Malichus found himself alienated from the Jews. Lacking the kind of enterprise which took Herod as far as Rome to secure recognition, Malichus confronted the future in strictly Near Eastern terms. With the Parthians in Jerusalem, he chose the path of least resistance and gave his support to the invaders.[42] He was by no means the only client of Rome to have chosen this course at the time;[43] but he found himself in an exceedingly vulnerable position when Herod returned triumphant from Rome as the recognized king of Judaea and as Rome's ally. The Roman general Ventidius Bassus succeeded in driving the Parthians back to their Iranian homeland; and in the process of restoring Roman authority in the region, he imposed a large fine on Malichus for his apparent disaffection from the Roman cause.[44] Since the Roman treasury was

[39] For the career of Herod, A. Schalit, *König Herodes: Der Mann und sein Werk* (1969), is indispensable.

[40] Josephus, *AJ* 14.370; *BJ* 1.246–47.

[41] Josephus, *AJ* 14.374–76; *BJ* 1.277–79 (through Egypt to Rome). On Roman recognition of his kingship, *AJ* 14.389; *BJ* 1.285.

[42] Cassius Dio 48.41.5.

[43] Sartre (above, n. 1), 47, fairly compares kings such as Antiochus of Commagene and Ptolemaeus of Chalcis, who also supported Labienus.

[44] Cassius Dio 48.41.5.

seriously depleted at this time of turmoil, it certainly cannot have escaped Ventidius that the Nabataeans were wealthy. He would have had good reason to turn the apparent treachery of Malichus to the financial advantage of the Romans.

It was Antony who acquired the eastern part of Rome's empire as his portion under the terms of the triumviral settlement. Arrived in the East, he was recognized by the old friends of Rome as the new patron to whom they had to give their allegiance. Most of those who cared about preserving such liberty as they had under Roman influence did so. It was at this time, however, that Antony came under the spell of the gifted and powerful beauty who was queen of Egypt. After decades of weakness in the Ptolemaic dynasty that seemed to mirror what had happened to the Seleucids, Cleopatra was a late and memorable reminder of what the Ptolemies once had been. She was not satisfied merely with Antony's infatuation: she fully intended to enlarge her dominions as queen and ultimately, through Antony, to lay claim to the government at Rome itself. Or so it seemed to the partisans of Octavian.[45] In any event, she made substantial requests for territory.

At Antony's side in Syria, she demanded no less than the two kingdoms of Judaea and Arabia.[46] At this the infatuated commander balked, and he protested that it would be rank injustice for him to do away with two kings, Herod and Malichus, about whom he had no reason to complain.[47] Antony did, however, oblige Cleopatra by executing Lysanias, the successor of the notorious Ptolemaeus, son of Mennaeus, in the brigand-infested territory of Ituraea, on the evidently specious charge that he had favored the Parthians.[48] (This is a charge that could have been levelled against a good many others, including Malichus himself.) In the Near East, Cleopatra also acquired from Antony extensive portions of Phoenicia, as well as the balsam groves of Jericho,

[45] See Horace's exultant ode I.37 (*Nunc est bibendum*) on the death of Cleopatra, esp. ll. 6–8: *dum Capitolio / regina dementis ruinas funus et imperio parabat.*

[46] Josephus, *AJ* 15.92: ᾔτει δὲ παρ᾽ Ἀντωνίου τήν τε Ἰουδαίαν καὶ τὴν τῶν Ἀράβων ἀξιοῦσα τοὺς βασιλεύοντας αὐτῶν ἀφελέσθαι. Cf. *BJ* 1.360: ἔτι δὲ ἐκτείνουσα τὴν πλεονεξίαν ἐπὶ Ἰουδαίους καὶ Ἄραβας ὑπειργάζετο τοὺς ἑκατέρων βασιλεῖς Ἡρώδην καὶ Μάλχον ἀναιρεθῆναι.

[47] Josephus, *BJ* 1.361: Ἀντώνιος τὸ κτεῖσθαι μὲν ἄνδρας ἀγαθοὺς καὶ βασιλεῖς τηλικούτους ἀνόσιον ἡγήσατο.

[48] Josephus, *AJ* 15.92.

which had formerly been among the treasured possessions of Herod, who was now required to rent them back from the new owner.[49]

It is also recorded that Antony turned over part of Arabia to Cleopatra,[50] but it is unfortunately by no means clear which part. Plutarch, writing over a hundred years later in his biography of Antony, includes among the gifts to Cleopatra the territory of Nabataean Arabia which inclines toward the outer sea (πρὸς τὴν ἐκτὸς θάλασσαν).[51] Since the inner sea in antiquity was the Mediterranean, the Nabataean possessions in the Negev are obviously not in question. It may be that the reference here is to the Dead Sea and the lucrative production of asphalt, which had long played a role in the Nabataeans' economic success. But it seems peculiar to describe a sea inside the Nabataean kingdom as the outer sea. The most plausible interpretation of Plutarch's phrase is the Gulf of ʿAqaba and its extension into the Red Sea, indicating a gift of the Nabataean settlement in the Ḥejāz in the northwest Arabian peninsula. This was precisely the region through which Nabataean commerce passed on its way to Petra. It included, in addition, coastal towns from which the Nabataeans had been able to launch their attacks on Egyptian ships in the second century.[52] For the queen of Egypt control of the opposite coast along the Red Sea and the Gulf of ʿAqaba would have been highly desirable. Hence this was probably the territory that Antony bestowed upon her.

In the late thirties Herod had to suffer the ignominy not only of renting his own former property around Jericho but also of serving as the guarantor of payments that were expected from the Arab king.[53] The arrangement was calculated to sow dissension between the Jewish and Arab rulers. Cleopatra finally compelled Antony to order Herod to launch a campaign against Malichus

[49] Josephus, *AJ* 15.96; *BJ* 1.361–62.

[50] Josephus, *AJ* 15.96: τῆς τε Ἀραβίας τὰ δοθέντα. Cf. Cassius Dio 49.32.5 on gifts to Cleopatra's children. Dio says that parts of the kingdom of Malchus and some Ituraean territory were presented to her offspring. The reference implies tracts in the Ḥawrān and Leja'.

[51] Plut., *Ant.* 36.2.

[52] See above, pp. 20–21.

[53] Josephus, *AJ* 15.107.

because of a default in his payments.[54] Josephus alleges that she was hoping thereby to have both kings destroyed in mutual conflict.[55] Since she had been unable to persuade Antony to eliminate them years before, she now excogitated this subtle means of putting them in opposition to one another. Her ultimate aim was undoubtedly the same as it had been before—the Ptolemaic annexation of both Judaea and Arabia. But the fortunes of Antony were soon to be determined at the battle of Actium in September of 31. Only a year after that, Cleopatra would take the asp to her bosom, and the great Egyptian kingdom of the Ptolemies would fall in its entirety to the first emperor of Rome. The kingdoms of Judaea and Arabia were destined to survive.

The war which Antony forced Herod to wage against Malichus early in the year of Actium was a desultory affair. Herod first invaded the Ḥawrān. It is by no means clear why he chose to enter the kingdom at this point, especially since the territory with its many hiding places was particularly difficult for any aggressive action. Because of earlier operations of his own in the adjacent territory of Galilee, it is possible that Herod felt more at home in this kind of terrain and had some knowledge of the ways of tribes in the area. The Jews won the first battle, which took place at Diospolis,[56] and then moved on to confront a substantial army of Arabs at Canatha,[57] the modern Qanawāt on the western slope of the Jebel Drūz. Here Cleopatra's representative in the region, a certain Athenion, fought on the side of the Arabs because of his own personal differences with Herod.[58] He succeeded in leading the Arab forces to victory. Stunning Arab success, combined with a major earthquake in Judaea, seriously weakened the authority of Herod in his own kingdom. In despair of prosecuting the war against the Arabs further, Herod finally sent ambassadors to Malichus to appeal for peace.

[54] Josephus, *AJ* 15.111; *BJ* 1.365.

[55] Josephus, *AJ* 15.110: *ἠξίου γὰρ ἡ* Κλεοπάτρα *ταῦτα λυσιτελεῖν αὐτῇ τὸν ἕτερον ὑπὸ θατέρου κακῶς πάσχειν ἡγουμένη*. The plan is given explicitly in *BJ* 1.365: *ἵν' ἢ κρατήσαντος* 'Αραβίας *ἢ κρατηθέντος* 'Ιουδαίας *γένηται δεσπότις καὶ θατέρῳ τῶν δυναστῶν καταλύσῃ τὸν ἕτερον*.

[56] Josephus, *AJ* 15.111; *BJ* 1.366.

[57] Josephus, *AJ* 15.112; *BJ* 1.366.

[58] Josephus, *AJ* 15.115–16; *BJ* 1.367–68.

The Arab king, however, savoring his recent good fortune, put the Jewish envoys to death and contemplated a conquest of Judaea.[59] Herod was accordingly obliged to reopen hostilities, and this time he chose to cross the Jordan Valley considerably farther south than in the previous expedition. He engaged an Arab force under the leadership of a certain Nabataean general Elthemos (*'lṭmw*, a good Nabataean name) in the vicinity of Philadelphia, the modern ʿAmmān.[60] In this battle the Nabataeans suffered a major defeat, and the conquered Arabs appealed to Herod to become their patron.[61] But nothing much seems to have come of this Jewish triumph in Transjordan. The outcome of the great struggle between Antony and Octavian at Actium was about to provide the occasion for a new dispensation in the Near East at the hands of the victorious Octavian.

As a partisan of Antony, Herod was understandably fearful that Octavian might depose him in favor of his long-time rival Hyrcanus. He therefore had this now aged friend of his father summarily put to death.[62] Hyrcanus had attempted to seek exile in the court at Petra, and Malichus had in fact agreed to receive him.[63] As another partisan of Antony, Malichus himself had reason to be concerned about the outcome at Actium. He succeeded, however, in securing the good will of Octavian by a master stroke. He sent forces to burn the ships which Cleopatra had managed to salvage from the debacle at Actium and had beached in the vicinity of Suez.[64] By contrast, the Jewish king used direct personal intervention, which had regularly been his most successful means of forging a career. Herod won the support of the victor of Actium by alleging that the loyalty he showed to Antony until the end was proof of the steadfast loyalty he was now prepared to offer Octavian.[65]

59 Josephus, *AJ* 15.124; *BJ* 1.371.
60 Josephus, *AJ* 15.147–52; *BJ* 1.380–81. For *'lṭmw*, see Cantineau (above, n. 27), p. 63.
61 Josephus, *AJ* 15.159 (προστάτης τοῦ ἔθνους).
62 Josephus, *AJ* 15.164; *BJ* 1.433.
63 Josephus, *AJ* 15.172.
64 Plut., *Ant.* 69.3. Cassius Dio 51.7.1 says that Q. Didius, governing Syria, incited the Arabs to burn the ships.
65 Josephus, *AJ* 15.193. Cf. *BJ* 1.390.

Cleopatra's dream of extending Ptolemaic sovereignty across the Near East, encompassing both Judaea and Arabia, was obliterated along with her Roman lover. Her own dramatic suicide finally left the Egyptian kingdom in a state of chaos not unlike that of Seleucid Syria in the sixties. The moment had come for Roman annexation of Egypt. This meant that from the year 30 B.C. the kingdoms of Judaea and Arabia, on the two sides of the Jordan Valley, confronted Roman legates to the north (in the province of Syria) and Roman prefects around the corner to the southwest (in the new province of Egypt). It was only a matter of time before the Roman government would feel obliged to close the gap in the circuit of provinces along the southern and eastern shores of the Mediterranean.

IV

THE EARLY PRINCIPATE

In a little more than four decades the first *princeps*, Caesar Augustus, laid the foundations of the Roman Empire. Despite his early claims to a restoration of the republic, he effectively organized the administration of the dominions of Rome so as to ensure a monopoly of power for himself and his designated successors. The momentous transformation of Roman government at this point touched every part of the Mediterranean world and many regions beyond. The Near East, and in particular the kingdoms of Judaea and Arabia, were profoundly affected by the new dispensation. It was not that Augustus knew from the start what he wanted to do with these regions. In this, as in other affairs, he proceeded by responding to crises and opportunities in the best interests of his grander design of control. By the time of his death in A.D. 14, Judaea was no longer a client kingdom but a province of the Roman Empire, under the administration of a Roman procurator, and Arabia entered upon a golden age of Nabataean civilization under the leadership of the long-lived monarch Aretas IV, "the lover of his people."[1]

This turn of events, by which the annexation of Judaea began to close the gap at the southeast corner of the Mediterranean while the resplendent rule of Aretas gave stability to the adjacent realm of the Nabataeans, could not have been foreseen by the first *princeps* in 27 B.C., when he received from the senate the name Augustus. At that time he had already accepted the loyalty of the energetic and ambitious Idumaean king of the Jews, Herod, and he had every reason to expect a strong and pro-Roman government in Herod's kingdom.[2] In Arabia, by contrast, Malichus' gesture of support in destroying Cleopatra's ships had borne no

[1] On coins and inscriptions the name of Aretas IV is often followed by the words *rḥm ʿmh:* cf. Y. Meshorer, *Nabataean Coins*, Qedem 3, Monographs of the Institute of Archaeology, Jerusalem (1975), pp. 43 ff.

[2] On the pro-Roman and Hellenic pretensions of Herod the Great, see, above all, A. Schalit, *König Herodes: Der Mann und sein Werk* (1969).

fruit, since he himself appears to have died not long after Cleopatra. His successor was a weak ruler with the royal name of Obodas, identified in modern works as Obodas II or Obodas III (according to whether a king of this name is recognized for the late sixties B.C.).[3] In 27 it seemed far more likely that the kingdom of the Jews would endure, whereas that of the Arabs might not. Not even Augustus could have anticipated the complete reversal in the balance of power on the two sides of the Jordan that was to take place by the conclusion of his long reign.

In the opening phase of his government, Augustus showed considerable interest in imperial expansion. The poets flattered him by intimations of extensive conquest, and military expeditions at the most distant frontiers bore witness to the emperor's aims.[4] The armies of Rome were advancing into the fastnesses of northwest Spain and along the Rhine and Danube. In the newly acquired province of Egypt legionaries were marching southward against Ethiopians. In this context of expansionism, it is not surprising that Augustus should also have considered the opportunities in Arabia. Even before he had instructed the prefect of Egypt to move, in the late twenties, against Ethiopia, he had ordered Aelius Gallus, his first prefect, to launch an expedition into the Arabian peninsula. This bold enterprise took place in about 26 B.C., with the auxiliary support of about 1,000 Nabataeans and 500 Jews.[5]

The target of the expedition was not the kingdom of the Nabataeans (which the Romans came to designate simply Arabia), but the kingdom of the Sabaeans in the southwest corner of the Arabian peninsula, known as Arabia Felix. The Sabaeans had grown rich with the proceeds of commerce in perfume and spices, homegrown and from the East. It had been from these people that the precious merchandise was passed on to the Nabataeans in its overland progress to the Mediterranean. With the help of the

[3] See above p. 34. Also Meshorer (above, n. 1), p. 28.

[4] Cf. H. D. Meyer, *Die Aussenpolitik des Augustus und die augusteische Dichtung* (1961), with the review by P. A. Brunt, *JRS* 53 (1963), 170–76.

[5] On this expedition, Dihle, *Umstrittene Daten* (1965), pp. 80–84, and S. Jameson, *JRS* 58 (1968), 71–84. Jameson proposes that the operation lasted from spring or summer 26 until autumn 25.

monsoons, some of the traffic in perfume and spices was already going directly from India across the Red Sea to ports on the east coast of Egypt,[6] although the Nabataeans were still enjoying a considerable success in their overland routes. Clearly Augustus intended in the middle twenties to win some kind of share in the operations of the Sabaeans on whom both the Egyptian and the Nabataean traffic depended.

The geographer Strabo was a personal friend of the leader of the Arabian expedition, Aelius Gallus, and took care to leave a relatively detailed account of it. In Strabo's view Augustus expected the expedition to be advantageous to the Romans, either by compelling the affluent Sabaeans to become Rome's allies or by conquering their territory outright.[7] But Gallus' expedition turned out to be a terrible disaster; and Strabo, unwilling to pin the blame upon his friend and patron, found in the Nabataean minister of Obodas, Syllaeus, a suitable scapegoat.[8] Syllaeus had served as a native guide for the Roman force, which he had led over a hard route to the outskirts of the capital of the Sabaeans. Strabo blames him not only for choosing a route which debilitated the Roman army but even for bringing the troops across from Egypt to the coastal port of Leuke Kome in the Ḥejāz.[9] Yet it would certainly have been foolish, despite Strabo's protestations, to have imported a Roman army into Petra and then to march overland through the wilderness of the Ḥismā into the inner Ḥejāz. Furthermore, there could have been no route to the capital of the Sabaeans which would have passed through country familiar or tolerable to Roman soldiers. Later events in Nabataean history show that Syllaeus was unscrupulously ambitious and cruel. Strabo must have known this and found it convenient to see in

[6] On the discovery of the monsoons, associated with a certain Hippalus, see *Periplus of the Red Sea* 57. Cf. Pliny, *NH* 6.84, for which A. Dihle (above, n. 5), p. 27, n. 24. The matter is also reviewed by M. Raschke, *ANRW* II.9.2 (1978), 660–63. See also p. 21, n. 33 above. For the difficulty of the monsoon voyage to and from India, see L. Casson, *TAPA* 110 (1980), 31–35.

[7] Strabo 16.4.22, C 780: *ἢ γὰρ φίλοις ἤλπιζε πλουσίοις χρήσεσθαι ἢ ἐχθρῶν κρατήσειν πλουσίων.*

[8] Strabo 16.4.24, C 782: *ὁ δ' αἴτιος τούτων ὁ Συλλαῖος*. . .

[9] Strabo 16.4.23–24, C 781. On Gallus' preparations for the expedition as possibly reflected in *Pap. Oxy.* 2820, cf. N. Lewis, *GRBS* 16 (1975), 295–303.

this character a willful saboteur in the army of Aelius Gallus. But, for all that, there is nothing in what happened to suggest that Syllaeus actually played such a role.[10]

On the contrary, when the expedition departed into the interior from Leuke Kome, Gallus and his men spent several days as guests of a relative of the Nabataean king. This person bore the royal name of Aretas and seems to have resided somewhere in the territory between Madā'in Ṣāliḥ and Medīna.[11] The area was destined to become an important part of the Nabataean kingdom in the decades ahead, and it must have served the Nabataean merchants as a base in the transfer of goods brought in by the Sabaeans. Syllaeus, the minister of Obodas, could have done no better for the troops in his charge than to have offered them, in the best Arab fashion, the hospitality of a member of the king's family. Indeed, it was for contacts like that that the Romans had taken on a Nabataean guide.

As the Roman expedition neared the Sabaean city of Mārib, they established a garrison in the area known as the Jawf of the Yemen at a place called Athloula.[12] Even as late as the early third century A.D., this garrison represented the southernmost penetration of Roman power in the East. A fragmentary inscription in both Greek and Latin from the site of Athloula seems to be the first concrete evidence of the Roman presence there.[13]

From Athloula the forces of Gallus pressed on to the city of Mārib in the hope of taking it by siege. Their hope was soon frustrated by a shortage of water, which compelled them to raise the siege and return whence they had come.[14] Once back in the Ḥejāz,

[10] The assessment here of Syllaeus' role in Gallus' expedition is different from that in G. W. Bowersock, *JRS* 61 (1971), 227. For another Roman failure blamed on Arab treachery, cf. Plut., *Crassus* 21–22 (where Ziegler's Teubner text persuasively reads the name of Abgar for Ariamnes).

[11] Strabo 16.4.24, C 781: *εἰς τὴν* Ἀρέτα *γῆν συγγενοῦς τῷ* Ὀβόδᾳ. A. F. L. Beeston, *BSOAS* 43 (1980), 453–58, argues from the Adulis throne inscription copied by Cosmas Indicopleustes that Gallus' expedition inspired the Hellenized Yaṣduq'il to repeat it—successfully under Augustus. *Non liquet.*

[12] Strabo 16.4.24, C 782, names the place Ἄθρουλα, whereas Cassius Dio 53.29.8 gives Ἄθλουλα. The latter appears to be correct if the identification of this site with ancient YṮL is to be accepted. See Appendix I.

[13] Paolo Costa, *Proc. Seminar for Arabian Studies* 7 (1977), 69–72. See Appendix I on this inscription and its interpretation.

[14] Strabo 16.4.24, C 782, where the name of the city seems to be Marisaba (perhaps

which was part of the territory of the Nabataean king, the Roman forces reached the sea at a town that Strabo calls Egra.[15] This may have been, in fact, the port for a better known city in the interior, also called Egra (or Hegra) in antiquity and known as Madā'in Ṣāliḥ today. From the coast the Romans took ship for the return voyage to Egypt. The whole business was ignominious for the invaders. As for the Arabs, both Sabaean and Nabataean, it is unlikely that they did not feel some sense of relief, if not actual pleasure. If any Arab had shared Gallus' regret over the expedition, it was—in spite of what Strabo alleges—probably Syllaeus, who would have expected prominent advancement from the Romans as a direct result of any success in the Arabian peninsula. It had been clearly established in the Near East during the late decades of the republic that anyone who wished promotion at home could be assured of it by service to the Romans abroad. From the incontestable fact that Augustus took no steps against the Nabataeans after the failure of Gallus' expedition, it would be reasonable to infer that they were not held accountable for it. Augustus simply turned his attention to another area in which a prefect of Egypt could launch a Roman invasion, namely Ethiopia.[16]

As far as the Nabataeans were concerned, their principal problem lay with the growing power of Herod in the kingdom of Judaea to the west. In the early years of his rule under the triumvirs, Herod had appreciated the crucial importance of the rough country, infested with brigands, at the northern edges of the Nabataean territories. This was the Jebel Drūz and the surrounding parts, which had been the portion of Lysanias before he

---

Mariaba). On the site of the siege, cf. J. Pirenne, *Le royaume sud-arabe de Qatabān et sa datation* (1961), pp. 110 ff. Also H. von Wissmann, *ANRW* II.9.1 (1978), 396–98.

[15] Strabo 16.4.24, C 782. Despite the failure of the assault on Mārib Augustus was later able to boast that his troops had gone so far: *Res Gestae* 26.5, *in Arabiam usque in fines Sabaeorum pro[cess]it exercitus ad oppidum Mariba.* Among the marble blocks at Aphrodisias in Caria which record the peoples conquered by Rome is one, found in the theater where it was evidently taken for reuse from the north portico of the Sebasteion, with the inscription ["E]*θνους* [—]*βων*: J. Reynolds, *ZPE* 43 (1981), 326–27, no. 21. Although the date of this text could be late first or early second century, Reynolds believes all the conquests commemorated in the series to be Augustan. She is inclined to accept the suggestion of M. Speidel to read ['Α*ρά*]*βων* here. She had originally thought of Suebi or Perrhaebi. (Information from Kenan Erim.)

[16] On the Ethiopian war of C. Petronius, see S. Jameson, *JRS* 58 (1968), 71–84.

had been removed to make possible one of Antony's gifts to Cleopatra. After the defeat of Antony, the victor of Actium had turned over the newly released territories to Lysanias' son, Zenodorus. And Zenodorus had put them up for sale.[17] It appears that the Nabataeans, who were at home in these regions and understood the strategic importance of controlling them, paid Zenodorus' price but neglected to secure official recognition of their possession from Rome. Herod, who appreciated the importance of this territory for the security of the northeast corner of Judaea, managed to gain possession of it himself as a gift from Augustus.[18] When Zenodorus died in 20, Augustus enlarged Herod's possessions to include the whole of the Golan.[19] This created a substantial Jewish buffer zone between Syria and Nabataean Arabia and must have constituted a singular embarrassment for the court of Obodas.

If Obodas was too ineffectual to do anything about all this, his minister Syllaeus was not. He understood the sources of power in the Roman Near East. Demonstrated loyalty in the Roman cause was one way to get it, but dynastic marriage was another. After all, Herod himself was the offspring of the union of a Nabataean noblewoman with the Hasmonaean Antipater. Syllaeus proposed nothing less than marriage to the sister of Herod, the notorious Salome.[20] Syllaeus was by all accounts handsome and personable, and Salome herself was keen on the marriage. But Herod, who must have appreciated the political implications of the union, refused Syllaeus' proposal and ultimately terminated the romance between Arab and Jew by marrying off his sister to a nonentity with the name of Alexas.[21]

During the course of these amorous transactions, Syllaeus was undermining the authority of Herod in his newly acquired territories along the northern frontier of the Nabataean kingdom. In 12 B.C., when Herod had been away currying favor in Rome, the

[17] Josephus, *AJ* 15.351–52: Auranitis went for 500 talents.

[18] Josephus, *AJ* 15.343.

[19] Josephus, *AJ* 15.360.

[20] Josephus, *AJ* 16.224. Notorious as she was (*RE* I.A.2, col. 1995, signals her "diabolical" influence), she must not be confused with the lady who danced.

[21] Josephus, *AJ* 17.10; cf. *BJ* 1.566. On Syllaeus' charm, Josephus, *AJ* 16.220: δεινὸς ἀνὴρ καὶ τὴν ἡλικίαν νέος ἔτι καὶ καλός.

natives of the Leja' came out of the caves in which they lived to raise a rebellion against the Jewish king. Officers of the king managed to put down the revolt. Some forty leaders escaped and found refuge with the Nabataeans.[22] Syllaeus saw to their warm reception and gave them a base from which they could make devastating incursions into Judaea. His deliberate encouragement of the experienced bandits of the Leja' in their attacks against Herod moved the king again to call for the intervention of Roman authorities. He made a formal complaint before the governor of Syria, C. Sentius Saturninus, in 9 B.C., and Saturninus found in Herod's favor.[23] Syllaeus, almost as adept as Herod at exploiting the Romans, determined to go himself to Rome and to Augustus, while Herod launched a punitive expedition into Nabataean country in order to take possession of the base in which the rebel chieftains had established themselves. A conflict between Nabataeans and Jews ensued, in which a Nabataean captain, Nakebos (*nqybw*), and some of his force were destroyed.[24]

When Syllaeus reached Rome, he was able to make an emotional plea on behalf of his people. He spoke of the deaths of some 2,500 Nabataeans during Herod's invasion, which, it seems, had been undertaken without Roman approval.[25] In this instance Syllaeus surpassed Herod at his own game. And this, in turn, would have encouraged him in any ambition he may have had to become the next king of the Nabataeans.

In fact, it happened that during Syllaeus' stay in Rome over the winter of 9/8 B.C., Obodas died. According to Josephus, the power passed to a certain Aeneas, who changed his name, upon proclaiming himself king, to Aretas.[26] Whatever Nabataean name is

[22] Josephus, *AJ* 16.130, 274–75.

[23] Josephus, *AJ* 16.276–81. A. Negev, *ANRW* II.8 (1977), 566, refers to "Sarturninus [*sic*] and Volumnius, the procurators of Syria." Saturninus was the governor (*legatus*) and Volumnius, also mentioned by Josephus, his procurator. Cf. E. Schürer, *A History of the Jewish People*, rev. Millar and Vermes (1973), p. 257.

[24] Josephus, *AJ* 16.284. For the Nabataean name, cf. J. Cantineau, *Le nabatéen* II (1932), p. 122.

[25] Josephus, *AJ* 16.288. See the two bilingual inscriptions left by Syllaeus on his way to Rome: one, at Miletus, to Dushara *'l ḥyy ʿbdt*, "for the life of Obodas," Cantineau (above, n. 24), p. 46; and the other at Delos, *Inscriptions de Délos* 2315, as revised by J. T. Milik and J. Starcky (cf. P. Bruneau, *Recherches sur les cultes de Délos* [1970], p. 244). For the coinage of Syllaeus, see Meshorer (above, n. 1), pp. 36–40.

[26] Josephus, *AJ* 16.294. The Nabataean name of Aeneas may have been *hn'w* (or

represented by Aeneas in Josephus' Greek, it seems clear that the new Aretas was not an immediate member of the royal family. Aeneas was certainly not a dynastic name among the Nabataeans. On the other hand, a recent Nabataean inscription suggests that this Aretas was related in some way to the royal house through Obodas' predecessor Malichus.[27] The dismay of Syllaeus at the succession in the Nabataean kingdom, as well as the anxiety of the new king, can be seen from the attempt which Aretas made to undermine Syllaeus' prestige with Augustus through a letter accusing Obodas' former minister of various crimes.[28] Not least of these was the death of Obodas himself, whom Syllaeus, according to Aretas, had poisoned. Augustus reacted angrily to the accession of Aretas, not only because of his newly found admiration for Syllaeus, but also because Aretas had not sought permission from Rome to rule.[29]

Ironically it was the Jewish advocate of Herod before Augustus, Nicolaus of Damascus, who was ultimately responsible for Augustus' decision to confirm Aretas on his throne. By diminishing the credibility of Syllaeus' testimony before the emperor, Nicolaus brought him over again to the side of Herod.[30] Augustus came to recognize that Aretas' characterization of Syllaeus was not so wide of the mark. On the other hand, he was still annoyed with the new king for failing to solicit Roman approval. He even thought seriously of turning over the entire kingdom of Arabia to Herod. Such a move would have doubled the size of Herod's kingdom and had the advantage of uniting the two sides of the Jordan Valley, which had for so long been rivals of one another. But

---

hny'w), for which Greek equivalents of Ἀνεος and Ἀναιος are attested: cf. Cantineau (above, n. 24), p. 87. But on this interpretation the initial diphthong in the name Aeneas is not easy to explain.

[27] N. Khairy, *PEQ* 113 (1981), 19–26: a dedicatory text from the Wādī Mūsā "with the largest number of names of the Nabataean royal family in Aretas IV's reign ever to be found in one single Nabataean inscription" (p. 21). The name of Malichus I (*mnkw*) appears in the first line. On Aretas and Malichus, J. Starcky, *Hommages à André Dupont-Sommer* (1971), p. 157.

[28] Josephus, *AJ* 16.296.

[29] Josephus, *AJ* 16.295: Augustus was angry τῷ μὴ τὸν Ἀρέταν ἐπιστείλαντα πρότερον αὐτῷ βασιλεύειν.

[30] Josephus, *AJ* 16.335–55.

Augustus was compelled to acknowledge that internal turmoil in the court of Herod made it unwise to add so substantial a responsibility to those which Herod already had. And so, reluctantly and with no great enthusiasm for the king himself, Augustus confirmed Aretas, known to modern historians as the fourth king of that name, in his rule over the Nabataeans.[31]

In anger and bitter disappointment Syllaeus returned to Petra and apparently engaged in a campaign of political assassinations. He is said to have eliminated a number of Nabataean nobles and even to have attempted the assassination of Herod himself.[32] As a result of further complaints lodged with Saturninus, who was still the governor of Syria, Syllaeus returned to Rome in an attempt to win back the favor of Augustus. This was in 6 B.C., and there is no record of the impression which Syllaeus made upon Augustus the second time. All we know is that at some stage, presumably not too much later, Syllaeus was executed by decapitation on the orders of the Roman emperor.[33] Strabo was pleased to believe that this was proper retribution for the miscarriage of the campaign of Aelius Gallus decades before.[34] But it seems evident that the more recent events in Arabia were the cause of Syllaeus' disgrace. During his first journey to Rome, Syllaeus had reason to think himself a figure of international importance. He took care to set up two inscriptions, each in both Nabataean and Greek, to the principal deity of the Nabataeans, Dushara (Dousares). The inscriptions were to invoke the deity's aid in support of the good health of Obodas the king. Syllaeus is described in these texts as the king's brother, confirming Strabo's statement that the principal ministers of the king were known as his brothers.[35]

When Herod died shortly thereafter, in the spring of 4 B.C., Augustus must have been confronted with a major dilemma in his

[31] Josephus, *AJ* 16.355.
[32] Josephus, *AJ* 17.54–55.
[33] Josephus, *AJ* 17.52–57; *BJ* 1.374–77. For the death of Syllaeus, Strabo 16.4.24, C 782 (*ἀποτμηθεὶς τὴν κεφαλήν*).
[34] Strabo, ibid.
[35] See the references in n. 25 above for the two inscriptions. On the use of brother (*'ḥ* or *ἀδελφός*), cf. Strabo 16.4.21, C 779: *ἔχει δ' ὁ βασιλεὺς ἐπίτροπον τῶν ἑταίρων τινὰ καλούμενον ἀδελφόν*. On the Miletus text of Syllaeus: *'ḥ mlk'* and *ἀδελφὸς βασιλ[έως]*.

Near Eastern policy. He was discontent with the situation under Aretas in the Nabataean kingdom, and he had no basis for confidence in the group of relatives to whom Herod had bequeathed the various parts of his kingdom. A multiplicity of Herodian tetrarchs was unlikely to ensure stability in Judaea, and the current Nabataean king had no particular reason to be grateful to Augustus. The literary sources are lamentably scarce for this crucial period after 4 B.C. The narrative history of Cassius Dio does not survive at this point, except in inadequate epitomes. Josephus' writings are no longer based on the detailed narrative of Nicolaus of Damascus and are therefore less well informed about relations between the Jews and Arabs. But there is one source which may be invoked to provide some illumination on this dark epoch.

The geographer Strabo stated unambiguously, in a passage that has been curiously neglected, that in his day (*νῦν δέ*) the Nabataeans, like the Syrians, were subjects of the Romans.[36] He makes this point in connection with the observation that before the Nabataeans were brought under Roman rule, they had been given to making incursions into Syrian territory. The words of Strabo can mean only one thing: the territory of the Nabataeans was, at the time he was writing, a province of the Roman Empire. Yet it is perfectly well known that Aretas IV ruled for some forty-nine years with great success and that the kingdom of the Nabataeans did not become a province of Rome until the age of Trajan. For all that, Strabo ought to have known what he was saying, and his remarks should perhaps be considered in the light of other possibilities than simple egregious error. It is worth asking whether the kingdom of Aretas was actually annexed for a brief interval and returned subsequently as a client state of Rome. Cases of kingdoms annexed and then returned are by no means unexampled in Roman imperial history.[37]

[36] Strabo 16.4.21, C 779: *νῦν δὲ κἀκεῖνοι* [i.e., Ναβαταῖοι] *Ῥωμαίοις εἰσὶν ὑπήκοοι καὶ Σύροι*. The demonstrative pronoun identifies the Nabataeans as distinct from the Sabaeans (also mentioned in the previous sentence) and introduces an account of Nabataean Petra.

[37] The most notable case is Commagene (annexed in A.D. 18, returned to a king in 37, annexed again soon afterward, returned to a king by Claudius, and annexed finally in 72). See Tacitus, *Ann.* 2.56; Cassius Dio 59.8.2 and 60.8.1; Suetonius, *Vesp.* 8; Josephus, *BJ* 7.7.1–3.

Strabo is known to have been at work on his *Geography* as late as 3/2 B.C., after which he seems to have abandoned the enterprise until the reign of Tiberius.[38] At that late stage of his life, he took the trouble to make a certain number of insertions about contemporary events, but seems not otherwise to have altered what he had written previously. In short, apart from the evidently Tiberian insertions, what stands in the *Geography* represents the state of affairs frozen in 3/2 B.C. It is certain that the reference to the Nabataeans as subjects of the Romans cannot be one of Strabo's Tiberian additions, since the coinage of Aretas establishes beyond doubt his kingship throughout the reign of Tiberius.[39] We have then to consider the possibility that in about 3 B.C. a province of Arabia might have been in existence. This is precisely the problematic time after the death of Herod. Josephus leaves us in no doubt that Augustus finally decided to accept the testament of Herod and recognize his son and brothers as the administrators of the various segments of Herod's kingdom. That was not an arrangement in which Augustus could have had great confidence, and so he would have had good reason to consider annexing the eastern side of the Jordan to have control over one part, at least, of the southeastern segment of the Mediterranean. His dislike of Aretas would have been encouragement to take the step of annexation.

Such an explanation of Strabo's explicit and by no means oblique statement about the Nabataeans' subjection finds striking confirmation in the abundant coinage of Aretas himself. This king, who reigned from 8 B.C. to A.D. 40, was the most prolific minter of Nabataean coins in the kingdom's history. The standard work on Nabataean coinage declares that eight of every ten known Nabataean coins are of Aretas IV.[40] On the extant coinage, specimens from virtually every regnal year of Aretas IV are known, with one notable exception. There are no known coins advertising Aretas as king in 3, 2, and 1 B.C. The three-year gap

[38] J. G. C. Anderson, *Anat. Studies Pres. to Ramsay* (1923), pp. 1–13, and G. W. Bowersock, *Augustus and the Greek World* (1965), p. 134. H. I. MacAdam has acutely observed that in a Tiberian addition recording the annexation of Commagene, Strabo (16.2.3, C 749) wrote νῦν δέ just as in the passage about the Nabataeans.

[39] See Meshorer (above, n. 1), pp. 103–4. Only the year A.D. 17 is unrepresented.

[40] Ibid., p. 41.

in the coinage of Aretas has been noticed but not interpreted.[41] It might have no significance at all, were it not for the very large number of coins surviving from the reign of this king and the extraordinarily thorough representation of all other years of his reign. The coinage may therefore be adduced as evidence for an interruption in the rule of Aretas during the years 3 to 1 B.C.

There is still more to be said in support of the notion that Augustus created a short-lived province of Arabia after the approval of Herod's testament. When Gaius Caesar, the emperor's grandson, was sent to the East with various missions on behalf of the Roman government, there was among them an *expeditio Arabica.*[42] To prepare the prince for his encounter with the Arabs, the erudite king of Mauretania, Juba, had prepared an edifying treatise;[43] and it is clear from the elder Pliny that Gaius and his forces made their way as far as the Gulf of ʿAqaba.[44] A reference in the inscription on a cenotaph for Gaius at Pisa leaves little doubt that this expedition took place in A.D. 1,[45] just before Gaius set out for Armenia, where he received the wound that cost him his life.

It is in A.D. 1 that the coinage of Aretas begins again after the three-year gap. It is likely, then, that the result of Gaius' expedition to Arabia was a renewal of the Nabataean kingdom under the auspices of Rome and the reinstatement of Aretas IV as king. Naturally, Aretas continued to count the years of his reign from the date of his original accession, 8 B.C. The Arabian expedition of Gaius, viewed in conjunction with the three-year gap in the Nabataean coinage, can accordingly supply an explanation of Strabo's explicit statement that the Nabataeans had become subjects of the Romans by the time he was writing.

Once the Roman government had determined to continue the reign of Aretas as a client king, it became possible to give closer

[41] Ibid., p. 49. There are no coins from regnal years 7, 8, and 9. (The first regnal year is 9/8 B.C.) The omission of one or two years might be an accident in the survival of the coins, but here we have an omission of three years in succession.

[42] Pliny, *NH* 2.168; 6.141, 160; 12.55–56; 32.10. Cf. G. W. Bowersock, *JRS* 61 (1971), 227, and F. E. Romer, *TAPA* 109 (1979), 205.

[43] Cf. *FGH* III.A.275, F 1–3.

[44] Pliny, *NH* 6.160, and references in n. 42 above.

[45] *ILS* 140, ll. 9–10: *consulatum quem ultra fines extremas pop. Romani bellum gerens feliciter peregerat.*

attention to the unsettled condition of Judaea as it was divided up among the heirs of Herod. The foregoing argument imposes the view that Augustus' first arrangement after Herod's death had been the continuation of Judaea in native hands, together with the annexation of Arabia on the other side of the Jordan. With the reinstatement of Aretas, Augustus seems now to have felt free to annex Judaea instead. At any rate, in A.D. 6 various tetrarchs were stripped of their authority and the province of Judaea came into existence under an equestrian procurator from Rome.[46] Meanwhile Aretas, now confident of Roman support, set about the development of his nation in an unprecedented manner.

The Nabataean settlement at Madā'in Ṣāliḥ (Hegra or Egra), near the port which the troops of Aelius Gallus had found in the hands of a relative of the Nabataean king, seems to have been deliberately converted into a major Nabataean city just at the time when Aretas was having his troubles with the court of Augustus. The spectacular rock-cut tombs which survive in that city and so vividly evoke the comparable rock-cut monuments at Petra bear, in most cases, inscriptions which permit dating of these great monuments. They all belong to the first century A.D., and the preponderance of them to the first half of it. The earliest inscriptions come from the year A.D. 1.[47] The sudden growth of Madā'in Ṣāliḥ at this time leads to the supposition that Aretas consciously dispatched settlers there to create a fall-back position in the Ḥejāz, should Romans persist in their takeover of Transjordan. Furthermore, the military character of the new settlement in the Ḥejāz is borne out by the unusually large number of military officers among the dead who are buried in the rupestrian tombs. Most of the titles are borrowed from Greek and Roman army terminology, but they are clearly employed by the Nabataeans for their own officers. Madā'in Ṣāliḥ has produced numerous *strategoi*, some hipparchs, a chiliarch, and a centurion.[48]

[46] Josephus, *AJ* 18.1.2; *BJ* 2.8.117. Cf. Schürer (above, n. 23), pp. 357 ff.

[47] Cantineau, (above, n. 24), p. 26: *šnt tšʿ lḥrtt mlk nbṭw* (the ninth year of Aretas IV).

[48] *'strtg'*: *CIS* II.319a; *'srtg'*: *CIS* II.213, 214, 224, 234. *klyrk'*: *CIS* II.201. *qnṭryn'*: *CIS* II.217. Cf. discussion, with regard to a *rb mšryt'* (*praefectus castrorum*, **στρατοπεδάρχης**) at Jawf, in J. Starcky and R. Savignac, *RB* 64 (1957), 200–4. On eparchs at Hegra, Starcky (above, n. 27), pp. 157–58.

Inscriptions from the oasis at Jawf far out in the desert at the southern end of the Wādī Sirḥān show similar military officers and again suggest a military encampment.[49] It is by no means impossible that the enlargement of the Nabataean presence at Jawf was related to the efforts of Aretas to strengthen the Nabataean position outside of Transjordan during the middle of the principate of Augustus. Jawf, like Madā'in Ṣāliḥ, would have been virtually impossible for the Romans to capture. As the elder Pliny observed, Gaius only looked into the Arabian peninsula but did not attempt to march into it.[50] He turned back at ʿAqaba. He undoubtedly had no desire to repeat the error of Aelius Gallus.

[49] See the *rb mšryt'* in the foregoing note, as well as the centurion in the text cited by M. Speidel, *ANRW* II.8 (1977), 694.

[50] Pliny, *NH* 6.160: *C. Caesar Augusti filius prospexit tantum Arabiam.*

V

THE FLOWERING OF NABATAEA

King Aretas IV is regularly described on coins and inscriptions as "the lover of his people" (*rḥm ʿmh*). To judge from the unprecedented prosperity and growth of the Nabataean kingdom during the long years of his reign, extending as far as A.D. 40, the appellation was richly deserved. With the newly won security in the central regions of Herod's former kingdom, Aretas had less to fear from the Jews. Moreover, in Galilee, which was one of the surviving Herodian tetrarchies after the formation of the Roman province of Judaea, the ruler, Herod Antipas, had taken as his wife a daughter of Aretas.[1] This marital bond renewed the diplomacy of Antipater in the days of the Hasmonaeans, and it effected a link such as Syllaeus had only recently attempted to forge in the Augustan age. Philip the Tetrarch continued to rule north of the Yarmūk, in the regions of Jebel Drūz, Leja', and Ḥawrān; but his rule seems not to have uprooted the Nabataean culture which had flourished there for well over a hundred years.[2] It is, in fact, more

[1] Josephus, *AJ* 18.109: *Ἡρώδης ὁ τετράρχης γαμεῖ τὴν θυγατέρα καὶ συνῆν χρόνον ἤδη πολύν*. J. Starcky (*SDB* 914) identified this daughter with the *šʿwdt* of *CIS* II.354. The same lady appears as *šʿdt* in the large family group of the new Wādī Mūsā inscription (*PEQ* 113 [1981], 22), and she is also the *šʿwdt*, daughter of Aretas, in a fragmentary text from ʿAvdat (*IEJ* 11 [1961], 127). A photograph of the latter inscription is given as no. 40 on plate XXX in A. Negev, *ANRW* II.8 (1977), but the inscription is shown there upside down.

[2] Josephus, *AJ* 17.319: Philip's portion consisted of *Βαταναία. . .σὺν Τράχωνι καὶ Αὐρανῖτις σύν τινι μέρει οἴκου τοῦ Ζηνοδώρου λεγομένου*. Auranitis, the Jebel Drūz (or Jebel Ḥawrān) and its foothills, must carefully be distinguished from the modern Ḥawrān, which is the plain of ancient Batanea: cf. R. Dussaud, *Topographie historique de la Syrie antique et médiévale* (1927), pp. 323, 346. For evidence of Nabataean culture in this area, see particularly *CIS* II.163, the dedication of the temple of Baʿalshamīn at Sīʿ between 33/32 and 2/1 B.C., and a later dedication from the time of Philip's tetrarchy (A.D. 29/30) in E. Littmann, *PAES* IV.A, p. 78, no. 101. For Sīʿ in the context of other sites in the area, note J. and J. Dentzer, *CRAI* 1981, p. 101. See also Littmann, pp. 81–82, no. 103 (bilingual): *Σεεῖα κατὰ γῆν Αὐρανεῖτιν ἑστηκυῖα* / *dʾ ṣlmtʾ dy šʿyʿw* (this is the statue of Sheʿīʿ). Sheʿīʿ will be the eponymous deity, whose name derives, as Littmann says, from *šʿyʿ*, "levelled square" (*πλατεῖα*).

than likely that Philip welcomed the Nabataean presence as a bulwark against the brigand tribes, which constituted the biggest problem in the area. In short, for about the first thirty years of the Christian era, Aretas was in a position to lead his nation in relative peace. It was only in the final decade of his life that serious troubles are known to have arisen.

From approximately A.D. 1 to 30 the literary record of historical events concerning the Nabataeans is silent. But the surviving remains of Nabataean civilization are eloquent. The succession of magnificent and, fortunately, dated tombs at Madā'in Ṣāliḥ bears witness to Aretas' encouragement of the growth of that outpost in the Ḥejāz. The pride he took in this achievement appears to be illustrated by a special coinage commemorating the city of Hegra on the site of Madā'in Ṣāliḥ.[3] Urbanization proceeded vigorously at other major points in the kingdom and appears to have been a significant part of Aretas' policy of economic growth. The major cities of the Negev—Oboda, Mampsis, Nessana, Elusa, and Sobata—all show signs of increased Nabataean settlement at this period.[4] Irrigation was obviously the prerequisite for settlements of this kind, and traces of a sophisticated system of reserving rain water and channeling it in terraces to the cultivable fields probably go back to the age of Aretas.[5] A comparable desert regime for agriculture in the Ḥejāz has been discovered in recent years at a Nabataean settlement at Qurayya, not far from the principal center at Madā'in Ṣāliḥ.[6] Nabataean urbanization in the north is most conspicuous at the site of Bostra, which was to become the capital of the Roman province.[7] It lay close to the boundary with the tetrarchy of Philip and commanded at the same time the

[3] Y. Meshorer, *Nabataean Coins*, Qedem 3, Monographs of the Institute of Archaeology, Jerusalem (1975), pp. 53–54: head of Aretas IV on the obverse, with an unexplained object on the reverse together with the word *ḥgr*'.

[4] For a review of the evidence for these cities, see Negev (above, n. 1), 621–35. The remains of Sobata (Sbeita, Shivta) still await a proper publication.

[5] See A. Negev (above, n. 1), 631–35, on the water problem at Mampsis, Sobata, and Elusa. For the irrigation system at Oboda see the account of a modern reconstruction there in M. Evenari, et al., *The Negev: The Challenge of a Desert* (1971; rev. ed., 1982).

[6] P. J. Parr, G. L. Harding, and J. E. Dayton, *Bull. Inst. Arch. Univ. London* 8–9 (1970), 225.

[7] On Bostra, see the fundamental work of M. Sartre, *Bostra, des origines à l'Islam*, forthcoming.

interior routes of the Wādī Sirḥān from the Nabataean post at Jawf northwestward toward Damascus. Bostra provided an increasingly important focus for Nabataean interests in the Ḥawrān, both inside and outside of Aretas' kingdom.

The royal court was, of course, established at Petra, where archaeological discoveries of the past three decades have revealed astonishing progress in urbanization under Aretas IV. Two of the major monuments in the city have now been anchored securely in his reign. Both have long been thought to belong to a much later era and to reflect Hellenized Roman taste well after the annexation of the territory of Arabia. These are the theater cut in the rock near the inside end of the Sīq and the free-standing temple in the center of the city with the popular name of Qaṣr al-bint.[8] The presumption of architectural historians that the temple could be no earlier than the second century A.D. was conclusively shattered by the discovery of an inscription from the time of Aretas in the *temenos* area of the building.[9] At last there could be no doubt that the Nabataeans, in the days of their independence, had developed a highly sophisticated style under the influence of the Hellenic tastes of the eastern Roman Empire. The theater is an even more obvious case of the Nabataean absorption of Graeco-Roman styles. The excavators' demonstration that this building belongs to the time of Aretas IV is another major step forward in the understanding of Nabataean culture. Petra was, after all, a cosmopolitan place. Strabo tells us that his friend and informant, Athenodorus of Tarsus, found the city full of foreigners.[10] Indeed, since the Nabataeans were such a tranquil people, it was the foreigners, according to Athenodorus, who supplied such litigation as was to be found in this peaceable city. It should scarcely be surprising that the tastes of the world to the west of Petra should have been absorbed by the Nabataeans.

[8] See P. Hammond, *The Excavation of the Main Theater at Petra, 1961–1962* (1965), pp. 55–65, and G. R. H. Wright, "The Structure of the Qasr Bint Far'un," *PEQ* 93 (1961), 8–37.

[9] J. Starcky and J. Strugnell, *RB* 73 (1966), 237. Cf. P. J. Parr, "The Date of the Qasr Bint Far'un at Petra," *Ex Oriente Lux* 19 (1965–66), 550–57.

[10] Strabo 16.4.21, C 779: *γενόμενος γοῦν παρὰ τοῖς Πετραίοις Ἀθηνόδωρος, ἀνὴρ φιλόσοφος καὶ ἡμῖν ἑταῖρος, διηγεῖτο θαυμάζων· εὑρεῖν γὰρ ἐπιδημοῦντας ἔφη πολλοὺς μὲν Ῥωμαίων πολλοὺς δὲ καὶ τῶν ἄλλων ξένων.*

As for the multitude of rock-cut tombs at Petra, which are mostly undated but bear a resemblance in style to those at Madā'in Ṣāliḥ, it would not be unreasonable to assume that they belong roughly to the same period as their dated counterparts. Furthermore, with an early first century A.D. date secured for the Qaṣr al-bint and theater, it becomes highly probable that the stunning façade of the so-called Khazneh ("treasury") belongs to the same age. The date and style of this miraculous façade, which greets the visitor to Petra just as he emerges from the Sīq, have been a subject of dispute for a long time.[11] Its strongly Hellenized architectural elements cannot be denied. But it is no longer necessary to believe that work of this kind could only have been accomplished after the Romans had put an end to the Nabataean kingdom. In fact, the design is most closely paralleled in Pompeiian wall paintings of the second period, perhaps reflecting architecture at Alexandria.[12] On balance the Khazneh, probably the most memorable of all the monuments in Petra, should also be numbered among the achievements of Aretas IV.[13]

Aretas seems to have fostered a new respect for the Nabataean royal house and accordingly to have encouraged the memory of his predecessors. An inscription at Petra from the time of his rule reveals a cult of an Obodas, presumably the first of that name. The text proclaims a statue of "Obodas the god," a deity known also to the Greek world (as a passage in Stephanus of Byzantium makes plain) and worshipped in his eponymous city, Oboda, several centuries later under the name of Zeus Obodas.[14] The Nabataeans'

[11] Cf. G. R. H. Wright, "The Khazneh at Petra: a Review," *ADAJ* 6–7 (1962), 24–54; see also *id.*, *PEQ* 105 (1973), 83–90.

[12] See the excellent analysis in Andreas Schmidt-Colinet, "Nabatäische Felsarchitektur," *Bonner Jahrbücher* 180 (1980), 189–230, esp. 217–33, on the Khazneh in relation to wall painting. A more traditional view of the Khazneh may be seen in the same number of the *Bonner Jahrbücher*, 231–36 (Adnan Hadidi). For other possibly Augustan monuments at Petra, David Graf notes helpfully F. Zayadine on Petra tomb 813 in *ADAJ* 23 (1979), 197, and P. J. Parr on the Conway High Place in *PEQ* 92 (1960), 124–35.

[13] A. Negev, *PEQ* 114 (1982), 125, supports the same dating.

[14] *CIS* II.354 (Petra). Steph. Byz., *s.v.* Ὄβοδα: Uranius is reported to have said, in his *Arabica*, that the city of Oboda was where the Nabataeans buried Obodas the king, ὃν θεοποιοῦσι. (The text is quoted above, p. 25, n. 47.) On Uranius, see J. M. I. West, *HSCP* 78 (1974), 282–84. For the worship of Zeus Obodas, see the inscriptions published for the first time by Negev (above, n. 1), 659, as well as a text discovered by

regard for the royal family of Aretas himself is amply attested on two important inscriptions from Petra, as well as on another from Oboda.[15] Thanks to these documents we know the names of Aretas' sons and daughter, as well as of his wives, who bore the title of queen. The wife of the heir-apparent, Malichus, also bore the title of queen—hence the occurrence of several queens during the reign of a single king in the Nabataean royal stemma. These queens were customarily called sisters of their husbands, but this is probably a court convention rather than an indication of kinship.[16] It will be recalled that ministers of the king were known as his brothers. Syllaeus, it has been noted, called himself a brother of his king, Obodas.[17] Aretas himself encouraged the publicity of the royal family and even issued coins bearing the name of his son Phasael, possibly indicating that this was the only one of his children born during the years of his kingship.[18]

One of the inscriptions listing the members of the royal household may allude at the beginning to Baʿalshamīn, "the god of Malichus."[19] If the reading is correct at this point, it provides another indication of the importance of the dynasty in Nabataea, even in its more remote cities. Just as the god Obodas calls to mind the city of Oboda, so too Baʿalshamīn evokes the one great Nabataean temple to that deity, in Sīʿ in the Ḥawrān. This edifice is

---

Musil and reprinted by Negev, 660. The major texts for Zeus Obodas are reproduced in *SEG* 28.1370, 1371, 1372. Negev's opinion, cited in *SEG*, that this Zeus may be a deity of the city rather than Obodas as Zeus is unlikely in view of the report in Uranius, not to mention *SEG* 28.1373 which calls Obodas a god.

15 *CIS* II.354 and *PEQ* 113 (1981), 22 (both from the Petra area); *IEJ* 11 (1961), 127 (Oboda).

16 For a discussion of the designation *'ḥt* (sister) for the wives of Nabataean kings, cf. Meshorer (above, n. 3), p. 61. It would be imprudent, however, to rule out the possibility of royal incest, as in Ptolemaic Egypt. On this matter, see K. Hopkins, "Brother-Sister Marriage in Roman Egypt," *Comp. Stud. in Society and History* 22 (1980), 303–54.

17 J. Cantineau, *Le nabatéen* II (1932), p. 46 [Miletus]. Cf. Strabo 16.4.21, C 779. See above p. 53, n. 35.

18 Meshorer (above, n. 3), pp. 48–49, on coins with the letters *fṣ*. On p. 49 one specimen is cited with *fṣ'l* written out in full.

19 *PEQ* 113 (1981), 22, with the restorations and commentary of J. T. Milik on 25–26. Milik reads the first line of the Wādī Mūsā text as *lbʿšmyn 'lh mnkw*. The reader should note that Milik here seems to prefer calling Malichus by the form Mank, but this is one and the same ruler (for whom *mlkw* and *mnkw* are both attested in Nabataean).

known to have been under construction during the last three decades of the first century B.C.[20] The temple, in other words, was projected and begun precisely during the reign of Malichus I. During the reign of Aretas, at least until the death of Philip the Tetrarch in 34, Sīʿ lay outside the boundaries of the Nabataean kingdom, but it could nonetheless serve the purpose of unifying Nabataea to recall the shrine there in conjunction with one of the earlier kings.

Overall the urbanization and unification of the Nabataeans under Aretas IV point to the increasing sedentarization of his people. The sophistication of irrigation systems indicates the growing importance of agriculture, as the old trade routes become less active and productive. Diversion of perfumes and spices across the Red Sea to coastal ports in Egypt had begun over a century earlier, and the impact of this change had already been reflected in the events of the first century B.C. The commercial activity of the Nabataeans had naturally not come to an end overnight, but it was evidently declining. There remained internal trade routes, especially the one up the Wādī Sirḥān from the interior of the Arabian peninsula, although this would certainly not have been in itself adequate to support a substantial nation. Aretas, "the lover of his people," pursued a deliberate and energetic policy of transforming the Nabataeans into a settled people with an agricultural economy, on which a network of strategically placed urban centers depended. It has long been observed that the principal road connecting Petra with Gaza begins to go out of use in the middle of the first century A.D. While it is unlikely that this road was closed down altogether, since it provided a reasonable access from southern Transjordan to the Mediterranean, there can be little doubt that it ceased to be a principal commercial artery from the mid-first century A.D.[21] The decline

[20] For the evidence see n. 2 above.

[21] On the continued, although obviously less heavy use of the Petra-Gaza road in the second and third centuries (*contra* A. Negev, *PEQ* 98 [1966], 89–98), see Rudolph Cohen in the *acta* of the *Eighth Archaeological Conference in Israel* and also in an important article on the Petra-Gaza road in *BiblArch* 45 (1982), 240–47. It is worth noting that Cohen's more nuanced conclusions are based on excavations, whereas Negev's view of complete disuse after the mid-first century A.D. depends upon surface surveys. Negev (above, n. 13) has fixed the end of the Petra-Gaza traffic in A.D. 7

of this road complements the rise in cities and farming under Aretas IV. But the leadership of this ruler, undoubtedly one of the greatest figures in the history of pre-Islamic Arabia, was seriously threatened by an impulsive act of Herod Antipas in the last years of the reign of Tiberius at Rome.

In about A.D. 27, Herod Antipas conceived a passion for a sensuous woman who happened to be his niece as well as the wife of Philip the Tetrarch. She was the notorious Herodias. To make way for her, Herod Antipas expelled his Nabataean bride, the daughter of Aretas, and had her returned to her father.[22] It is not known at exactly what point during the course of Herod's infatuation with Herodias the Nabataean was returned to Arabia; but it is clear from the account in Josephus that whenever this happened, Aretas was enraged. He launched an invasion to punish Herod and was able to win a major victory over his new enemy.[23]

In view of the importance of the event, it is regrettable that there is confusion concerning both its location and its date. The transmitted text of Josephus states that the victory occurred in the territory of Gamala, north of the Yarmūk. Now this region was part of the tetrarchy of Philip until his death in 34, and it is not immediately obvious why Aretas would have invaded Philip's domain in order to punish Herod Antipas. After Philip's death Tiberius annexed the region—Jebel Drūz, Leja', and Ḥawrān—to the province of Syria, and there is some reason to believe that Aretas' campaign occurred at that time. For after his defeat Herod brought formal complaint to Tiberius, who then instructed Vitellius, the governor of Syria, to take action. Vitellius did not arrive in Syria until 35, one year after Philip's death.[24] While it is of course possible to emend the text of Josephus so as to relocate Aretas' invasion in a territory farther south that was known to belong

---

because of a drop in the silver content in some Nabataean coins of that year. But this is a frail reed: the tables reproduced by Negev from Meshorer (above, n. 3), pp. 73–74, show that within the emission of the year 7 alone silver contents of 62%, 54%, and 41.5% have been noted. In 6 B.C. some Nabataean coins already had 54%.

[22] Josephus, *AJ* 18.109–112. On Herodias, cf. Matt. 14.3–12.

[23] Josephus, *AJ* 18.112–14.

[24] For Gamala as the site, observe Josephus, *AJ* 18.113 (ἐν γῇ τῇ Γαμαλικῇ or Γαμαλίτιδι). On Tiberius' order to Vitellius, *AJ* 18.115. L. Vitellius, consul A.D. 34, went to Syria in the following year as legate of the province: Tac., *Ann*. 6.32.

to Herod Antipas,[25] it probably makes better sense to follow the chronological indications provided by Vitellius' governorship and to assume that Aretas did indeed march over the Yarmūk into the former lands of Philip, so as to take advantage of the new instability there and to threaten Herod's own territory by control of the Golan and the regions to the east of it.

Herod would certainly not have relished a hostile power at his borders in the Golan, which has always tended to provide a control over Galilee. Once Aretas had moved northward, not only in the hope of menacing Herod but also in anticipation of recovering sites with Nabataean traditions (such as Suweidā', Qanawāt, and Sīʿ in the Ḥawrān), Herod would have felt obliged to move into the area with his own troops. One good indication that these movements took place after the death of Philip is the presence, attested by Josephus, of exiles (*φυγάδες*) from Philip's tetrarchy in Herod's army.[26] Such exiles would not make much sense in Herod's army during the lifetime of Philip, his relative and ally, but they could reasonably show up there once their homeland had been annexed to the province of Syria. The exiles, however, were the cause of Herod's defeat. They betrayed their commander and cast their fortune with the Arabs.[27] They may have welcomed the prospect of returning to their homeland under the sympathetic and benevolent rule of the Nabataean king.

It seems, therefore, as if Aretas calculated very carefully the occasion on which to take his revenge against Herod for the return of his daughter. Although it is impossible to say exactly when she came back, it is clear on any accounting that Aretas did not act immediately. His opportunity came with the death of Philip, the annexation of his tetrarchy to the province of Syria, and the existence of discontented exiles in the army of Herod. The rupture with Herod provided an ideal opportunity for Aretas to

[25] A. Negev (above, n. 1), 568–69, assumes erroneously that the text of Josephus shows *Γαβαλίτιδι* and then goes on to attack Starcky (*SDB* 914) for transferring the episode to Gamala. It is Negev, not Starcky, who had made the transposition by unnecessary emendation. For the location of Gamala at Jamle, see Dussaud (above, n. 2), p. 386.

[26] Josephus, *AJ* 18.114.

[27] Josephus, *AJ* 18.114: *προδοσίας αὐτῷ γενομένης ὑπ' ἀνδρῶν φυγάδων, οἳ ὄντες ἐκ τῆς Φιλίππου τετραρχίας Ἡρώδῃ συνεστράτευον.*

attempt to regain the areas of former Nabataean influence in the north. After so long and successful a reign, he might well have contemplated the recovery not only of Philip's tetrarchy but even of Damascus itself, where the last king named Aretas had once issued coins. The concern of Aretas IV with the achievements of his predecessors, such as Obodas I and Malichus I, would make it reasonable to suppose that he had some regard for Aretas III, whose domains, if not fully organized, had certainly been more extensive than those of any other Nabataean king. When Philip died in 34, there was probably no governor at all in Syria, and if there was, he was probably no great threat to Aretas. For one thing, his residence was far away in Antioch on the coast, and for another Tiberius had, for reasons best known to himself, kept the governor of Syria out of his province for ten years.[28] Aretas can have had no reason to think that the Romans would worry excessively about the newly acquired and difficult terrain in the south of the Syrian province.

By the time that Herod had managed to persuade Tiberius to take action against Aretas for Herod's ignominious defeat, the old emperor at Rome had not much longer to live. He instructed Vitellius to move against Petra, and with some reluctance the governor undertook to do so.[29] But fortunately Tiberius' death intervened, and Aretas was spared a confrontation with the Syrian legions. The death of Tiberius brought the unstable Gaius Caligula to the throne, who immediately obliged his friend and client, Herod Agrippa I, by turning over to him the former tetrarchy of Philip and thus terminating its brief association with the province of Syria.[30] Aretas himself was to die only three years later, and

[28] On the ten-year governorship of L. Aelius Lamia *in absentia*, cf. Tac., *Ann.* 6.27. Lamia's successor in A.D. 32 appears to have been L. Pomponius Flaccus, consul A.D. 17. In *Ann.* 6.27 Tacitus records his death under the year 33. Whether this means (as it obviously should) that Flaccus died in that year or whether Tacitus recorded his death in the wrong year for artistic purposes cannot be determined. No governor after Flaccus is known before L. Vitellius takes office in 35. On all this, see W. Orth, "Die Provinzialpolitik des Tiberius," diss. Munich (1970), pp. 82–85.

[29] Josephus, *AJ* 18.115, 120–24.

[30] Josephus, *AJ* 18.237. The grant to Herod Agrippa also included *τὴν Λυσανίου τετραρχίαν*, which seems to have meant at this time Abila, west of Damascus (cf. *AJ* 19.275 and 20.138). The Lysanias must be the great figure of the triumviral age.

he evidently made no further move to the north during those final years.

A celebrated and perplexing allusion to Aretas in the city of Damascus is best connected with the events immediately before Tiberius' death, rather than immediately after. This reference may well signal the fulfillment, if only for a short time, of Aretas' desire to take back the ancient city in which his homonym once had ruled. In his second letter to the Corinthians, the apostle Paul describes the unorthodox means by which he escaped from Damascus.[31] He was let down the side of a city wall in a basket suspended from a window. He declared that he found it necessary to make such an exit because in Damascus at that time the ethnarch of Aretas the king (*ὁ ἐθνάρχης Ἀρέτα τοῦ βασιλέως*) had garrisoned the city so as to catch the apostle.

The chronology of Paul's adventures precludes a date before the last years of the reign of Tiberius, while the existence of Aretas the king provides a terminus of 40, the final year of Aretas' reign. It has long seemed obvious from Paul's remark, as well as from an oblique account of this incident in the Acts of the Apostles,[32] that the ethnarch of Aretas was in charge of the security of Damascus as a whole. Yet, in the absence of any other evidence for Nabataean control of Damascus in the later years of Aretas, it has seemed prudent to some to view the ethnarch as an officer in charge of the Nabataean community in Damascus, rather than an officer of the city as a whole. This is a counsel of despair. Paul's language is very explicit: "in Damascus the ethnarch of Aretas the king was guarding the city of the Damascenes."[33]

It may be that after his remarkable defeat of Herod Antipas Aretas decided to push still farther north. With Vitellius newly arrived in Antioch and the former tetrarchy of Philip probably without any appropriate Roman administration, Aretas would have had a relatively easy march on to Damascus. There is no need to assume that the ethnarch installed by Aretas remained there for long. Once it had become known that Tiberius had

[31] 2 Cor. 11.32–33. Cf. Gal. 1.15–17.

[32] Acts 9.23–25.

[33] 2 Cor. 11.32: *ἐν Δαμασκῷ ὁ ἐθνάρχης Ἀρέτα τοῦ βασιλέως ἐφρούρει τὴν πόλιν Δαμασκηνῶν.*

instructed the governor of Syria to launch an expedition against the Nabataeans, Aretas is unlikely to have wasted time in relinquishing his new territory. A confrontation with Roman forces was certainly not in the Nabataeans' best interest, and operations on two fronts, in the north and in the vicinity of Petra, would not have been prudent. If the Nabataean recapture of Damascus under Aretas IV lasted for a relatively short time, perhaps less than a year, the absence of coinage attesting this event would not be very disturbing.

The attention that Aretas had given to publicizing the Nabataean dynasty led to a smooth succession upon his death. The new king, Malichus II, was his son, presumably the eldest. From all indications the new king continued Aretas' policy of urban growth and a peaceful transition from commerce to agriculture. Caligula's friend, Herod Agrippa I, who seemed to have a rare talent for cultivating improbable persons with bright futures, was rewarded for supporting the elevation of Claudius to the throne upon the destruction of Caligula in 41. Before his death, Caligula had added to his original gift to Herod Agrippa—which had been the territory of Philip's tetrarchy—by deposing Herod Antipas and turning over the Galilee to Agrippa as well. A grateful Claudius extended his dominion still further by turning over to him the whole of the Roman province of Judaea and thereby reconstituting for a brief moment the original kingdom of Herod the Great.[34]

The resurrection of the Jewish kingdom on the western side of the Jordan must have taken the new Nabataean king by surprise, but there is no evidence that the situation led to hostilities. There was, in any case, not much time for troubles to develop, since Herod Agrippa died just three years later, in A.D. 44, whereupon the province of Judaea reappeared; and the old territory of Philip's tetrarchy was joined to the province of Syria yet again.[35] That the Roman administration in Syria had no ability or desire to control this wild region is suggested by its transmission to another

[34] Josephus, *AJ* 18.252 (Galilee); 19.351 (Judaea). On the direct succession of Malichus II after Aretas IV, without any intervening king (such as Abias in Josephus, *AJ* 20.77), see Starcky, *SDB* 916.

[35] Josephus, *AJ* 18.108.

native ruler only ten years after its second annexation to the province. In 53 Claudius saw fit to bestow the territory upon the son of Agrippa, Herod Agrippa II, whose remarkable longevity relieved the Romans from worrying about the area until the end of the century.[36]

An allusion to a Malichus, king of the Nabataeans, in the anonymous treatise on the circumnavigation of the Red Sea (the *Periplus*) fixes that important document for the Indian trade securely in the middle of the first century A.D.[37] The Malichus mentioned in this text could not possibly be the only other Nabataean king of that name. The treatise provides an absorbing account of the emergent traffic from India to the coast of Egypt, while demonstrating that commerce also continued along the old routes through the land of the Nabataeans. Although the author knows about the impact of the discovery of the monsoons upon the pattern of sea trade, he notes that the Nabataeans still conveyed goods up to Petra and from there on to the Mediterranean.[38] He notes further that there was a customs station at the port of Leuke Kome on the coast of the Ḥejāz, with a centurion (ἑκατοντάρχης) in charge of the city.[39] With the great Nabataean settlement inland at Madā'in Ṣāliḥ, as well as other Nabataean installations in the Ḥejāz, it is inconceivable that the port of Leuke Kome was being administered by Roman officials. The customs officer, collecting a tax of twenty-five percent, must have been a Nabataean official employing rates that can be paralleled in the customs

[36] Josephus, *AJ* 20.138; *BJ* 2.247. On Herod Agrippa II, see E. Schürer, *The History of the Jewish People in the Age of Jesus Christ*, rev. Millar and Vermes (1973), pp. 471–83.

[37] *Periplus*, ch. 19: εἰς Πέτραν πρὸς Μαλίχαν, βασιλέα Ναβαταίων. For the textual transmission of the last word, see above p. 17, n. 19. An old effort to find a later Malichus III is now completely ruled out by the papyri in the Babatha archive, on which see Y. Yadin, *IEJ* 12 (1962), 227–57. See also M. Raschke, *ANRW* II.9.2 (1978), 549 ("only a mid first-century date [for the *Periplus*] is possible"). It is a pity that N. Groom, *Frankincense and Myrrh* (1981), p. 89, is so out of touch with discoveries made in the last twenty years.

[38] *Periplus*, ch. 19. For the discovery of the monsoons, see above p. 21, n. 33.

[39] Ibid.: φρούριον ὃ λέγεται Λευκὴ κώμη. Note also παραφυλακῆς χάριν ἑκατοντάρχης μετὰ στρατεύματος. The location of Leuke Kome is still unclear. L. Kirwan has proposed the area of ʿAinūna: "Where to Search for the Ancient Port of Leuke Kome," *Second International Symposium on the History of Arabia, Pre-Islamic Arabia*, mimeographed (Riyadh, 1979).

regulations at Palmyra.[40] The presence of a centurion is no indication of a member of the Roman army. On the contrary, it is clear from the Nabataean terminology for military officers that "centurion" had been taken over by the Nabataeans as a title, so that a Nabataean *qnṭryn*ʾ at Leuke Kome would make perfect sense.[41]

The author of the *Periplus* knew of only one time in which the Romans penetrated into Arabia Felix. Since there was only one time in which the Romans ever did this, the allusion must certainly be to the expedition of Aelius Gallus. The recollection of that event, some three quarters of a century later, in the text of the *Periplus* shows an imperfect knowledge of what actually happened. If the Romans sound more like successful invaders in the *Periplus* than they do in the pages of Strabo, it is only because any Roman incursion into so remote a place would have been remarkable enough to impress the natives. But for the Romans themselves, the fact that they had to turn back could only be viewed as a humiliation. It is good that the tremendous advances in our knowledge of Nabataean history, especially the king lists, have made it possible to speak now with confidence about the date and context of the *Periplus* of the Red Sea.

The most conspicuous oddity in the evidence for the reign of Malichus II is the apparent cessation of all Nabataean coinage, after annual issues over many decades, during the last six years of his life.[42] A Nabataean inscription with double dating, according to both the Seleucid and the Nabataean systems, has put beyond all question the accession of Malichus' successor Rabbel II in the year A.D. 70.[43] Furthermore, Josephus reports that Malichus was the Nabataean ruler who sent 1,000 cavalry and 5,000 infantry to

[40] Ibid.: *παραλήπτης τῆς τετάρτης τῶν εἰσφερομένων φορτίων*. Cf. H. Seyrig, *Syria* 22 (1941), 263–66 (Palmyra).

[41] Note the *qnṭryn*ʾ at Madāʾin Ṣāliḥ: *CIS* II.217. It is perhaps also worth comparing the words *παραφυλακῆς χάριν* in *Periplus*, ch. 19, with the phrase on another Nabataean inscription at Hegra (A. Jaussen and R. Savignac, *Mission arch. en Arabie* II [1914], no. 246), *fršy*ʾ *nṭryn*, "horsemen who are on guard."

[42] See Meshorer (above, n. 3), p. 67. The cessation of minting can only be seen from the dated silver coinage. It is theoretically possible that bronze coins continued to be issued.

[43] *CIS* II.161. The first regnal year is 70/71. A Rabbel I in the distant past is deduced from *CIS* II.349 (cf. Starcky, *SDB* 905).

Titus when he was rallying his forces against the Jews at Acre in 67.[44] But, at the present time, there are no coins of Malichus later than his twenty-fifth regnal year (64/65).

Since the coinage of Malichus generally is by no means abundant, it would be dangerous to put great weight on this gap, but it is perhaps worth observing that it coincides with the period of Rome's war against the Jews. The Romans may conceivably have requisitioned bullion for minting to pay the troops during this time of crisis. The city coinage of Damascus begins again after a substantial interval at just about the same time as the Nabataean coinage stops.[45] Arab support for the Roman war effort is amply apparent in the contingent sent, doubtless at Roman request, to Titus in 67.[46] Some recent writers have suggested that the reign of Malichus II saw a decline in Nabataean prosperity, but there is really very little to support such a view. Levels of destruction at the city of Oboda, which were once invoked to justify the hypothesis of a major disaster in the Negev, are unfortunately neither datable nor explicable.[47] There is no reason to think that the Negev was lost to the Nabataeans under Malichus, nor that the cessation of the coinage in the last years implies some singular weakening of his rule.

Perhaps the most powerful evidence for postulating some kind of decline in Malichus' reign is the phrase which came to be normally attached to the name of his successor, Rabbel, "who brought life and deliverance to his people."[48] Yet the exact meaning of this phrase is far from clear. It is not attached to Rabbel from the beginning of the reign, nor need it be anything more than an expression of satisfaction and flattery. Assessed coolly on

[44] Josephus, *BJ* 3.68.

[45] This observation is made by Meshorer (above, n. 3), p. 67.

[46] See n. 44 above.

[47] For postulated decline or disaster under Malichus, see Negev (above, n. 1), 570 and 637, as well as *id.*, *PEQ* 108 (1976), 125–33.

[48] E.g., in Cantineau (above, n. 17), p. 9: *dy ʾḥyy wšyzb ʿmh*. It is conceivable that this phrase may be connected with the suppression of the revolt of Damasī: see Appendix II. Whatever it was from which Rabbel delivered his people may also explain the somewhat surprising appearance of a Roman official in charge of the Decapolis under Domitian: B. Isaac, *ZPE* 44 (1981), 67–74. The Decapolis included several cities in Nabataean territory (cf. above, p. 30, n. 12).

the basis of the available evidence, the reign of Rabbel is distinguished on two counts in particular: the increased use of irrigation in the Negev for the development of terraced agriculture and the transference of the royal capital from Petra to Bostra. Nabataeans in the Negev could well have looked to Rabbel as their deliverer, in view of the increased prosperity there during his reign. The transference of the capital to Bostra had been long coming and was a reflection of the ever increasing sedentarization of the Nabataeans in the north as the commerical role of Petra was diminished. On an inscription from A.D. 93, Rabbel is described as "our lord who is at Bostra."[49] This is a text in honor of the local deity of Bostra, Aʿra, who had been assimilated with the Nabataean god Dushara, and hence became Dushara–Aʿra. By contrast, in a much earlier inscription from the reign of the first Malichus in the middle of the first century B.C., there is another dedication to Aʿra, not yet identified with Dushara but described simply as the god who is at Bostra,[50] rather than, as in the text of A.D. 93, the god of "our lord who is at Bostra."

The surviving Nabataean remains at Bostra give ample proof of the efflorescence of that city in the reign of the last of the Nabataean kings. The arch at the western end of the city and the arch near the *medreseh* are both good examples of Nabataean design and decoration.[51] The location of the city in the fertile Ḥawrān with its communications north to Damascus, south through the interior along the Wādī Sirḥān, and southwest along the King's Highway down to Petra and the Gulf of ʿAqaba, gave it a crucial position within a kingdom for which the trade route from the Arabian peninsula was no longer so important. The rise of Bostra to such preeminence did not, however, mean that Petra ceased to be an international metropolis, or that Madā'in Ṣāliḥ did not continue to be an important outpost of Nabataean power in the

[49] Cantineau (above, n. 17), p. 21: *mr'n' dy bbṣr'*.

[50] *CIS* II.218: *l'ʿr' dy bbṣr'*. Since this text is dated to the first year of Malichus, the reference to a Rabbel (*'lh rb'l*, "the god of Rabbel") must either be connected with Rabbel I or, preferably, with Rabbel II before his accession. It is notable that he is not described as a king.

[51] Cf. the catalogue of the Museum of Lyon, *Pétra et la Nabatène* (1978), p. 82 (section written by J. M. Dentzer and S. Mougdad).

Ḥejāz. It is salutary to note that the one inscription which we possess from Rabbel's final year as king—therefore the very year in which Nabataea was annexed as a Roman province—comes from the Ḥejāz in the vicinity of Madā'in Ṣāliḥ on the route from Teimā'.[52]

Like Aretas IV, Rabbel seems to have given publicity to his entire royal household, and an inscription from the area of Petra preserves the names of the members of the dynasty with a fullness reminiscent of the texts of Aretas IV.[53] And it is not only the fullness which recalls that earlier monarch: the names themselves do. As in the earlier reign, one sees here a multiplicity of Nabataean queens during the reign of a single king and the generous use of the term "sister" for royal spouses and relatives. In fact, in this late text from the Nabataean kingdom the two consorts of Rabbel II, presumably in succession (to judge from the coinage), are described explicitly as the children of Malichus II.[54] In this case, therefore, we may have to do with genuine sister-queens. Incest in the Nabataean royal house remains an open question. The purely honorific use of such words as brother and sister cannot, of course, preclude their use in a more strict genealogical sense.

Whatever the explanation of Rabbel's saving and delivering of his people, these last years of the Nabataean kingdom brought the remarkable work of Aretas IV to fruition. The Nabataeans were prosperous and at peace. They had developed an effective system of desert agriculture and built up a group of strategically placed cities throughout the reign. The trade routes of former times had ensured that the kingdom would be well knit together by a royal road system that provided easy communication. By now the frontiers with the Jews were untroubled. A cache of papyri hidden away in the caves above En Geddi during the time of the Bar Kokhba rebellion under Hadrian includes documents of the reign of Rabbel II, in which complex legal negotiations involving both Arabs and Jews in the border territories at the southern tip of the

[52] Jaussen and Savignac (above, n. 41), no. 321. For another text of Rabbel in the same year: *RB* 8 (1911), 273–77 (Ḥawrān).

[53] Cantineau (above, n. 17), pp. 9–10. Cf. the discussion of this text in Meshorer (above, n. 3), pp. 78–79.

[54] Cantineau (above, n. 17), text cited in the preceding note, lines 7–8: [*w*ʿ]*l ḥyy gmlt wḥgrw* ʾ*ḥwt*[*h m*]*lkt nbṭw bny mlkw* [*mlk*]ʾ *mlk nbṭw*.

Dead Sea can be traced in detail.[55] As we shall see, these documents, belonging to a certain Babatha, make clear that this was a society in which Arabs and Jews associated freely and in trust.

[55] Reported, but not published in full: H. J. Polotsky, *IEJ* 12 (1962), 258–62, and Y. Yadin, *Ex Oriente Lux* 17 (1963), 227–41. Cf. H. J. Wolff, *ANRW* II.13 (1980), 763–806. Three documents were published by Polotsky, *Eretz Israel* 8 (1967), 46–50, and republished, with English translation, by N. Lewis, *Ill. Class. Stud.* 3 (1978), 100–14.

VI

THE NEW PROVINCE

In A.D. 132, after Hadrian's grand tour of Syria and Palestine, and in the earliest phase of the great Jewish rebellion of Bar Kokhba against the Romans, Babatha, a Jewess, daughter of Simeon, retreated into the caves west of the Dead Sea to protect herself and her precious archive of family documents. Her life had been seriously disturbed by legal complications arising from the deaths of her two husbands. The thirty-five documents, which pertain to the property of her father, the guardianship of her son, and the demands of the family of her second husband, were carefully taken into the cave in 132, where Babatha hoped to survive during the revolt. She did not. And, as a result, nearly two thousand years later, excavators were able to recover, from the mass of textiles, baskets, and leather utensils also stored in the cave, Babatha's remarkable archive.[1] The documents, in Greek, Nabataean, and Aramaic, illuminate the whole period of transition from the Nabataean kingdom to the new Roman province of Arabia. Even as late as 132, the province could still be described as new, although it was in 106 that the Nabataean kingdom had been replaced by the government of Rome.[2]

These were times of rapid change in the Near East. It has never been easy to determine the precise circumstance which led to the annexation of the kingdom of Rabbel II. He himself had been an innovator in shifting the center of his realm from Petra to Bostra and in providing, as his inscriptions record, "life and deliverance to his people" from unnamed tribulations and threats. The

[1] Y. Yadin has recounted the story of the discovery and examination of Babatha's archive in his book, *Bar Kokhba* (1971), pp. 222–53. Cf. his summary of the substance of the documents in *Ex Oriente Lux* 17 (1963), 227–41. Only three documents (one in two copies) have been published so far, despite the passage of over twenty years: see the additional references in the final note to the preceding chapter.

[2] On a document dated 19 August 132 *κατὰ τὸν τῆς νέας ἐ̣[πα]ρχίας Ἀραβίας ἀριθμόν*. The text was first published by H. J. Polotsky, *Eretz Israel* 8 (1967), 50, and republished by M. Lemosse, *The Irish Jurist* 3 (1968), 365; by N. Lewis, *Ill. Class. Stud.* 3 (1978), 112; and by H. J. Wolff, *ANRW* II.13 (1980), 771.

first four documents in the archive of Babatha all belong to the last years of Rabbel. The earliest is dated to A.D. 93 and the latest to A.D. 99.[3] For the most part they reveal a stable and peaceful society in which a modest Nabataean bureaucracy can be seen accommodating the efforts of a Jewish family to establish itself within the Nabataean kingdom in a neighborhood of Arabs. Babatha's father, Simeon, the son of Menaḥem, acquired land in the town of Maḥoza in the region of Zoar, in an area that is explicitly described: "to the south is the garden of our lord, Rabbel the King, king of the Nabataeans, who maintained life and brought deliverance to his people, and to the north the swamp."[4] Since date palms were growing on Simeon's property, the Zoar in question is probably to be found in the region south of the Dead Sea, precisely where date palms are represented on the mosaic map at Mādabā several centuries later.[5] Simeon made his purchase through a Nabataean registry, and penalties for violation of the contract had to be paid to the Nabataean king as well as to the injured party. The buyer was guaranteed the right to sell the property, pledge it, transfer it, or make it over in any way he pleased, from the day on which the deed was written in perpetuity. Irrigation rights were guaranteed, with a detailed statement of the hours and days of the week in which the land could be watered.[6] The whole sale shows a surprisingly sophisticated legal

[3] Y. Yadin, *IEJ* 12 (1962), 239–41; *Ex Oriente Lux* (above, n. 1), 229–32.

[4] Yadin, *Ex Oriente Lux* (above, n. 1), 231: *wlymyn' gnt mr'n' rb'l mlk' mlk nbṭw dy 'ḥyy wšyzb ʿmh wlšmwl' rqq'*. The last word is presumably the Nabataean equivalent of Syriac *my' rqyq'*, "shallow (or standing) water."

[5] See Josephus, *AJ* 1.204, on Ζωώρ (the orthography is uncertain) in the vicinity of Sodom. Because little grows there, at least without irrigation, Josephus claims the name was given because it represents the Jews' word for τὸ ὀλίγον (the Semitic root is *zʿr*, cf. Aramaic *zʿyr* "small"). For Zoara registered among the cities of Moab, Josephus, *AJ* 13.397, 14.18 (Zoira). The name is placed by conjecture in *BJ* 4.454. It appears in Ptolemy, *Geog*. 5.17.5. The location of Zoara in Ptolemy's list (after Ἄδρου, southeast of Petra), together with Josephus, *BJ* 4.454 (if rightly emended), may possibly mean that there was another Zoara south of Petra. The Greek documents specify the site of Simeon's property as ἐν Μαωζα περὶ Ζοάραν or as κώμη Μαωζα (Yadin, *IEJ* [above, n. 3], 242; *Ex Oriente Lux* [above, n. 1], 231), whereas the Nabataean texts read *mḥwz ʿgltyn*. A Hebrew document discovered in the same cave as Babatha's material mentions "ha-Luḥit in the district of ʿAgaltain," and this serves to confirm the location of Maḥoza southeast of the Dead Sea. For ha-Luḥit, cf. Isa. 15.5 and Jer. 48.5. Zoar would be at modern Ṣāfī.

[6] For the penalties, guarantees, and regulations, see Yadin, *IEJ* (above, n. 3), 241,

organization within the Nabataean kingdom and a willingness to accept in perpetuity a new resident from the Jewish communities across the valley. The quality of the land for the successful growth of date palms is guaranteed by its proximity to the royal domain of Rabbel just to the south of it.

There are no documents in Babatha's archive from the year in which the Nabataean kingdom was brought to an end, or indeed from the years immediately thereafter; but it seems clear from a document of 120 that the rights of Simeon to his land, as guaranteed by the Nabataean contracts, were still in force under the Roman government. In 120 he was able to make over to his wife Miriam, Babatha's mother, all of his property in his own lifetime.[7] The document of 120 is dated to the reign of Hadrian by consular year as well as by provincial era (from the beginning of the province of Arabia). The definition of the boundaries of Simeon's property reveals that more Jews had moved into the region of Zoar in the period between 99 and 120. Where the neighbors' names had been exclusively Nabataean, they are now obviously Jewish.[8] Since the region can be seen, from several documents in the collection, to fall under the general administration of Petra, it may be suspected that, with the transference of the Nabataean central authority from Petra to Bostra and the Roman preservation of Bostra as the capital of Arabia, opportunities for the purchase of land in the territory northwest of Petra may have increased. Members of the Nabataean bureaucracy and nobility presumably moved to Bostra with Rabbel and made possible the acquisition of desirable lands. One thing is clear: there were no visible difficulties about the new residents in Zoar.

Apart from the documents concerning Simeon's property, most of Babatha's archive is concerned with the complex legal maneuvers whereby she endeavored to secure better maintenance for her

---

and *Ex Oriente Lux* (above, n. 1), 231–32. The allowed watering periods are called *ʿnymy*.

[7] Yadin, *IEJ* (above, n. 3), 242–44; *Ex Oriente Lux* (above, n. 1), 232–33.

[8] Yadin, *Ex Oriente Lux* (above, n. 1), 232. Whereas Simeon's neighbors in 99 had been Habiba, daughter of [ ] Illahi and Ṭaḥa, daughter of ʿAbdobdat, there appear in 120 the heirs of Joseph bar Babba, the heirs of Menaḥem, and the heirs of Joseph bar *drmns*.

son after the death of her first husband and subsequently protected herself against the claims of another wife of her second husband. All of the complex litigation, which provides a rich treasure of material for the administration of law in a Roman province, comes from the period after the annexation of Arabia. And perhaps the most striking feature of the evidence is the thoroughly Roman character of the law which is being applied in this frontier territory of Semitic and Hellenic traditions.[9] The designation of guardians for the son of Babatha was made by the *boulē* of Petra in the form of a *datio tutoris*, and one of Babatha's documents provides two copies of a Greek text of the Roman formula of *actio tutelae*.[10] The litigation of Babatha under Roman law, in Greek translation but in a Semitic environment, provides new and vivid support for what had once seemed a simple periphrasis for annexation in the text of Ammianus. Writing of the creation of the province of Arabia, that fourth-century historian, who came from Syrian Antioch and should therefore have known, wrote *obtemperare legibus nostris Traianus conpulit imperator*.[11] It seems clear that in the most literal sense Trajan's annexation involved submission to the Roman legal system. The trickiest point about the annexation, however, and one which Babatha's archive unfortunately fails to illuminate, is the nature of the annexation itself.

It is not clear whether Ammianus' verb *conpulit* implies armed force or simply moral suasion. All that we have of the account of Cassius Dio for this period is a Byzantine abridgment, which may or may not contain some of his actual vocabulary. This abridgment reports that the governor of Syria, Cornelius Palma, τὴν Ἀραβίαν τὴν πρὸς τῇ Πέτρᾳ ἐχειρώσατο καὶ Ῥωμαίων ὑπήκοον ἐποιήσατο.[12] Making Arabia a subject of Rome could

[9] See above all the extensive treatment by H. J. Wolff, *ANRW* II.13 (1980), 763–806, which is the book publication eight years later of an article issued as a preprint in 1972 with pagination 1–44; the same author, in French, in *RIDA* 23 (1976), 271–90.

[10] On these formulae, Lemosse (above, n. 2), 367–69.

[11] Amm. Marc. 14.8.13.

[12] Cassius Dio 68.14. On 106 as the date of the annexation, instead of 105 (as some had formerly believed), see G. W. Bowersock, *ZPE* 5 (1970), 39. Bardaiṣan, *Book of the Laws of Countries* (ed. F. Nau [1931], p. 27 Syriac text), states that the Romans have recently conquered Arabia (*ʾtmly ʾḥdw rhwmyʾ lʿrb*) and forbidden circumcision there. This cannot refer to Trajan's province, since Bardaiṣan lived in the second half

certainly have been accomplished peacefully; on the other hand, the verb ἐχειρώσατο does imply some kind of defeat or humiliation on the part of the Nabataeans.[13] In fact, the activity of the governor of Syria in bringing about the annexation would suggest that some force was indeed necessary. Two cohorts were transferred from Egypt to Judaea in the year before the annexation and, as they are soon to be found in Arabia, look like units in a larger plan to take over the area.[14] The peaceful annexation of other kingdoms in the early Roman Empire does not seem normally to have involved the agency of an outside governor. The Babatha documents from the time of Rabbel II have revealed that Rabbel had a son by the name of Obodas who was presumably the heir-apparent.[15] So it cannot be argued that there was an end of the royal stock.

---

of the second century and early in the third. Furthermore, the sentence immediately preceding makes plain that the Arabia referred to is in the neighborhood of the participants in the discussion (*qryb' lkwn*), and they were in Edessa. The allusion is undoubtedly to Septimius Severus' annexation of Mesopotamia, which is often described in the ancient sources as an Arabian province (Eutropius 8.18.4; Festus 21; *HA*, Sept. Sev. 18; Zosimus 1.8; not to mention the confused remarks in Herodian 3.9.3).

[13] Two Safaitic graffiti mention a "year of the Nabataean war," *snt ḥrb nbṭ: AAES* IV (1904), p. 143, no. 45; and F. V. Winnett and G. L. Harding, *Inscriptions from Fifty Safaitic Cairns* (1978), p. 325, no. 2113, where the editors associate the war in question with the revolt of Damasī in 71 (*BASOR* 211 [1973], 54–57). Obviously there is no reason to think that a Nabataean war for tribes of the Ṣafā had anything to do with Rome. More important is the graffito in Winnett and Harding, pp. 406–7, no. 2815, mentioning "the year the Nabataeans revolted against the people of Rome," *snt mrdt nbṭ ʿl ʾl rm*. This would certainly seem to suggest at least some military action.

[14] These are the cohorts *I Hispanorum* and *I Thebaeorum:* see M. Speidel, *ANRW* II.8 (1977), 709–10 and 719. R. Syme has suggested that the adlection of Ti. Claudius Quartinus (*praet. ca.* 113, *cos. suff.* 130) to senatorial rank may well have been for merit shown in the annexation of Arabia. Quartinus had served as military tribune in III Cyrenaica (*CIL* 13.1802): R. Syme, *Historia* 14 (1965), 353, n. 53, reprinted in *Danubian Papers* (1971), p. 237, n. 53.

[15] Yadin, *IEJ* (above, n. 3), 239–40; *Ex Oriente Lux* (above, n. 1), 230: *wʿl ḥyy ʿbdt br rbʾl mlkw mlk nbṭw dy ʾḥyy wšyzb ʿmh.* In both publications Yadin argues that the papyrus text proves that the familiar phrase *ʿl ḥyy* in Nabataean inscriptions does not mean, as is usually assumed, "for the life of" but rather "in the times of" (a chronological indicator). This is a most unsatisfactory hypothesis: cf., to take but one example, *CIS* II.354 (Petra), which records the erection of a statue to Obodas the god *ʿl ḥyy* Aretas IV, his sister, his six children (all named), and one grandchild "in the year 29" of Aretas IV. Nine members of the royal family scarcely needed to be listed by name to provide a date that is then rendered precisely by the king's regnal year. For an acute analysis of *ʿl ḥyy*, arguing that the phrase is very similar to *lyqrh* ("in honor of"), see H. J. W. Drijvers, *Le muséon* 95 (1982), 183–88.

In the very first year after the annexation in 106, papyri from Karanis have shown the presence of legionaries at work on construction in the southern part of the province.[16] If these legionaries were there in 107, it is by no means improbable that they were brought in the previous year during the process of taking over the country. The coin legend which later appears in commemoration of the new province declares, as has often been noted, *Arabia adquisita* and not *Arabia capta.*[17] Furthermore, Trajan never takes the title Arabicus in his titulature, although he does add Dacicus to commemorate another annexation of about the same period as the Arabian one. Obviously there was no major war for Arabia which could be compared in any way with the war in two phases for the conquest of Dacia. On balance the evidence for the annexation of Arabia implies a military presence and perhaps even some military skirmishes, but no major conflict. Since the army in the south near Petra has been shown to be the Third Cyrenaica, which had formerly been in Egypt, there may have been a two-pronged invasion of the kingdom with the legionaries from Egypt entering from the south by way of the Sinai or ʿAqaba, and the forces with Cornelius Palma coming down from Syria in the north. There is some reason to believe that the Sixth Ferrata, which had formed part of the Syrian garrison, was present, at least in part, in the Arabian province in the early period.[18] Presumably the presence of Roman legionaries at the principal centers of the Nabataean kingdom was sufficient to persuade the Nabataeans not to undertake a major war which they

[16] *Pap. Mich.*, 8 (1951), no. 466 (cf. 465). See also E. Husselman, *Papyri from Karanis*, 3rd ser. (1971), no. 562. The date of *Pap. Mich.* 466 is 26 March 107, and it names Claudius Severus as governor (ὑπατικός, the unofficial term, since Severus did not become consul until 112). The work is stone-cutting all day (perhaps for building the Via Nova). The writer says that he has been enrolled in the cohort going to Bostra, which is said to be eight days' journey from Petra.

[17] E.g., H. Mattingly and E. A. Sydenham, *Roman Imperial Coinage* II (1926), pp. 278 and 287.

[18] On the movements of VI Ferrata, see the excellent study by D. L. Kennedy, "*Legio VI Ferrata:* the Annexation and Early Garrison of Arabia," *HSCP* 84 (1980), 283–309. Kennedy believes that the initial legion, III Cyrenaica, was taken out of Arabia ca. 117–123 and replaced by VI Ferrata. It may be suggested, then, that this particular legion was used to fill the gap because of some prior experience with Palma during the annexation. I now accept, however, Speidel's argument from *Pap. Mich.* 466 that III Cyrenaica was the initial garrison of the province: (above, n. 14), 691–93.

had no hope of winning. It is highly likely that the date of the operation was due to the decease of Rabbel, who had been on the throne since A.D. 70.

The war in Dacia was still going on at this time, and one would be hard put to believe that Trajan was then giving any serious thought to launching a major operation in the East. He knew the Near East well from his service there in the company of his father, who had been governor of Syria during the reign of Vespasian.[19] He must have understood clearly that the Nabataean kingdom represented the final piece—the missing piece—in securing Roman control throughout the entire Mediterranean. With Egypt, Judaea, and Syria all part of the Roman Empire, the Nabataean kingdom, civilized and pacified by its enlightened monarchs, was ripe for annexation. He may therefore have determined early in his reign that whenever Rabbel should die, the forces of Rome would take the opportunity to bring in his kingdom as a new province. This kind of standing policy, to be implemented at whatever moment nature determined, could well account for an operation at a time when Trajan was so heavily occupied with the Balkans.

Similar considerations may also explain another mysterious and often unremarked feature of the history of the province's first years: the failure of the Roman government to advertise the annexation of 106 before the year 111.[20] There are no inscriptions and there are no coins before this date in celebration of the annexation of Rabbel's kingdom. The time, however, was not wasted. As we have already observed, legionaries were hard at work on construction, possibly of roads, in the year after the kingdom was incorporated, and the governor of the new province is already recognized as such in a Nabataean inscription dated to the third year of the provincial era.[21]

[19] G. W. Bowersock, "Syria under Vespasian," *JRS* 63 (1973), 133–40.

[20] This point is made in a review of A. Spijkerman, *The Coins of the Decapolis and Provincia Arabia* (1978): G. W. Bowersock, *JRS* 72 (1982), 197–98. P. L. Strack had already recognized the problem of the late issuance of the Arabia coinage in his *Untersuchungen zur römischen Reichsprägung des zweiten Jahrhunderts: I, Die Reichsprägung zur Zeit des Traian* (1931), p. 194.

[21] J. T. Milik, *Syria* 35 (1958), 244: "in the year three of the eparch (governor) of Bostra" (*bšnt tlt lhprk bṣr'*), for which the Greek on this bilingual text reads simply

Throughout those five years of public silence about the annexation, the Romans were establishing their control of the former Nabataean kingdom. The most conspicuous monument to their endeavors is the great road that extends down to the head of the Gulf of ʿAqaba along the line of the King's Highway. This is the Via Nova Traiana commemorated on numerous milestones, all of which are dated to the year 111 or later.[22] Throughout the period of building and for some years afterward, the governor was C. Claudius Severus, whose lengthy tenure may be taken to imply a mission of organization and building that he had to complete before relinquishing office. He appears to have succeeded Cornelius Palma directly after the formal annexation and to have stayed in office as governor throughout his consulate (which he will have held in absence) and down to at least 115.[23]

By a coincidence that can scarcely be fortuitous, the public announcement of the Via Nova Traiana on milestones throughout the length of the province begins in the same year as the Trajanic coinage advertising the acquisition of Arabia. The first Arabia coins are dated to Trajan's fifth consulate and anticipate the series of provincial coins which begin to appear in 112 and continue through 114. The coins of the fifth consulate, therefore, whether they be judged provincial or Roman, must have been struck in the last year in which the emperor could be designated *cos.* V, and that is 111.[24] The provincial Arabia type, minted in either Antioch or Bostra, with a bust of Trajan on the obverse and a standing figure of Arabia with a camel on the reverse, echo eloquently the milestones of Trajan's road.[25] Trajan may not have wished to

---

ἔτους τρίτου ἐπαρχίας. The earliest inscription dated by the era of the new province was found at ʿAvdat in the Negev: *IEJ* 13 (1963), 117–18, no. 11 (year 2).

22 For a conspectus of milestones with the name of Claudius Severus: *PIR*² C 1023. The fullest treatment is P. Thomsen, "Die römischen Meilensteine der Provinzen Syria, Arabia, und Palaestina," *ZDPV* 40 (1917), 1–103.

23 On the evidence for Severus in Arabia, see now M. Sartre, *Trois études sur l'Arabie romaine et byzantine* (1982), pp. 78–80.

24 *BMC* Roman Empire III, p. 185, no. 877; cf. p. 203. For the date of the Arabia coins with *cos* V: W. Metcalf, *Amer. Num. Soc. Mus. Notes* 20 (1975), 104. For the tridrachms with *cos* V, cf. M. Weder, *Schweizer Münzblätter* 27 (1977), 60–61. See below, plate 16.

25 For a full discussion of these coins, see Metcalf (above, n. 24), 39–108, proving

call particular attention to his work in Arabia until it was done. There might have been reason for others to interfere with it if it had been too widely publicized. The long delay in announcing the annexation through coinage and inscriptions may be seen as a deliberate effort to wait until the work was completed—in short, to confront the Near East with a fait accompli. By 111, as the milestone inscriptions put it, the province had been *redacta in formam provinciae*.

In the year 114 the provincial Arabia coins come to an end, but just at this time a new issue appears, in the form of drachms with representations of a camel.[26] This camel, however, is not the same beast as we have seen on the provincial Arabia coins, but rather a two-humped Bactrian camel. The Arabia coins showed exclusively a dromedary, which is appropriate, since this was the kind of camel to be seen in Arabia. The Bactrian camel belongs to regions farther east and somewhat to the north, to the territory of Afghanistan and Iran. Since Trajan was already in the Near East in 114, in the early stages of his Parthian expedition, it seems more than likely that the issue of drachms displaying a Bactrian camel from that year is programmatic. By 114 there was no doubt that the emperor intended to march farther east, against the great empire in the Iranian heartland.[27] And it was obviously important to him to secure the countries behind him as he moved eastward. The organization of Arabia with the great road linking Syria to the Gulf of ʿAqaba and the establishment of Roman authority at Bostra may well have been part of Trajan's master plan for conquest of the Parthians.

It is perhaps no accident that the greatest memorial to Trajan in Roman Arabia was on the triumphal arch at Petra, where the city honored him with a magnificent inscription and showed that it was at the same time honored by him as metropolis of the province.[28] The text of this inscription, only recently made known

---

that the mint was not Cappadocian Caesarea. Metcalf opted for Bostra. Weder (above, n. 24), 57–61, prefers Antioch.

[26] Metcalf (above, n. 24), 96. See below, plate 16.

[27] On Trajan's plans and operations, F. A. Lepper, *Trajan's Parthian War* (1948), is still valuable.

[28] I have published the complete text of the inscription on the Petra arch thanks to the kindness of John Strugnell in providing photographs and drawings: *JRS* 72

in full, shows that the honorific title of the city, long associated with Hadrian's visit later, is Trajanic. Furthermore, Arabia's legion, the Third Cyrenaica, which contributed to Trajan's expedition, itself commemorated the emperor with a great arch in the following year at Dura Europus near the Euphrates.[29] It looks very much as if the mission of Claudius Severus in the province of Arabia over the course of nearly a decade was to provide continuity in preparations for the fulfillment of Trajan's great dream to reenact the conquests of Alexander the Great and conquer the kingdom in Iran. Trajan could not have known exactly when Rabbel would die, but he must have had good reason to judge from Rabbel's age that it would happen at some point in his own imperial rule. When the occasion arose, the arrival of Roman troops forced the Nabataeans into submission and allowed the Romans to accomplish a thorough organization of the region while the attention of the Roman world was directed to the brilliant conquests in Dacia. By 120 when our reports of the private life of the family of Babatha resume, Trajan is already dead, his great expedition a failure. But the province of Arabia remained as his legacy in the Near East, with its Roman troops, its Roman governor, and its Roman law.

It had become clear from Trajan's grant of the title of metropolis to Petra by 114 that it was not his intention, in placing the capital of the province at Bostra, to diminish the role of Petra as a center for the southern part of the Arabian territory. We have seen that the guardians of Babatha's son were appointed by the *boulē* of Petra, and it is evident from a document of 124 that a record of the arrangements was maintained in the *acta* of the city council.[30] The document of that year is described explicitly as

---

(1982), 198. Since the text is new and important, it may be useful to reproduce it here: [Αὐτοκράτορι Καίσα]ρι Θεοῦ [Νέρουα υἱῷ] Νέρουα Τρ[αϊανῷ] / ['Αρίστῳ Σεβαστῷ Γερμανικῷ Δακικ]ῷ ἀρχιερεῖ μεγίστῳ δ[ημαρ]χικῆς ἐξουσίας τὸ [ι]η' αὐτοκράτορι τὸ ζ' ὑπ[άτῳ τὸ ϛ'] / [*vac.* ἡ τῆς 'Αραβίας μη]τρόπολις Πέτρα ἐπὶ Γαΐου Κλ[αυδίο]υ Σεουήρου πρεσβευ[τ]οῦ ἀντιστρατήγου *vac.* The date is A.D. 114.

[29] *Exc. Dura-Europus* 4 (1933), 57–65; 6 (1936), 480–82.

[30] H. J. Polotsky, *IEJ* 12 (1962), 260; Yadin, *Ex Oriente Lux* (above, n. 1), 234: ἀπὸ ἄκτων βουλῆς Πετραίων τῆς μητροπόλεως. There is a photograph of these words in the document of 124 in Yadin's *Bar Kokhba* (above, n. 1), p. 240. The document as a whole remains unpublished.

having been issued ἐν Πέτρᾳ μητροπόλει τῆς Ἀραβίας. In the following year we find Babatha herself summoning a guardian to be judged by the governor of the province of Arabia, Julius Julianus, at Petra.[31] The presence of the governor in that city on such an occasion does not prove, as some have surmised, that the city was the provincial capital as late as the reign of Hadrian. It simply shows that, in this province as in others, the governor traveled to the major cities outside the capital in order to hold assizes and administer justice.[32] The assizes to which Babatha had recourse at Petra do indicate that the city was considered among the most important in the province.

There are additional indications that Petra continued to flourish under the Roman administration. Not least of these is the magnificent tomb for T. Aninius Sextius Florentinus, whose name was recorded in a Latin inscription on the tomb.[33] This person now appears in the archive of Babatha, and his governorship can be securely anchored to the year 127.[34] That the city of Petra should have been thought an appropriate place for the construction of a tomb for a major Roman official in the province is sufficiently eloquent testimony to the preeminence of the city in the Hadrianic age.

Furthermore the careful excavation of the domestic area of Petra has provided evidence of unbroken habitation through the Roman period, down to the great earthquake of the mid-fourth century A.D.[35] A recently uncovered temple with winged lions and fragments of a dolphin has proven to be the shrine of the goddess whose image was found there and already known from Teimā' and Ramm in the south: al-ʿUzzā, identified with the Syrian

[31] Yadin, *Ex Oriente Lux* (above, n. 1), 238. On Julius Julianus, now known to be Ti. Iulius Iulianus Alexander, honored at Gerasa (*ADAJ* 21 [1976], 105–8), see Sartre (above, n. 23), pp. 81–82.

[32] On the travels of provincial governors for giving judgment, see A. J. Marshall, "Governors on the Move," *Phoenix* 20 (1966), 231–46; G. P. Burton, "Proconsuls, Assizes, and the Administration of Justice under the Empire," *JRS* 65 (1975), 92–106.

[33] R. E. Brünnow and A. von Domaszewski, *Die Provincia Arabia* I (1904), p. 382. See also Appendix III.

[34] Polotsky *IEJ* (above, n. 30), 259; Yadin, *Ex Oriente Lux* (above, n. 1), 238.

[35] Philip C. Hammond, "Cult and Cupboard at Nabataean Petra," *Archaeology* 34.2 (1981), 27–34. Cf. *id.*, "New Evidence for the Fourth-century A.D. Destruction of Petra," *BASOR* 238 (1980), 65–67.

Atargatis—in other words, the Arabian Aphrodite.[36] The discovery of this temple may provide an explanation of one of the more elusive phrases in the Babatha archive. A document is said to have been issued ἐν τῷ ἐν Πέτρᾳ Ἀφροδεισίῳ.[37] Although one scholar proposed that this building was the Qaṣr al Bint,[38] the discovery of a temple to the Arabian Aphrodite (al-ʿUzzā) makes it more probable that we have here on the north bank of the Wādī Mūsā in the center of the city the site of the Aphrodeision.[39] The principal difficulty with this identification is that the excavator has determined from his stratigraphy that the temple was burned in the last years of Rabbel II and left without a roof thereafter.[40] It may be, of course, that a wooden roof was placed on the building in the early decades of the province. Or it may be suspected that the devastation, from whatever cause, came somewhat later, perhaps at the same time as the devastation recorded at ʿAvdat (if that can be dated to the middle second century A.D.)[41]

Nor was Petra the only other major city of the province apart from Bostra. It is clear from seal impressions which have been discovered from the time of Hadrian at Mampsis in the Negev that Characmoba was an important center with its own official seal.[42] Furthermore, the archive of Babatha records that this troubled lady had to declare her property to a Roman commander

[36] Hammond, *Archaeology* (above, n. 35), 32–34; *AJA* 86 (1982), 268. On the Petra image of the goddess and her antecedents: J. Starcky, in *Pétra et la Nabatène*, Musée de Lyon cat. (1978–1979), pp. 42–43; and Hammond, "Ein nabatäisches Weiherelief aus Petra," *Bonner Jahrb.* 180 (1980), 265–69. For the Teimā' stone, see L. A.-W. Yehya, *al-ʿarab fī al-ʿuṣūr al-qadīma* (1978), plate 9. For the identification of Aphrodite and al-ʿUzzā see the Greek-Nabataean bilingual inscription from Cos: G. Levi della Vida, *Clara Rhodos* 9 (1938), 139–48, with, for the Nabataean text, F. Rosenthal, *Die aramäistische Forschung* (1939), p. 91, n. 4. Cf. also J. and L. Robert, *Bull. épig.* 1940.89, and Starcky, *SDB* 1003.

[37] Yadin, *Ex Oriente Lux* (above, n. 1), 235.

[38] Yadin, *Ex Oriente Lux* (above, note 1), 235–37, and again in his *Bar Kokhba* (above, n. 1), p. 240.

[39] Starcky already proposed this identification in his catalogue entry for the Petra stone: (above, n. 36), p. 43.

[40] Hammond, *Archaeology* (above, n. 35), 34.

[41] On the burnt level at ʿAvdat, see A. Negev, *Archaeology* 14 (1961), 125; *IEJ* 13 (1963), 121, and 17 (1967), 46; *PEQ* 101 (1969), 6. Negev's dating of this burnt layer has ranged from mid-first to mid-second century A.D. He now favors the earlier date: *ANRW* II.8 (1977), 659.

[42] A. Negev, "Seal Impressions from Tomb 107 at Kurnub (Mampsis)," *IEJ* 19 (1969), 89–106.

who was based at Rabbathmoba (or Rabba), ἐν Ῥαββαθμωβοις πόλει.[43] It is worth observing by contrast that there is no sign of a major Roman administrative center in the Ḥejāz. The golden era of Hegra (Madā'in Ṣāliḥ) seems to have passed, and it may be suspected that Philadelphia, a city of the Decapolis, went on to claim special exemption from Roman interference because of its traditional membership in the local district of Coele Syria.[44] So far as can be told, then, the principal Roman centers in the new province were Bostra, Petra, Characmoba, and Rabbathmoba.

As Ammianus says, Trajan forced the people of Nabataean Arabia to obey Roman laws. Babatha and her fellow litigants had not only to appear before the governor of the province and to deal with Roman bureaucrats when they swore their oaths: they had now to swear by the fortune of the emperor. The phrase can be seen in one of Babatha's documents, where she says, ὄμνυμι τύχην Καίσαρος καλῇ πίστει ἀπογεγράφθαι.[45] And in the later contracts, where in former times a violator had to pay a penalty both to the injured party and to the Nabataean king, he must now pay to the injured party and to the emperor of Rome.[46]

Among the other Jews who had property in the province of Arabia in the early years were the relatives of Babatha's second husband. The family seat appears to have been at En-Geddi, in Judaea on the west coast of the Dead Sea; but they were also established in the fertile Lisān on the Jordanian side of the Sea and were, like Babatha, subject there to Roman magistrates of Arabia.[47] The latest document in Babatha's possession is dated to August of 132,[48] and it may be assumed that she fled with her most precious things very soon thereafter as the rebellion of Bar Kokhba began to gather momentum. She may have tried at first to join the relatives of her husband at En-Geddi before resolving

[43] Polotsky, *IEJ* (above, n. 30), 260; Yadin, *Ex Oriente Lux* (above, n. 1), 239.

[44] Observe that the coins of Philadelphia show Φιλαδελφέων Κοίλης Συρίας throughout the second and early third centuries A.D.: Spijkerman (above, n. 20), pp. 242–57.

[45] Polotsky, *IEJ* (above, n. 30), 260; Yadin, *Bar Kokhba* (above, n. 1), p. 245.

[46] Yadin, *IEJ* (above, n. 3), 246: *wlmrn' qysr'* ("and to our lord the emperor").

[47] Yadin, *Ex Oriente Lux* (above, n. 1), 240.

[48] Published by Polotsky, *Eretz Israel* (above, n. 2), 50, and republished by Lemosse (above, n. 2), 365; Lewis (above, n. 2), 112; and Wolff (above, n. 2), 771–72.

to hide in a cave that was in the immediate vicinity. One supposes that the Jewish settlers in the Lisān as well as some of Babatha's neighbors in Zoar may, like her, have decided to flee from Roman Arabia at the same time. The Jewish uprising across the valley must have endangered the security of Jews in the adjacent province, and to avoid reprisals they returned to their own country to conceal themselves and wait. As of now there is no sign that they ever returned to the palm groves of Arabia. Babatha cannot have been the only refugee who died in the caves of the Judaean desert.

VII

BOUNDARIES AND DEFENSES

THE EXACT BOUNDARIES of the province from which Babatha fled constitute a thorny problem. Her repeated dealings with governors of Arabia leave no doubt that the property which her father had acquired in the vicinity of Zoar formed an integral part of the new province, just as it had formerly of the Nabataean kingdom. The disappearance of the Nabataean kings and the organization which they had created throughout both the desert and the sown would suggest that the Romans annexed the totality of their kingdom. This does indeed seem to have been the case, but the matter must be demonstrated in detail.

Unfortunately the second-century geographer, Claudius Ptolemaeus, can provide no guidance in the determination of Roman administrative boundaries. His work, detailed as it is and equipped with measurements of longitude and latitude, is clearly based upon regional geographical concepts rather than those of the Roman administration. It may be surmised that the ultimate source of his maps, which accompanied the text we now have, was also the source of the Peutinger Table.[1] But whether this was so or not, he does not register places by Roman provinces. This is immediately apparent from a cursory glance at his treatment of the cities in Transjordan: some are assigned to Arabia Petraea (which, naturally, describes the area in the general vicinity of Petra and the south of Transjordan), while others are assigned to Coele Syria, which did not become the name of a Roman province until well after the composition of Ptolemy's geography.[2] Coele Syria was, however, an important local geographical unit, to which a city such as Philadelphia (ʿAmmān) belonged. Philadelphia was at one and the same time a city of the province of Arabia and a city, in local terms, of Coele Syria. The affiliation to the

[1] See Appendix IV.

[2] Ptolemy, *Geog.* 5.15 (Coele Syria) and 5.17 (Arabia Petraea).

local geographical unit is remarkably the one that is most conspicuous on the coinage of Philadelphia.[3] Since Ptolemy was not operating with Roman provincial units in writing his great work, it is unreasonable to assume, as one excellent scholar has done lately, that from time to time he became confused by the multiplicity of geographical designations for various cities. If he enters Adraa and Adrou under separate headings, this should not be ascribed to confusion but to the presence of two cities with a similar name.[4] Adraa, modern Derʿā in the north, was a major place, as was the military camp at Adrou, modern Udhruḥ, in the south. It would be legitimate therefore to consult Ptolemy for guidance on the existence of cities, but not on the location of Roman provincial boundaries.

No one would wish to dispute that the core of the Nabataean kingdom was likewise the core of the Roman province. This is amply apparent from the creation of the Via Nova Traiana along the route of the old King's Highway. Bostra, the capital, and Petra, the former capital, were the two principal cities of the province, just as they had been in the later years of the Nabataean kings. But it is at the edges, where the province bleeds into the desert or even into other Roman provinces, that problems arise. For one thing, the old conglomeration of Hellenized cities known as the Decapolis came to an end with the annexation of Arabia. The ten cities of the Decapolis were distributed among the adjacent Roman provinces, with Adraa, Gerasa, and Philadelphia definitely going into the province of Arabia, while Gadara, Pella, and Capitolias seem to have been assigned to Judaea.[5] The more

[3] See above p. 88, n. 44.

[4] M. Sartre, *Trois études sur l'Arabie romaine et byzantine* (1982), p. 42, argues that Ἄδρα (Ptolemy, *Geog.* 5.15.23) in Coele Syria and Ἄδρου (5.17.5) in Arabia Petraea actually are the same city: "il s'agit à coup sûr de la même ville," and that is Derʿā. He also thinks that Adrama (5.15.26) in Batanea is the same place.

[5] For the Decapolis generally, H. Bietenhard, *ZDPV* 79 (1963), 24–58, and *ANRW* II.8 (1977), 221–61; S. T. Parker, *JBL* 94 (1975), 437–41; and on the individual cities see the invaluable collection of evidence: A. Spijkerman, *The Coins of the Decapolis and Provincia Arabia* (1978). Cf. also B. Isaac, *ZPE* 44 (1981), 67–74, proving that the Decapolis was a Roman administrative unit under Domitian. On Gadara, Pella, and Capitolias, note the judgment of Sartre (above, n. 4), p. 45. For current excavations at Pella: R. H. Smith, *Archaeology* 34.5 (1981), 46–53, and the same author's *Pella of the Decapolis* (1973).

northerly cities of the Decapolis formed a part of the province of Syria until at least one of them was reassigned to Arabia when the province's boundaries were changed at a later date.[6]

The elimination of the Decapolis as a formal association of major cities in the Near East may not have meant any practical difference in the way in which their affairs were conducted. The prestige of being a Decapolis city continued into later times, just as Philadelphia proclaimed itself a city of Coele Syria while actually forming a part of the province of Arabia. The city of Abila could describe itself as a member of the Decapolis while it belonged to the so-called Peraea of Judaea.[7] It is perhaps not an accident that, in creating the province of Arabia, the Roman administration divided up those important regions that had been outside the Nabataean kingdom, so that they were accommodated in no less than three distinct provinces and would therefore find it difficult ever to take concerted action in times of crisis. Membership in the Decapolis became an empty, though not forgotten honor.

The disposition of the Decapolis cities meant that the western boundary of Arabia lay not in the obvious place, along the Jordan Valley and the Dead Sea. On the contrary, Judaea extended to the eastern side of the valley, down as far as the beginning of the Wādī Mūjib and the plains of Moab. Since the city of Mādabā was conspicuously not a part of the Judaean Peraea in Transjordan, the line of demarcation may be set to the west of Mādabā and extending down to the intersection of the Wādī Mūjib with the Dead Sea. Ḥesbān also will have lain within the confines of the Arabian province.[8] South of the Wādī Mūjib it is clear that the province, like the Nabataean kingdom, extended along the edge of the Dead Sea and then south through Edom.

As the documents of Babatha demonstrate, the fertile region of Zoar south of the Dead Sea constituted a part of the province, as it had of the kingdom; and there is no doubt that the whole of the

[6] Canatha (Qanawāt) became a part of Arabia under Septimius Severus. See below, pp. 114–16.

[7] Waddington, *IGLS* no. 2631: Ἀβιληνὸς τῆς Δεκαπόλεος [*sic*] (in A.D. 133–134).

[8] Cf. Spijkerman (above, n. 5), pp. 122–23. The site, ancient Esbous, has been recently excavated under the auspices of Andrews University, and important remains from the second-century city have been uncovered: L. A. Mitchel, *AJA* 84 (1980), 224.

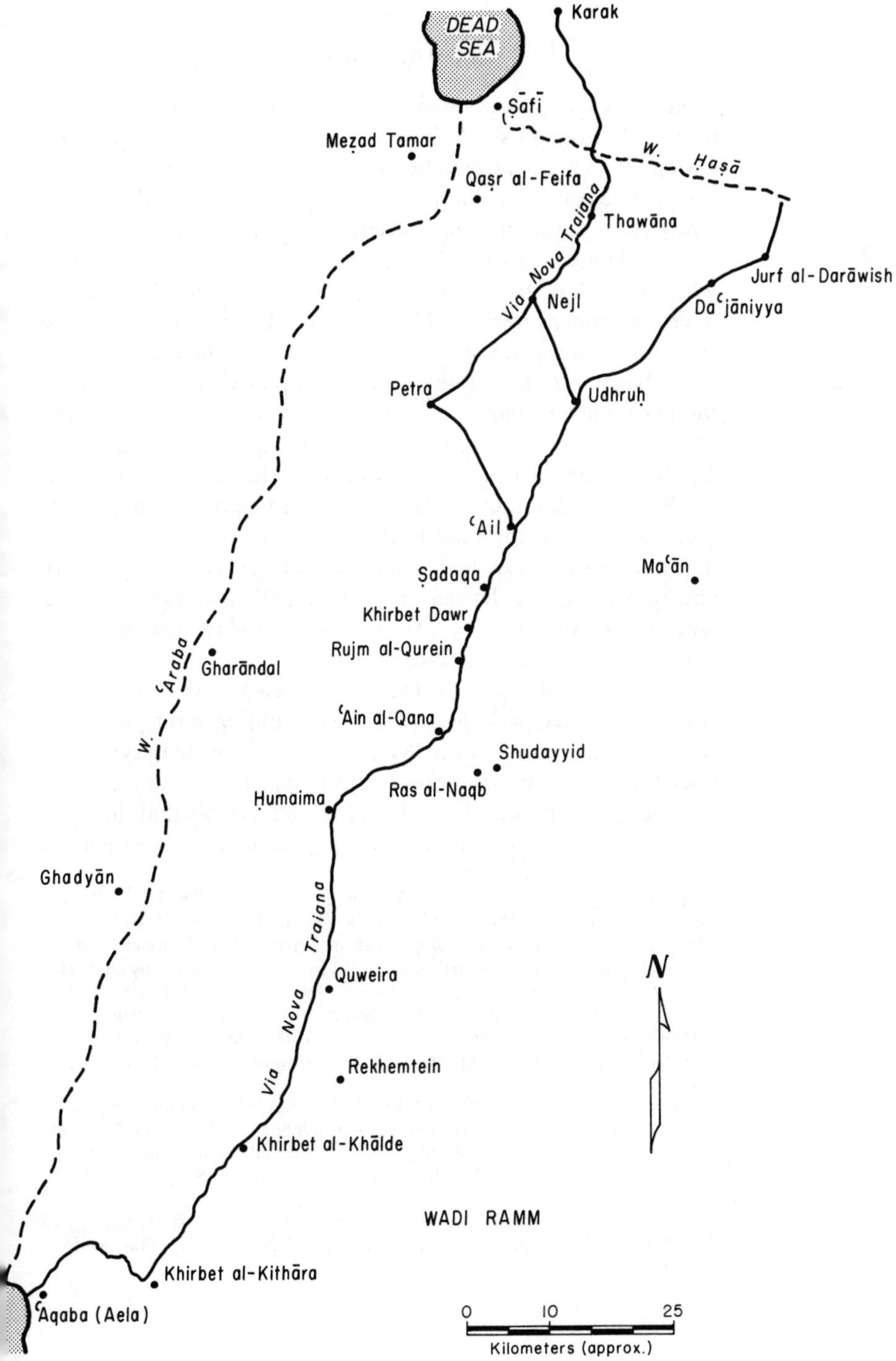
DEAD SEA
Karak
Ṣafi
Mezad Tamar
W. Ḥaṣā
Qaṣr al-Feifa
Thawāna
Via Nova Traiana
Jurf al-Darāwish
Daʿjāniyya
Nejl
Petra
Udhruḥ
ʿAil
Maʿān
Ṣadaqa
Khirbet Dawr
Rujm al-Qurein
Gharāndal
W. ʿAraba
ʿAin al-Qana
Shudayyid
Ras al-Naqb
Ḥumaima
Ghadyān
Via Nova Traiana
Quweira
N
Rekhemtein
Khirbet al-Khālde
WADI RAMM
Khirbet al-Kithāra
ʿAqaba (Aela)
0 10 25
Kilometers (approx.)

Negev was also incorporated by Rome. The great cities of Nabataea in that region show their adhesion to the new province by dating their public records henceforth according to the era of the province. Meanwhile, on the eastern side of the Wādī ʿAraba, which stretched south from the date-palm groves of Zoar, the Nabataean kingdom had included the whole region of the Ḥismā, which lay below the escarpment south of Petra and Maʿān at the lower extremity of Edom. The Via Nova Traiana descended the escarpment at a point somewhat to the west of the modern road. From Ṣadaqa it reached the Roman camp at Ḥumaima through the place known today as Baiḍā' and then descended along the Wādī Yutm, past further Roman camps at Quweira, Khālde, and Kithāra.[9] There is good reason to believe that all of these southern Roman installations were set at points where the Nabataeans had also guarded the road to the head of the Gulf of ʿAqaba.[10] There is, accordingly, no reason to doubt that the new province was constructed on the central part of the Nabataean kingdom, with the addition of a few Decapolis cities and the deliberate inclusion of the Nabataean Negev as well.

As for the Sinai, the Nabataeans are known to have been active in this region and perhaps involved in the mining of turquoise and copper in the vicinity of the Wādī Feirān.[11] They may even have introduced roads in this area. Graffiti and inscriptions dated according to the provincial era of Arabia would imply that the Sinai was also included in the new province.[12] Although this evidence is

[9] See the important new survey by David F. Graf, *ADAJ* 23 (1979), 121–27. For earlier attempts to trace the road between Ṣadaqa and Ḥumaima, cf. especially A. Musil, *The Northern Heǧâz* (1926), p. 58, and Aurel Stein, in D. L. Kennedy, *ArchExplor* (1982), pp. 271–87. Sartre (above, n. 4), pp. 22–23, inadvertently omits Ḥumaima from his list of major sites along the Via Nova in the Ḥismā. David Graf tells me that he believes the path of the Via Nova as it came down the escarpment was probably close to that of the new modern highway west of the old highway.

[10] Graf (above, n. 9), and for Quweira, Khālde, and Kithāra, S. T. Parker, *ADAJ* 21 (1976), 19–31.

[11] Nabataean graffiti in the Wādī Mukattab and the Wādī Feirān are abundant: cf. B. Rothenberg, "An Archaeological Survey of South Sinai," *PEQ* 102 (1970), 4–29. For a brief review of pertinent dated graffiti, cf. Sartre (above, n. 4), pp. 38–39. See also A. Negev, "Nabataean Inscriptions in Southern Sinai," *BiblArch* 45 (1982), 21–25.

[12] See the texts adduced by Sartre (above, n. 4), p. 38. Note, for example, *CIS* II.1325 (year 45 of the province, A.D. 150–151), *CIS* II.964 (year 85 of the province,

not conclusive proof of incorporation (since there is no reason why visitors to the region should not have dated according to a formula familiar to them), it is unlikely that the Roman government would have neglected to administer this valuable link between Egypt and the Negev. An inscription in Latin from the vicinity of the Wādī Umm Sidaira shows the presence of at least some kind of detachment of the Arabian legion, the Third Cyrenaica.[13] Another text from the region records a victory of Augusti and again implies some kind of official Roman military presence.[14] Therefore, although there is no conclusive evidence that the Sinai formed an official part of the province, it can be said with certainty that the persons responsible for administering the province took care to attend to the regulation of the peninsula. It would obviously be most reasonable to assume, on balance, that the region was, in fact, part of the province.

For the Ḥejāz in northwest Saudi Arabia, lying across the Gulf of ʿAqaba from the Sinai peninsula, there is far more secure evidence for Roman annexation. This territory had been indisputably a part of the Nabataean kingdom, as can easily be seen from the tombs at Hegra (Madā'in Ṣāliḥ). Recent explorers have also found decisive evidence for Nabataean presence at Qurayya to the northwest of Madā'in Ṣāliḥ.[15] Between the oases of al-ʿUlā (ancient Dedan) and Madā'in Ṣāliḥ, a substantial number of graffiti have been recorded which establish the presence of soldiers from the Nabataean army and subsequently the army of Rome.[16] On present evidence this seems to represent the southernmost point of

---

A.D. 190–191), and esp. *CIS* II.963 (year 100 of the province, with a prayer for "three emperors," A.D. 205–206). Sartre's date of 211–212 for *CIS* II.963 is shown to be untenable by de Vogüé's commentary *ad loc.*

[13] From the Wādī Tuweiba, *AE* 1972.671 (cf. M. Speidel, *ANRW* II.8 [1977], 694–95, and Sartre [above, n. 4], p. 39): *T. Atilius Turbo m(iles) leg(ionis) III Cyr(enaicae)*. The text was found near a copper mine, which may explain the soldier's presence. For further discussion of this inscription, E. D. Kollmann, *IEJ* 22 (1972), 145–47.

[14] *ZPE* 7 (1971), 152, n. 3, with the correction noted by Speidel (above, n. 13), 695, n. 23: *Victoria Augg.*

[15] P. J. Parr, G. L. Harding, and J. E. Dayton, *Bull. Inst. Arch. Univ. London* 8–9 (1970), 226–38.

[16] H. Seyrig, "Postes romains sur la route de Médine," *Syria* 22 (1941), 218–23. The texts are reproduced by Sartre (above, n. 4), pp. 30–33.

military patrol under the Nabataean kings and the Roman province. Until recently, however, it could not be asserted with confidence that these patrols were anything more than members of military outposts beyond the proper boundaries of the kingdom or province. But it is beyond question that they belonged to units of the central authority in the Transjordanian heartland. One of the Nabataean graffiti records the name of a certain Ṣabru, who is explicitly described as a native of Ṣalkhad in the Ḥawrān.[17] The Greek graffiti attesting soldiers of the Roman army give, in several cases, the names of the units to which they belonged, such as the *ala Gaetulorum* and the *ala dromedariorum* (a camel-riding unit).[18] And a new stele from Madā'in Ṣāliḥ has revealed a painter who belonged to the Third Cyrenaica.[19]

The presence of a temple to the Roman emperors Marcus Aurelius and Lucius Verus at the remote site of Ruwwāfa, to the northwest of Madā'in Ṣāliḥ and to the south of Qurayya, has been known since Musil's exploration of the region early in this century.[20] But the great bilingual inscription on that building, in Greek and Nabataean, has been published completely only in the last decade.[21] It is a document of the greatest importance for the

[17] First published by A. Jaussen and R. Savignac, *Mission archéologique en Arabie* II (1914), p. 193, no. 226 (the text is no. 19 in Sartre's list [above, n. 4], p. 32, but given only in translation): *ṣbrw br 'wšw dy mn ṣlḥdw.*

[18] Jaussen and Savignac (above, n. 17), pp. 647–48, nos. 14 and 16 (ἄλα Γετουλῶν), reproduced in Speidel (above, n. 13), 705; and Sartre (above, n. 4), pp. 30–31, nos. 1 and 3. For the *ala* of *dromedarii*, see Jaussen and Savignac, p. 645, no. 6 (Speidel, 704; Sartre, p. 31, no. 9).

[19] T. C. Barger published my reading of the inscription, but with an inaccurate sketch, in *Archaeology* 22 (1969), 139–40. A photograph may be seen in *Archaeology* 19 (1966), 218, and *JRS* 61 (1971), plate XIV.1. The text: Τύχῃ Βόστρων Ἁδριανὸς ζωγράφος σὺν λεγ. III Κυ. For the work of military painters, see G. M. A. Hanfmann, without knowledge of the Madā'in Ṣāliḥ inscription, in *AJA* 85 (1981), 87–88: "A Painter in the Imperial Arms Factory at Sardis." A legionary painter would have decorated shields.

[20] Musil (above, n. 9), p. 185. Cf. G. W. Bowersock, *JRS* 61 (1971), 230–31.

[21] J. T. Milik, in P. J. Parr, G. L. Harding, and J. E. Dayton, *Bull. Inst. Arch. Univ. London* 10 (1972), 54–57. The texts have been reproduced and discussed by G. W. Bowersock, *Le monde grec: Hommages à Claire Préaux* (1975), 513–22; David F. Graf, *BASOR* 229 (1978), 9–12; Sartre (above, n. 4), pp. 27–29 (but with the Nabataean text given only in translation). The early text published in F. Altheim and R. Stiehl, *Die Araber in der alten Welt* V.2 (1969), pp. 24–25, is useless, although the photographs on plates 2–5 are good.

history of the Arabian province. The dedicators of the shrine prove to have been a confederation of the Arab Thamūd, and their dedication is dated to the governorship of Claudius Modestus, governor of the province of Arabia. Modestus' name appears in one of the Greek inscriptions in a dating formula; and his predecessor, Antistius Adventus, also a governor of the province of Arabia, is mentioned explicitly in the Nabataean text, because of his good offices in restoring peace to warring factions within the Thamūdic confederation. So this text establishes the official role of a Roman governor in the Ḥejāz during the second century A.D. and puts beyond all doubt the incorporation of this region in the province as a whole. It would be inconceivable to find the names of Roman governors, as we do in the Ruwwāfa dedicatory inscription, if the site were not an integral part of the province they were administering.

The Ruwwāfa texts show furthermore that Nabataean culture was so firmly implanted in the Ḥejāz that another confederation of Arabs, the Thamūd, used in this territory the Nabataean language and script rather than their own (which is attested elsewhere). The existence of an Arab confederation in the confines of a Roman province is in itself worth remarking. The Greek designation is not as precise as one might wish, *ἔθνος Θαμουδηνῶν*; but the Nabataean language is exact: *šrkt tmwdw*. Although the Greek term *ἔθνος* could be used to describe either a tribe or a confederation, the Nabataean word is not ambiguous. The reference must be to a confederation, and not simply a tribe of the Thamūd. It may well be that the Roman authorities relied upon the presence of such confederated Arabs to assist in the administration of so inaccessible a territory, and indeed such reliance may explain the governors' efforts to assure peace among the various tribes of the confederation.[22] The use of such groups anticipates, at a far earlier date than one might have guessed, the role of Arab

[22] The Nabataean text ends *wḥfyt 'nṭsṭys 'dwnts hgmwn'* [- - *ca.* 10] *wrmṣhm*. The role of Antistius Adventus which is *ḥfyt* in Nabataean appears as *μετὰ προτρο[τῆς] καὶ ἐκ πẹι̣[θοῦς]* in Milik's text. I have proposed ([above, n. 21], 516) that *ἐκ π̣ρ̣ο̣[νοίας]* is preferable. The verb *rmṣ* shows that Adventus was making peace between tribes. The word does not appear, e.g., in Cantineau's lexicon; but classical Arabic *ramaṣa* (*baina*), "to make peace (between)," is decisive. For a recent study of Ruwwāfa and the Thamūd see J. Beaucamp, *SDB* 9 (1979), 1467–75.

confederations in the management of the Near East during subsequent centuries—and especially, of course, in the Byzantine age.

It is clear that the Nabataeans made good use of the Wādī Sirḥān in the desert to the east of the cultivated part of their kingdom.[23] This internal route from the central parts of Saudi Arabia up through the oasis of Jawf to the oasis of Azraq at the head of the wadi was an important means of communication and trade in antiquity, as it is today. The Roman administration, once it had terminated the rule of the Nabataean kings, could scarcely have afforded to neglect the Wādī Sirḥān. And it did not. The evidence of Roman troops of the Third Cyrenaica, not only at Azraq itself but at adjacent sites in the region, such as Qaṣr Asaikhin and Qaṣr ʿUweinid, imply a concern for the traffic along the Wādī Sirḥān.[24] By an agreeable coincidence, a Nabataean text attesting a Nabataean stratopedarch at Jawf, near the southern end of the Wādī Sirḥān, can be paralleled by a text from the time of the Roman province.[25] A Latin inscription at Jawf records a dedication *pro salute domm(inorum) nn(ostrorum) Augg(ustorum)*, who would appear to be either the emperors Marcus Aurelius and Lucius Verus or Septimius Severus and Caracalla.[26] The dedication is made to the gods *Juppiter optimus Hammon* and *sanctus Sulmus* by a centurion of the Third Cyrenaica, Flavius Dionysius. Since both deities are Arab, with known associations at Bostra and Umm al-jimāl in the region of Bostra, we may be certain that this centurion had been sent out from the garrison legion of the province for duty in Jawf.[27] He is probably an Arab

[23] See Appendix II; also G. W. Bowersock, on the work of Nelson Glueck and F. V. Winnett, in *JRS* 61 (1971), 221.

[24] See D. L. Kennedy in *Roman Frontier Studies 1979*, BAR International Series 71 (1980), 879–87, and the same scholar, *ArchExplor* (1982), chap. 4, on Azraq and its environs.

[25] The Nabataean *stratopedarch* (*rb mšryt*ʾ) at Jawf: R. Savignac and J. Starcky, *RB* 64 (1957), 215.

[26] For the Latin text at Jawf, still not formally published but now available in full, Speidel (above, n. 13), 694, and Kennedy, *ArchExplor* (1982), p. 190, no. 39: *Pro salute / domm. nn. Augg. / I.o. m. Ham/moni et san/cto Sulmo / Fl. Dionysi/us 7 leg. III Cyr. / v.s.* See plate 14 below (courtesy of Mahmud Ghul).

[27] For the close association of Zeus Hammon with Bostra and its legion, see the coinage bearing the legion's name and the image of Zeus Hammon (A. Kindler, *IEJ* 25 [1975], 144, and *SNG*, Amer. Num. Soc., part 6, Palestine-South Arabia [1981], nos. 1222–26 [Bostra]). See also D. Sourdel, *Les cultes du Hauran à l'époque romaine*

with a Roman name, and accordingly the kind of soldier who might be expected to know how to live in a place like Jawf.

The evidence for Roman interest in the Wādī Sirḥān at its southern and northern extremities would imply that this region, like the Ḥejāz, was considered a part of the province of Arabia. It would be folly to seek any clear boundary line in the eastern part of the province. Just as the Romans did not have provincial boundaries within the waters of the Mediterranean, they were not likely to have defined clear boundaries within the wastes of the great Syrian desert. But it is reasonable to assume that the governor of Arabia considered the territory, at least as far as the Wādī Sirḥān, to be within his area of responsibility and jurisdiction. Beyond that there is no way of telling. To the north of the Azraq oasis and, indeed, far to the north and east of the settled part of Roman Arabia, there lies a remote Roman fortification, the Qaṣr Burquʿ. If, as now seems probable, this represents a Roman installation with a surviving Roman tower, we can gain some notion of how far into the desert the Romans were willing to establish themselves in order to guarantee the security of the more settled region to the west.[28]

The definition of the northern boundary of the province of Arabia is facilitated by the mass of inscriptions from a wide variety of sites in the area. In general, it is reasonable to assume that sites which register dates according to the era of the Arabian province belonged at that time to the province, whereas those which date by the Seleucid era, or simply by the regnal year of the emperor, belonged in all probability to the adjacent province of Syria.[29] It is clear that the plain of the Ḥawrān, within which lay

(1952), p. 89, citing inscriptions at Bostra mentioning Zeus Hammon. For Sulmus, see *PAES* III.A, no. 239 (Umm al-jimāl): θεῷ Σόλμῳ, reprinted in Sourdel, p. 87.

[28] Kennedy, *ArchExplor* (1982), p. 300, affirms that the tower is "Romano-Byzantine." On the Greek inscription there, see S. Dow, in H. Field, *North Arabian Desert Archaeological Survey 1925–1950* (1960), pp. 161–63. On the remains at Burquʿ, see H. Gaube, *ADAJ* 19 (1974), 93–100.

[29] The evidence has been carefully studied and catalogued by E. Kettenhofen, "Zur Nordgrenze der *provincia Arabiae* im 3. Jahrhundert n. Chr.," *ZDPV* 97 (1981), 62–73, and independently by Sartre (above, n. 4), pp. 48–54. Both Sartre and I have had access to the valuable analysis of the evidence for the northern frontier in chap. 4 of the unpublished dissertation, "Studies in the History of the Roman Province of Arabia" (Univ. Manchester, 1979), by H. I. MacAdam. By the third century, as Sartre shows

the capital city of Bostra, was an integral part of Arabia, as was the southern slope of the Jebel Drūz to the east of the plain. The major city of Ṣalkhad to the east of Bostra and south of the Jebel Drūz was, together with neighboring villages, included within the Arabian province.[30] By contrast, cities to the north, such as Ḥabrān, ʿAtīl, Mushannaf, Suweidā', and Qanawāt, were all part of the province of Syria after the annexation of Arabia.[31] It would naturally be expected that still more northerly territories, such as the rough country of the Leja', would likewise lie in the Syrian province, and inscriptions prove that they did.[32] Therefore, in the second century A.D., the Romans evidently drew a northern boundary for the new province a little to the north of Bostra and due east.

The problem as to what was incorporated to the north and west of Bostra is a difficult one, since there is virtually no epigraphic testimony from this region, the so-called Nuqra. There is one stone that is relevant, discovered early in this century at the site of Sijn in the northeast corner of the Nuqra, just to the south of the Leja' and near the northwestern slopes of the Jebel Drūz.[33] The text, which is fragmentary and far from transparently clear, seems to record a date of A.D. 179–180 by the provincial era.[34] It is, however, difficult to believe that the Romans would have absorbed into Arabia the whole region of the Nuqra bordering on the western slope of the Jebel Drūz, when they so carefully

---

(p. 55), dating by the regnal year of the emperor no longer shows anything about provincial affiliation.

[30] See the sites in this region in Kettenhofen (above, n. 29), 71–72, and the discussion in Sartre (above, n. 4), pp. 49–50.

[31] Ḥabrān: *PAES* III.A, nos. 661–63 (*IGR* 3.1292, 1294–95); ʿAtīl: *AAES* 427a (*IGR* 3.1237); Mushannaf: *AAES* 380a (*IGR* 3.1261); Suweidā': Waddington, *IGLS* 2306, 2308, 2309 (*IGR* 3.1274, 1276–77); Qanawāt: Waddington, *IGLS* 2330–31 (*IGR* 3.1224, 1226). For other cities and villages in this area see Sartre (above, n. 4), p. 51.

[32] See the listing for Kettenhofen's region A2 (above, n. 29), 65–66.

[33] R. Savignac and A. Abel, *RB* 14 (1905), 95, no. 10, reprinted in R. E. Brünnow and A. von Domaszewski, *Die Provincia Arabia* III (1909), p. 318 (cf. p. 267). MacAdam (above, n. 29) attends carefully to this inscription. Kettenhofen unfortunately misses it altogether, but Sartre (above, n. 4) treats it on pp. 50–52.

[34] The editors restored as follows: *ἔτους τοῦ ἑβδο[μηκόστου καὶ τετ]άρτου τῆς ἐπα[ρχείας]* But on the copy (with lunate sigma and epsilon) from which they worked, *ἔτους* appears as *σιους* and *ἑβδο* as *οβδο*.

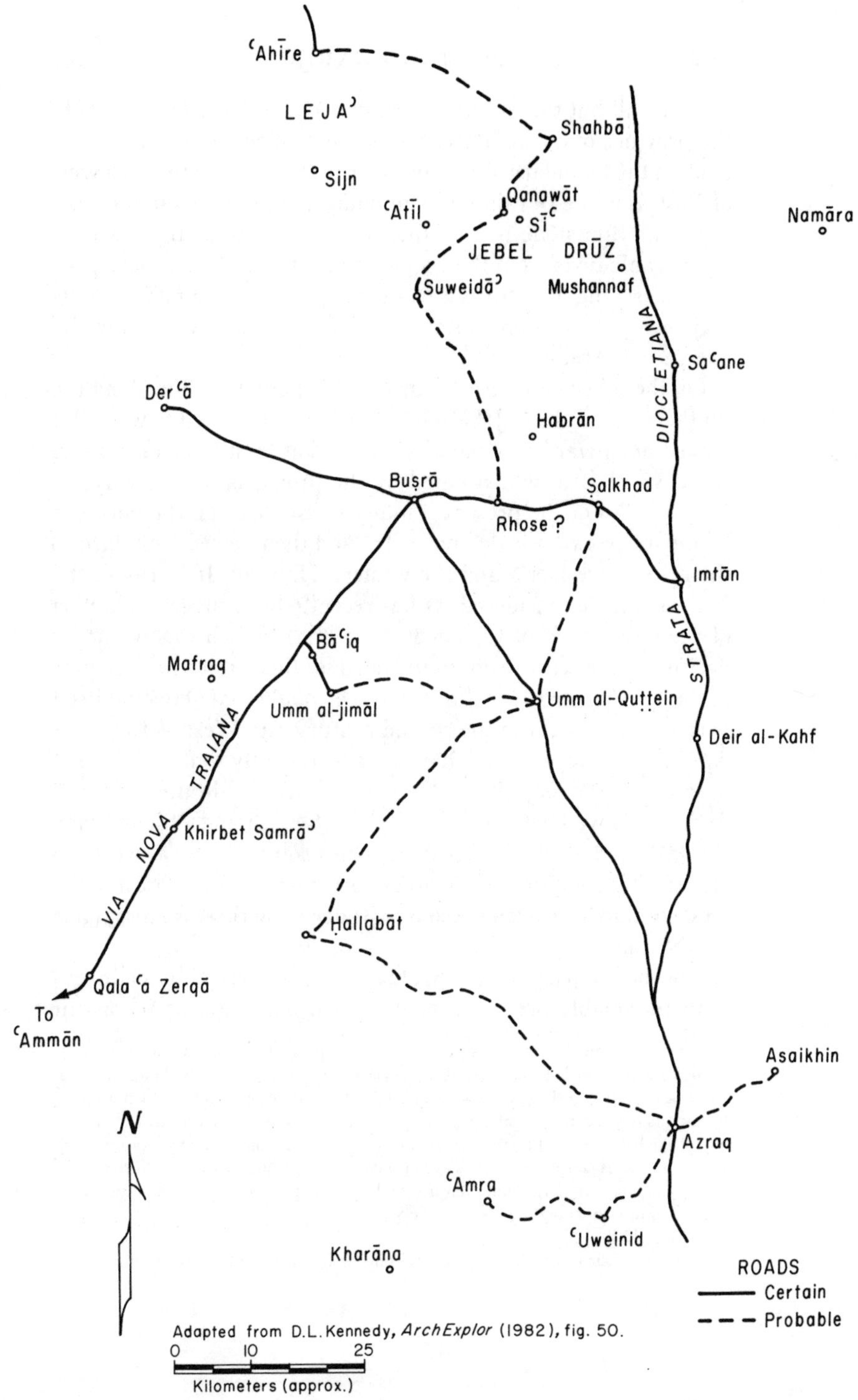

ᶜAhīre
LEJAʾ
Shahbā
Sijn
Qanawāt
ᶜAtīl
Sīᶜ
JEBEL DRŪZ
Namāra
Suweidāʾ
Mushannaf
DIOCLETIANA
Saᶜane
Derᶜā
Habrān
Buṣrā
Ṣalkhad
Rhose ?
Imtān
STRATA
Bāᶜiq
Mafraq
Umm al-jimāl
Umm al-Quṭṭein
Deir al-Kahf
VIA NOVA TRAIANA
Khirbet Samrāʾ
Ḥallabāt
Qalaᶜa Zerqā
To ᶜAmmān
Asaikhin
N
Azraq
ᶜAmra
ᶜUweinid
Kharāna
ROADS
Certain
Probable
Adapted from D.L. Kennedy, *ArchExplor* (1982), fig. 50.
0 10 25
Kilometers (approx.)

assigned all but the southernmost part of the Jebel Drūz itself to the province of Syria. There would be no obvious reason for extending the boundary abruptly so far to the north in the area west of Bostra, while refraining from doing so in the area to the east. Since the Sijn stone is a unique testimony, and as there are no comparable texts from the region at all, it is probably more prudent to assume that this is a wandering stone which had made its way to Sijn from some other place that was actually within the province of Arabia.[35]

On the other hand, it is clear that the boundary line along the southern slope of the Jebel Drūz was not extended due west, but curved northward to some degree, so as at least to accommodate the town of ʿIrā, which dated by the provincial era as early as 176–177.[36] For the present it may be assumed that the northern boundary passed a little above ʿIrā and then moved westward to the area above Derʿā and the western Ḥawrān. If Karak in the Nuqra is to be considered, as has recently been suggested, a part of the territorium of Qanawāt (Canatha),[37] then this would be decisive for rejecting Sijn, to the north of this territorium, as part of the Arabian province. For there is no doubt that Qanawāt itself was a part of Syria in the second century A.D. West of Derʿā the Arabian frontier seems to have turned abruptly southward, so as to have left the majority of Decapolis cities within the Peraea of Judaea. As we have seen earlier, only Gerasa and Philadelphia, the easternmost of the Decapolis cities south of Derʿā, were accommodated within the Arabian province, while those farther west seem to have been taken into Judaea and those further north into Syria.

The boundaries of the Arabian province are thus delimited with reasonable precision on the north and west, as far as the

[35] This is the conclusion of Sartre (above, n. 4), p. 52. Confronted with the Nabataean inscription of Deir al Mashqūq (*PAES* IV.A, no. 27) dating by Hadrian's regnal year, Sartre rightly acknowledges that even in the second century such a dating formula is not absolutely unknown in Arabia (p. 52). The site, southeast of Ṣalkhad, must have belonged to the province. As far as the erased name of a governor on *PAES* III.A, no. 155 is concerned, this does not have to be Avidius Cassius, as Sartre interestingly observes (p. 54). And, even if it is, Littmann properly evokes Avidius' *maius imperium* in publishing the text in *PAES*.

[36] *SEG* 7.1149.

[37] See the article of M. Sartre, "Le territoire de Canatha," *Syria*, forthcoming.

west coast of the Negev. Where the province abutted on the desert, there is no clear line of demarcation, nor should anyone expect to find one there. In the Sinai, in the Ḥejāz, and in the great Syrian desert to the east, we can only distinguish the areas that fell within the responsibility of the governor of Arabia. It is impossible to say at just what point those responsibilities evaporated. On the other hand, this kind of imprecision in desert terrain should not be interpreted to mean that such outlying parts were not considered within the province of Arabia. The frontier at these points was an open one, as it had been during the reigns of the Nabataean kings. When necessary, the forces at Jawf or Madā'in Ṣāliḥ could obviously venture beyond these distant places when dangers threatened, but they found it adequate to base themselves at the principal oases along the principal routes.

This situation constituted, particularly in the south and in the east, what has been aptly described as a frontier in depth.[38] Detachments of infantry, cavalry, and camel riders were placed at strategic points in the more remote parts of the province, while nearer to the settled and cultivated areas, there were more substantial forces and a more intricate network of watchtowers and forts. It was this kind of deep frontier in Arabia that became known much later as the *limes Arabicus*.[39] It must be emphasized that the term *limes* is nowhere applied to the fortified frontier of Arabia in the second and third centuries. The word was, of course, traditionally used to describe a fortified line of defense, such as could easily be seen in Germany or in the Balkans, along the Rhine or the Danube, or across the tops of mountains. Fortifications in Arabia were of a very different kind and scarcely fit the usual Roman sense of *limes* at the time the province was incorporated. By the time the expression *limes Arabicus* appears in our sources, the word itself had already changed meaning, perhaps

[38] E. Luttwak, *The Grand Strategy of the Roman Empire* (1976), chap. 3, "Defenses in Depth," pp. 127–90.

[39] The sole appearance of this expression in ancient texts is in Rufinus, *HE* 2.6: *Palestini et Arabici limitis oppida atque urbes*. Misconceptions can easily arise from using the term for an earlier period. The eastern Arabian frontier was a defense in depth well before the word *limes* was used to denote such a defense. The expression "Central Limes Arabicus Project" currently applied to the valuable excavations of S. T. Parker in Jordan is dangerous. The Arabian frontier did not change as the word *limes* changed: it was a frontier in depth from the start.

under the influence of the constraints of desert defense. It becomes the designation for fortified regions, rather than fortified lines; and in this sense it can be attested for North Africa and for the Near East from the third century onward.[40]

In fact, the phrase which Ammianus Marcellinus used of the more remote parts of the Syrian frontier, *interiores limites*, can now be seen simply to mean regions with fortifications in parts of the province that lay upcountry (*interior*).[41] Unfortunately past misapprehension about the sense of both *limes* and *interior* has led to some confusion in discussion of the eastern frontier. Two of the great explorers of Roman Arabia, Brünnow and Domaszewski, were misled into thinking that a *limes* in Arabia should be a fortified line of the traditional kind and were influenced by Ammianus' words to believe that, if there were such a thing as an *interior limes*, there could be an *exterior* one as well. They postulated accordingly inner and outer *limites* in the Arabian province. Subsequent investigation has demonstrated that this interpretation is untenable, in the light of the evidence on the ground of the province. There is no clear line, apart from the Via Nova Traiana, which is for the most part so far back in the settled area as to be of little use for frontier protection, and which is also not the site of the major military installations.[42] These are located farther to the east, in a dotting pattern which took account of elevations of the land for signaling purposes, and naturally also took account of the availability of water. In most cases, well before the Romans the Nabataeans had already determined the ideal spots for military encampments.

[40] In demonstration of *limes* as a fortified zone, see G. W. Bowersock, "Limes Arabicus," *HSCP* 80 (1976), 219–29. For a third-century example of this sense (in North Africa), see *Inscr. Rom. Tripol.*, no. 880, reprinted with helpful commentary by R. Goodchild, *Libyan Studies*, ed. J. Reynolds (1976), pp. 27–28: *regionem limi*[*tis Ten*]*theitani partitam*.

[41] This important point about the meaning of *interior* was made recently and independently by M. Malavolta, "*Interiores Limites*," *Ottava miscellanea greca e romana* (1982), 587–610, and by B. Isaac, "Bandits in Judaea and Arabia" (to appear in *HSCP*). Both take note of Velleius Paterculus 2.120.2: *penetrat interius, aperit limites*. Festus 21 uses *interior* in this same sense in writing of the more remote Arabs whom Septimius Severus conquered in Mesopotamia: *Arabas interiores*. Similarly in the Syriac life of Rabbūla the great man is said to go away into the more remote wilderness, *madbrā gawāyā* ("the inner desert").

[42] On all this see Bowersock, *HSCP* (above, n. 40).

When we speak of the *limes Arabicus* in reference to the fortified frontier of Arabia, we are speaking of a fortified zone with in-depth protection. That zone extended all the way from the great legionary camp that lies at Lejjūn in the vicinity of Karak (near the Dead Sea) to the detachments in the Wādī Sirḥān and the camel riders south of Madā'in Ṣāliḥ. Obviously the closer to settled land in the province, the more dense the network of fortifications. As one moves westward from Azraq toward the Via Nova that proceeded from Philadelphia to Bostra, there is increasing military protection, including the major outposts at Umm al-jimāl and at Qaṣr al-Ḥallabāt. Similarly, along the approaches from the east into the Wādī Ḥaṣā and the Wādī Mūjib, there are thick clusters of forts and watchtowers that protect the settled land in the western part of the province and also protect access from the south along the edge of the desert.[43]

Evidence abounds for the establishment of the new province's legion, the Third Cyrenaica, at a camp in the capital city of Bostra. It is less clear when the other major camps that lie in the province were built and exactly how many soldiers they were meant to accommodate. The camp at Lejjūn can be seen in outline from air photographs and is now under excavation, but the absence of inscriptions, as of this writing, leaves the date and nature of the camp still open to discussion. Sherds imply that it belongs to a much later phase in the life of the province. It may not have been constructed before the time of the Tetrarchy.[44] On the other hand, the camp that lies at modern Udhruḥ and is undoubtedly the site of ancient Adrou (in what the geographer Ptolemy calls Arabia Petraea) may well be an installation of the first years of the province. It is also under excavation at this time; and

[43] See the result of a surface survey: S. T. Parker, "Archaeological Survey of the *Limes Arabicus:* a Preliminary Report," *ADAJ* 21 (1976), 19–31; and the same author, "The Central *Limes Arabicus* Project: The 1980 Campaign," *ADAJ* 25 (1981), 171–78. On the project's name, see above, n. 39. Announcement of an exciting discovery at the eastern extremity of the Wādī Ḥaṣā can be expected from Burton MacDonald in *ADAJ*.

[44] S. T. Parker, *Roman Frontier Studies 1979*, BAR International Series 71 (1980), 871, and *ASOR News* 8 (June 1981), 8–20. The evidence of surface sherds is not, however, sufficient to justify Parker's assumption of a major general strengthening of Arabian defenses under the Tetrarchs. Such a military operation, connected with the foundation of Lejjūn, remains a possibility (even a probability) but is not yet proved.

the evidence of coins and stratigraphy points to a Trajanic date.[45] If this is the case, Udhruḥ may have served as the site of the protecting forces for the southern part of the province, just as Bostra provided protection for the north. It would certainly make sense to have a major garrison in the south, in addition to the forts and watchtowers, since in this period the port city of Aela was not yet the seat of a legionary force (as it was in the fourth century).

Overall the arming of Arabia was entrusted to the legion Third Cyrenaica, whose chief commander was at the same time the governor of the province. Although traces of the legion can be found outside on several occasions after its annexation, there can be little doubt, after extensive scholarly debate in recent years, that this was the legion assigned to the province from the beginning.[46] The Sixth Ferrata may have been on loan from Syria at one point or another during the years of organizing the province, but it was transferred finally to Palestine relatively early, perhaps in A.D. 123.[47] It is evident that until the time of Diocletian no legion, apart from the Third Cyrenaica, was assigned to Arabia on a permanent, or even temporary basis.[48] For some two hundred years this was a single-legion province.

[45] I owe this information to a preliminary report generously sent to me by A. C. Killick, who is directing the excavation at Udhruḥ.

[46] See the thorough discussion in D. L. Kennedy, "*Legio VI Ferrata:* the Annexation and Early Garrison of Arabia," *HSCP* 84 (1980), 283–309. III Cyrenaica has vexillations at Dura in 115 (*Exc. Dura-Europus* 4 [1933], 57–65; 6 [1936], 480–82) and at Jerusalem in 116–117 (*CIL* III.13587). Cf. the tribune of III Cyrenaica who is decorated by Trajan for service in the Parthian War: D. J. Blackman, in J. Schäfer, *Phaselis: Beiträge zur Topographie und Geschichte der Stadt und ihrer Häfen*, Istanbuler Mitt. Beiheft 24 (1981), p. 155.

[47] The problem has been that III Cyrenaica seems obviously located in Egypt in A.D. 119: *BGU* I.140. Hence earlier assumptions that this was not the initial Arabian garrison. But *Pap. Mich.* 465 and 466 must be taken to prove that III Cyrenaica was in Arabia from the beginning: M. Speidel (above, n. 13), 691–94. On VI Ferrata in Arabia, see the inscriptions in C. H. Kraeling, *Gerasa* (1938), p. 435, no. 171, as revised and reinterpreted by Kennedy (above, n. 46), 297–99, plus a new text published by Kennedy (299–300) and another published by M. Sartre, *ZPE* 13 (1974), 85–89. Kennedy argues that VI Ferrata was in Arabia from 116 to 123, while III Cyrenaica provided vexillations during Trajan's Parthian expedition and for Jerusalem and then was reinstated briefly in Egypt before returning to Arabia.

[48] For the arrival of IV Martia, perhaps in the late fourth century, see Speidel (above, n. 13), 699. Legio I Parthica Philippiana accompanied the Arab emperor in Arabia after his Persian campaign, but it was not a legion of the province: Speidel, 698–99.

For the auxiliary units, no military diploma from the province yet exists to provide help. But it is possible to determine from inscriptions and papyri the composition of the initial garrison. There appear to have been some twelve units,[49] including the *ala dromedariorum* and the *ala veterana Gaetulorum*, known from the graffiti between Madā'in Ṣāliḥ and al-ʿUlā in the Ḥejāz. The *cohors I Hispanorum* and the *cohors I Thebaeorum* seem to have been transferred from Egypt precisely in 105, with a view to participation in the organization of the Arabian province.[50] The *cohors VI Hispanorum* has reasonably been thought to have entered the province near the beginning from a station on the Syrian frontier between Damascus and Palmyra.[51] Likewise, two other Syrian units appear to have been transferred early into Arabia, the *cohors I Augusta Thracum equitata* and the *cohors I miliaria Thracum*.[52] An inscription at Imtān indicates that the *cohors I Augusta Canathenorum equitata* was also present in the province near the beginning.[53] Presumably there were at least four other units, as yet unknown, to fill out the auxiliary garrison in numbers which would match that of the provincial legion.

It has been well observed that Arabia's initial armed force was by necessity an army of foreigners.[54] The occupying legion, as well as several cohorts, came from Egypt; the *ala* of Gaetuli came from Palestine; and several other cohorts presumably came from Syria. On the other hand, outside the Arabian province but still within the Roman Near East, at least six *cohortes Ulpiae Petraeorum* turn up in numbers that come to 4,000 or 5,000.[55] It seems

[49] Cf. the authoritative register of known units, together with an opinion of the overall number, in Speidel (above, n. 13), 699–717.

[50] See p. 80, n. 14: Speidel (above, n. 13), 709–10 and 719.

[51] Speidel (above, n. 13), 709. For the Ḥallabāt inscription attesting this cohort in 212–213, see now Kennedy *ArchExplor* (1982), pp. 39–40, no. 3.

[52] Speidel (above, n. 13), 710–11. For the *cohors I Augusta Thracum equitata* see R. Mellor and E. Harris, *ZPE* 16 (1975), 121–24 (in Syria in 88), and A. Negev, *IEJ* 17 (1967), 54 (in Mampsis in the early second century). For the *cohors I miliaria Thracum*, this might be the Syrian unit attested in 88 and 91 (Speidel, 711) and the Arabian one mentioned on the Ḥallabāt inscription (n. 51 above).

[53] *CIL* III.14379 (cf. Speidel [above, n. 13], 709). Canatha was a city in the Syrian province in the second century A.D., and so this unit would have had to cross over into Arabia.

[54] Speidel (above, n. 13), 719.

[55] For the *cohortes Ulpiae Petraeorum*, see C. Cichorius, *RE* 4.1.324–25; also Speidel (above, n. 13), 719.

obvious that these cohorts with the *gentilicium* of Trajan and a home base of Petra must be the Nabataean cavalry sent outside the new province for service in the Roman army. These Nabataeans, serving with the inferior status of *equites cohortales* rather than *alae*, will have been sent out of the country, perhaps for reasons of security. Able and young, they served to replace the units which were withdrawn from other provinces in order to garrison their own. It was not long, however, before the Arabian army began to recruit locally both for its *auxilia* and for the legion, as well as for other units to serve outside the province.[56]

The defenses of Arabia in the second century A.D. seem to have served adequately for the protection of the frontiers, for both the linear ones in the north and west, and the open ones in the south and east. There is some evidence of destruction in ʿAvdat, in the middle part of the century, but it is impossible to associate this with any known invasions or disturbances. There are only hints of other difficulties. Of these the most mysterious is the recent revelation that the name of the governor Haterius Nepos was carefully erased from inscriptions at Gerasa.[57] Since he was governor in 130 and may possibly have stayed on beyond that year, his disgrace may have had something to do with conduct in Arabia during the course of the troubles fomented by Bar Kokhba. And we know that part of his legion was dispatched to Judaea to aid in crushing the uprising. In view of the swift and unhappy retreat of Babatha from her residence within the province of Arabia into the war zone in Judaea, it is perhaps not excessive to speculate whether Haterius Nepos was responsible for some kind of pogrom in the Roman interest at the time of the Jewish revolt.

In any event, the erasure of a governor's name in the province is a rare occurrence; but it is not altogether unique. An inscription

[56] See Speidel (above, n. 13), 720. For local recruitment to III Cyrenaica, note particularly *IGR* 3.1257: *Μεσάμαρος ἱππεὺς Κυρ. γένο*[s] Νάβας.

[57] The inscriptions at Gerasa have been known for some time: Kraeling (above, n. 47), nos. 58 and 143–44, dated to Hadrian's visit in 130. Thanks to the Babatha archive we now know the name of the governor of Arabia in that year (*IEJ* 12 [1962], 259), and it must accordingly be his name that was erased on the Gerasa stones. Sartre (above, n. 4), pp. 54 and 82, was the first to make this observation.

from Ṣalkhad of A.D. 169 shows once again the same phenomenon.[58] It has normally been assumed that this inscription carried the name of Avidius Cassius, who suffered a general *damnatio memoriae* as a result of the revolt which he raised in Syria against Marcus Aurelius some years later. Ṣalkhad, however, lies well south of the border of Syria, which was the province entrusted to Avidius Cassius. The disgraced governor on the Ṣalkhad inscription ought to be someone other than Avidius; and, if so, the erasure would provide an interesting parallel to the disgrace of Haterius Nepos. Apart from such indications of turbulence and improper conduct, the early decades of the new Arabian province seem to have passed in relative tranquillity.

[58] *PAES* III.A, no. 155. See n. 35 above. Sartre (above, n. 4), p. 54, made the comparison with Haterius Nepos.

VIII

THE IMPACT OF SEPTIMIUS SEVERUS

In his travels through Syria and Palestine during the years 129 to 130, the emperor Hadrian took care to recognize by his presence the importance of the new province of Arabia. Since Bostra had already taken the epithet Traiana from the founder of the province and proclaimed itself Nea Traianē Bostra, it was to Petra that Hadrian turned to confer his name, and henceforth Petra rejoiced in the epithet Hadrianē.[1] Hadrian may be presumed at least to have visited Bostra, which would have caused no difficulty on his itinerary.[2] There is no question that he passed through the Decapolis city of Gerasa on his way to Palestine and Jerusalem. Gerasa commemorated the event by erecting a massive triumphal arch, just as so many other cities had done along Hadrian's route in the East.[3] Even the considerably less important town of Karak, near the Dead Sea, appears to have celebrated the advent of Hadrian by issuing special seals celebrating Arabia and perhaps even coins that matched the seals.[4]

One honor which the emperor did not confer during his travels was the title of metropolis for Petra. It is now firmly established from the inscription on the Trajanic arch there that Hadrian's predecessor had already guaranteed this title for the old capital of the Nabataean kingdom.[5] Inasmuch as Hadrian felt no constraint

[1] Coins provide ample evidence of the epithets of Bostra and Petra. See A. Spijkerman, *The Coins of the Decapolis and Provincia Arabia* (1978), pp. 68–77 (Bostra), pp. 220–35 (Petra); and *SNG*, Amer. Numis. Soc., part 6 (1981), nos. 1178–91, 1193–96, 1202–5 (Bostra), nos. 1360–67, 1369–71 (Petra).

[2] W. Weber, *Untersuchungen zur Geschichte des Kaisers Hadrianus* (1907), p. 239, assumes that Hadrian stopped at Bostra.

[3] C. H. Kraeling, *Gerasa* (1938), pp. 73–83 (by A. H. Detweiler); for the inscription on the arch, see no. 58 in Welles's corpus in the Kraeling volume, pp. 401–2. For arches in other cities, see the discussion in G. W. Bowersock, "Hadrian and Metropolis," *Bonner Historia-Augusta-Colloquium 1982*, forthcoming.

[4] A. Negev, "Seal Impressions from Tomb 107 at Kurnub (Mampsis)," *IEJ* 19 (1969), 89–106.

[5] See the text printed above, p. 85, n. 28.

in the matter of bestowing the title of metropolis upon more than one city in a single province, he must have made a conscious decision not to honor Bostra in this way.[6] Bostra was perhaps too obviously Trajan's city. Furthermore Hadrian was a traditionalist and something of a romantic: despite the establishment of the provincial capital at Bostra, he may well have seen Petra as having the edge in dignity and antiquity.

The magnificence of the imperial tour was, of course, soon to be obliterated by the devastating war in Judaea that broke out in 132 and lasted until 135. The city of Jerusalem, which might once have taken pride in the name of Aelia Capitolina—simultaneously commemorating the family of the emperor and the capitol at Rome—now found in this new name a great humiliation.[7] But across the depression of the Jordan, Traianē Bostra and Hadrianē Petra were still pleased in the decades that followed to recall the honor which the province's first emperors had done them and to continue using the epithets they had acquired from them.[8]

The prosperity and quiet of second-century Arabia are best documented in the post-Hadrianic buildings at Gerasa and Bostra. In the middle of the century, the architects at Gerasa undertook a massive reorganization of the city plan by the construction of a great new shrine for Artemis, which effectively shifted the center of the city northward from the old forum.[9] Not long after the completion of the Artemis temple, the Gerasenes constructed a new temple of Zeus as well as a new theater in the northern quarter of town.[10] All of this, documented to some degree by inscriptions, attests eloquently the vigor of the city in this period and the wealth at its disposal. By contrast, the growth of

[6] On Hadrian's policy in assigning the title of metropolis, see Bowersock, "Metropolis" (above, n. 3).

[7] On the foundation of Aelia Capitolina as a glorious moment during Hadrian's tour of the Near East, see G. W. Bowersock, "A Roman Perspective on the Bar Kokhba War," in *Approaches to Ancient Judaism* II, ed. W. S. Green (Brown Judaic Studies no. 9, 1980), pp. 131–41, esp., on Aelia Capitolina, pp. 135–36.

[8] The epithets appear on the coins of the two cities down to, but not including, the reign of Elagabalus: see A. Spijkerman and *SNG* (both above, n. 1).

[9] Kraeling (above, n. 3), pp. 52–53 (cf. pp. 125–38, by C. S. Fisher, on the temple building). For a plan of Gerasa, see below, p. 188.

[10] Kraeling (above, n. 3), p. 54.

Bostra was less imposing, just as the city itself was less distinguished. It had never been a member of the Decapolis; and even now its principal importance was as the legionary headquarters. Nevertheless magnificent arches and a splendid theatre were commanding buildings in this northern city of the province. Some of these may have been Nabataean in origin, but there can be no doubt that the Romans in the second century enhanced them, if they were not actually responsible for their construction in the first place.[11] Furthermore, the Romans enlarged the city on the western side of the *cardo maximus*.[12]

The momentous events which disturbed the peace of Syria under Marcus Aurelius seem to have had little effect on the province to the south. The Parthian war of Lucius Verus provided no more than a cause for celebration in Arabia.[13] We do not even know that any troops from the Third Cyrenaica were recruited for this campaign. And the revolt of Avidius Cassius in Syria against Marcus Aurelius seems in no way to have compromised the province of Arabia. It may be that the rough territory of the Leja' and the Jebel Drūz provided a sufficient buffer to prevent Avidius from soliciting support in Transjordan. It may also be that there was some natural suspicion between the inhabitants of Transjordan and the more Hellenized and ambitious Syrians. This kind of suspicion between the two territories is not unknown even today.

With the civil wars that swept Septimius Severus to the throne, the history of provincial Arabia enters a new phase. Another governor of Syria had had himself proclaimed emperor. This was Pescennius Niger, who was proclaimed at Syrian Antioch in A.D.

[11] S. A. Mougdad, trans. by H. I. MacAdam, *Bostra: Historical and Archaeological Guide* (1978). See below, p. 189, for a plan of Bostra. Above all one will consult M. Sartre, *Bostra, des origines à l'Islam*, forthcoming. On the theater at Bostra: H. Finsen, *Le levé du théâtre romain à Bostra, Syrie* (1972).

[12] Mougdad (above, n. 11). For a valuable treatment of the city plan at Bostra, see F. E. Peters, "City Planning in Greco-Roman Syria: Some New Considerations," forthcoming.

[13] Cf. the Ruwwāfa inscription, for example: *Le monde grec: Hommages à Claire Préaux* (1975), pp. 514–15; also the Palmyrene inscription at Qaṣr al-Ḥair, which I published in *Chiron* 6 (1976), 349–55. Ritterling's speculations in *RE* 12.2.1512 that III Cyrenaica participated in Verus' war and later in Avidius Cassius' revolt are without any foundation.

193 and supported by that great metropolis.[14] Once again the province of Arabia, behaving as it had done at the time of the rebellion raised by Avidius Cassius, refused to follow the lead of Syria. The fidelity of the province and its legion toward Septimius Severus can be detected in two vital scraps of evidence. The province's governor in 193, during the brief reign of Pertinax, P. Aelius Severianus Maximus, was continued in his post by Severus.[15] There can be only one reason for this prorogation, and that is an unquestioned loyalty toward the antagonist of Niger. In addition, the Third Cyrenaica received the honorific epithet Severiana, clear proof of the legion's loyalty and the emperor's gratitude.[16]

With the defeat of Niger, the principal cities that had supported him suffered humiliation and punishment. Chief among these was Antioch itself, as well as Nicaea in Asia Minor.[17] Those who had risked the displeasure of Niger now reaped their reward. Antioch's great rival, Laodicea, received the title of metropolis, which was taken away from Antioch; and to avert yet another repetition of the crime of Avidius Cassius, Septimius Severus chose immediately to divide the province of Syria into two parts. These were Syria Coele and Syria Phoenice.[18] In constituting the frontiers of Syria Phoenice, which was the immediate neighbor of Arabia in the north, Severus may already have contemplated removing the dangerous area of the Leja' and the

[14] Herodian 2.8.6; cf. *HA*, Pesc. Niger 2.1. See also G. Downey, *A History of Antioch in Syria* (1961), p. 286.

[15] Severianus is attested as governor on milestones in Arabia under Pertinax (e.g., *ZDPV* 80 [1964], 126) and Septimius Severus (e.g., *CIL* 3.13612; Kraeling [above, n. 3], p. 464, nos. 261–63). Cf. *PIR*² A 260. Note that he is *cos. desig.* on a Bostra stone: *IGLS* 13.9069. H. Halfmann, *Die Senatoren aus dem östlichen Teil des Imperium Romanum bis zum Ende des 2. Jh. n. Chr.* (1979), pp. 205–6, no. 149, gives full documentation on Severianus and argues for Perinthus as his city of origin. Since Perinthus was the base of Severus' support in the war against Niger's forces at Byzantium (Cassius Dio 75.6.3 and 14.3), Severianus' loyalty in Syria may have had something to do with his roots in Perinthus.

[16] *CIL* 3.94 and p. 969.

[17] For Nicaea, see L. Robert, "La titulature de Nicée et de Nicomédie: La gloire et la haine," *HSCP* 81 (1977), 1–39. For Antioch, Downey (above, n. 14), pp. 239–43, and Bowersock, "Metropolis" (above, n. 3).

[18] The division had already taken place by late 194 or early 195; cf. H. Ingholt, *Syria* 13 (1932), 278–86. For the governors of Coele Syria, see J. F. Gilliam, *AJP* 79 (1958), 225–42. On the geographical concept of Coele Syria, see E. Bikermann, "La Coelé-Syria: Notes de géographie historique," *RB* 54 (1947), 256–68.

northern Jebel Drūz from the control of a Syrian governor. First, however, he will have perceived the need to improve communications between the Ḥawrān and the northern Leja', in which brigands had always found a secure refuge.[19]

It is certain that by the early third century Septimius Severus had already enlarged the Arabian province in the north. Cities and towns which had belonged indisputably to Syria in the second century can be seen as integral parts of Arabia by the time of Caracalla. At Qanawāt, for example, an inscription in honor of Julia Domna was set up by a centurion of the Third Cyrenaica, and at ʿAtīl there is a monument also erected by a centurion of that legion at about the same time.[20] Such activity on the part of centurions of the Arabian legion would not in itself be decisive, if we did not have clear indications of dating by the era of Bostra at Ḥabrān, also in territory that had formerly belonged to Syria.[21] Even more striking than these documents is an inscription from ʿAhīre in the central Leja' which shows a date according to the era of Bostra in the year 225.[22] From the time of its first publication, this inscription has been considered incontrovertible proof of the enlargement of Arabia into the Leja'.

Yet if Severus had planned this adjustment of the northern frontier at the time he divided Syria into Coele and Phoenice, it is nonetheless clear that he did not carry out the extension at that moment. For in 194–195 the governor of Syria Phoenice, Manilius Fuscus, is found commemorated on milestones south of Mismīye;[23] he seems to have been active in the repair of the Roman road across the Leja' plateau. Although it has sometimes been assumed from this evidence that Severus had annexed the southern Leja' along with the northern part of the Jebel Drūz (including Qanawāt and Suweidā'), while leaving the northern Leja'

[19] Cf. B. Isaac, "Bandits in Judaea and Arabia," *HSCP*, forthcoming. On the Roman road that had been laid across the Leja', see M. Dunand, "La voie romaine du Ledja," *Mém. Acad. Inscr. et Belles-Lettres* 13.2 (1930), 521–57.

[20] Qanawāt: Waddington, *IGLS* no. 2331b (*CIL* 3.121 and p. 970). The legion is called *Antoniniana*, therefore after Geta's death. ʿAtīl: Waddington, *IGLS* 2374b (*IGR* 3.1239), also with the legion called *Antoniniana*.

[21] Waddington, *IGLS* no. 2287 (*PAES* III.A, no. 664; *IGR* 3.1298).

[22] R. Mouterde, *Mél. Univ. St. Joseph de Beyrouth* 16 (1932), 79–82 (*SEG* 7.980).

[23] Dunand (above, n. 19), 543. Cf. Ingholt (above, n. 18), 283–84.

still in Syria, it makes little sense to postulate such a division of the Leja' plateau. There is simply no evidence at all for Manilius Fuscus south of ʿAhīre as far as Suweidā', and it is therefore impossible to say with certainty whether the region between ʿAhīre and those cities for which there is proof of Severan annexation belonged to Syria or to Arabia.

Inasmuch as the earliest evidence for the Arabian extension comes from the early third century, it would perhaps be reasonable to assume that Severus prepared for the change of frontiers by the work in the Leja' accomplished under the direction of Manilius Fuscus. When this was accomplished, perhaps towards the very end of the second century, Severus could then have annexed the entire territory of the northern Jebel Drūz and the Leja' in one reasonable stroke.[24] The redistribution of frontiers, to the advantage of Arabia, may be conveniently assigned to the period of Severus' second Mesopotamian war, which led to the annexation of the area between the Tigris and the Euphrates. This is the war which is known in literary sources as an Arabian war.[25] The successful outcome of that campaign would have provided an appropriate moment for readjusting the boundaries of the provinces lying to the west of the newly created province of Mesopotamia.

The role of Severus in transforming the boundaries of Syria and Arabia is reflected in the epithet which the city of Qanawāt, ancient Canatha, received at about this time. The city became Septimia Canatha. This epithet can be seen on a funerary inscription of an Arab buried at Thasos, as well as on the remarkable bilingual epitaph at Lyon in commemoration of a certain

[24] Such is the very attractive hypothesis of M. Sartre, *Trois études sur l'Arabie romaine et byzantine* (1982), pp. 59–61. Against the notion of a partial extension of the Arabian northern frontier, to include the Jebel Drūz and the southern (but not northern) Leja', observe Sartre's sagacious comment in regard to Manilius Fuscus: "Le fait qu'aucun milliaire à son nom n'ait été retrouvé au Sud d'ʿAhiré ne prouve en rien que sa province ne s'étendait pas jusqu'à Suwaydā': aucun autre milliaire n'a été découvert sur cette portion de la route."

[25] Cf. Aur. Victor 20.15: *Neque minus Arabas, simul adortus ut est, in dicionem redegit provinciae modo.* Also Herodian 3.9.3 (erring in naming Arabia Felix); *HA*, Sept. Sev. 18.1; Eutrop. 8.18.4; Festus 21; and Zosimus 1.8. Note also the speech of Marcus Aurelius in Cassius Dio 72.25.2, where Lucius Verus' eastern campaigns are described as τὸν Ἀραβικὸν τόν τε Παρθικὸν ἐκεῖνον πόλεμον.

Thaim, son of Saʿad, from Septimia Canatha.[26] Some have seen difficulties in the incorporation of Canatha into the Arabian province by Severus on the evidence of this latter inscription, on which Canatha is described as ἐπὶ Συρίας. But the term Syria as used in this general way is scarcely a reference to a Roman provincial unit.[27] It is a vague expression that reflects local geographical designations, such as one finds in the geography of Ptolemy and, in particular, in the striking Oxyrhynchus fragment on which Bostra is described as a city of Syria.[28] The use of Severus' *gentilicium* in the naming of Canatha is unambiguous testimony not only to the Severan date of the epitaph of Thaim but to the special regard which the city had for the man who restored it to the community of northern cities of Nabataean culture. It will be recalled that from the days of the Nabataean kingdom the cities of the northern Jebel Drūz with strong Nabataean traditions (such as Suweidā', Sīʿ, and Qanawāt) had been included in the province of Syria, despite their natural affinity with Bostra and the cities of the Ḥawrān plain.

Among the evidence from which an account of the Severan organization of Syria and Arabia can be assembled is a singular item in the *Historia Augusta* concerning the Third Cyrenaica.[29] We are told that during the course of Severus' war against his western rival, Clodius Albinus, he received a report that the Arabian legion (*legio Arabica*) had defected to Albinus. It is difficult to credit such testimony in view of this legion's loyalty to Severus during the much more immediate threat of the revolt of Pescennius Niger, and also in view of its epithet Severiana. It is perhaps easiest simply to discount the report of the defection to Albinus as another of the fabrications of the author of the *Historia Augusta*, but it is just possible that there may be some explanation of so bizarre a story.

[26] L. Robert, *Hellenica* 2 (1946), 43 (Thasos); *CIL* 13.2448 (Lyon) with J. and L. Robert, *Bull. épig.* 1976.800.

[27] As was suggested by J. Rougé, *Actes du 96ᵉ Congrès des sociétés savantes, Toulouse 1971* I (1976), p. 214, n. 12. Cf. the comments of Sartre (above, n. 24), p. 62.

[28] *Pap. Oxy.* 42.3054: ἀπὸ Βόστρας τῆς Συρίας. H. I. MacAdam has drawn my attention to a parallel in *PSI* 771 (Oxy.): ἀπὸ Βόστρων Συρίας. The inflections of Bostra as feminine singular and neuter plural are both attested.

[29] *HA*, Sept. Sev. 12.6.

Severus defeated Albinus in a battle at Lyon in southern Gaul. Naturally that city had espoused the cause of his rival and may be expected to have done everything possible to ensure victory for him. Lyon was a center of international trade by virtue of its location on the Rhône River, with access by water to the Mediterranean. Syrian traders, such as Thaim, can be observed in the city and were presumably part of a representative group of Near Easterners that frequented the marketplace.[30] In the final days of the struggle with Albinus, it is entirely conceivable that as a desperate measure Syrian adherents of Severus' enemy may have put out the news that his most faithful army in the East, the army that had withstood the blandishments of Pescennius Niger, had now defected. Such news would certainly have been as demoralizing as it was improbable. It was certainly false. But it was perhaps not false that a report to this effect was circulated. One will note that the *Historia Augusta* is uncharacteristically circumspect: *legio Arabica defecisse ad Albinum nuntiata est.*

The triumphant conclusion of Septimius Severus' wars against his rivals, together with the annexation of Mesopotamia and the reorganization of Syria and Arabia, opened a new era of splendor for the Near East within the context of the Roman Empire. It was not merely that Severus had taken great interest in this region; it was the important fact that he had taken as wife an aristocratic lady of Syrian Emesa. Julia Domna was a person of high education and ambition, and it is scarcely surprising that within a generation several new Syrian families appear in the roster of Roman senators, while the grandchildren of her sister, Julia Maesa, become emperors of Rome. Maesa's husband, C. Julius Avitus Alexianus, was adlected by Septimius Severus out of the equestrian order into the senate, and he advanced to the consulate.[31] The husbands of the two daughters of Maesa were likewise raised up from equestrian status to senatorial and in the process gave new luster to their native cities, Syrian Apamea and

[30] Cf. C. P. Jones, "A Syrian in Lyon," *AJP* 99 (1978), 336–53.

[31] On Syrian families in the senate, see G. W. Bowersock, "Roman Senators from the Near East," *Acta* of the colloquium *Epigrafia e ordine senatorio*, Rome (forthcoming). See also H.-G. Pflaum, "La carrière de C. Iulius Avitus Alexianus, grand'père de deux empereurs," *REL* 57 (1979), 298–314.

Arca-Caesarea. One of these was the father of the emperor Elagabalus and the other of the emperor Severus Alexander.[32] And thus, in an astonishingly short time, through the influence of the house of Septimius Severus, Arabs reached the pinnacle of Roman government.

The families which profited most from Arab influence in the imperial court were naturally Syrian and, for the most part, from the greater cities, such as Antioch, Emesa, Berytus, and Heliopolis.[33] But the desert Arabs were not neglected, and Septimius' favor to the caravan city of Palmyra is reflected in the spread of his *gentilicium* in the nobility of that city. A Septimius Odaenathus was already a senator in the early years of the third century, and his descendants constituted the family of the husband of the Palmyrene queen Zenobia.[34] A few Arabs of uncertain provenance, emerging in the senate during the third century, may also have come from the more outlying parts of the Syrian and Arab territories. A youth of senatorial family, with the impeccably Roman name C. Annius Fundanus, had as a sister Annia Maleca Avita.[35] The sister's name Maleca is undoubtedly Arab and, in view of its prevalence as a name in the Nabataean kingdom, might possibly imply a family in *provincia Arabia*. Again possibly, though not necessarily, the senator with the grandiloquent name L. Julius Apronius Maenius Pius Salamallianus, who is known as a consul designate in the early third century, suggests an Arab family of the province.[36]

In taking note of the merchants of Palmyra, Severus showed his appreciation of desert outposts and inner trade routes. He cannot have missed the increasing importance of the Wādī Sirḥān in Arabia after the shift of the region's center from Petra to Bostra, and it was entirely consonant with his policy for him to attend to the protection of that interior passage through the desert from the Arabian peninsula. Recent exploration of the region in and around

[32] Sex. Varius Marcellus and Gessius Marcianus respectively: nos. 8 and 9 in the Register provided by Bowersock, "Senators" (above, n. 31).

[33] See the persons listed for the cities in Bowersock, "Senators" (above, n. 31).

[34] *CIS* II.4202. Cf. J. T. Milik, *Dédicaces faites par des dieux* (1972), pp. 316–17.

[35] *CIL* 6.37060 = 11724 with p. 3509. Cf. Milik (above, n. 34), p. 321.

[36] *ILS* 1196; *CIL* 3.14184, 8.17639, 19131, 8782 with 18018; *AE* 1917–1918.51, 1942–1943.93. Adlected to the senate before 222: cf. *PIR*² I 161.

the important oasis at Azraq, lying at the northern end of the Wādī Sirḥān, has demonstrated clearly Severus' attention to this growing area of the province. At Qaṣr ʿUweinid, to the southwest of Azraq, an inscription known hitherto only in part has now been read in full.[37] It documents the establishment of a *praesidium Severianum* with a vexillation of the legion Third Cyrenaica. The inscription has a consular date of 201. This forms accordingly a pendant to another inscription from Qaṣr ʿUweinid with a clear reference to a *castellum novum Severianum*.[38] It is a building inscription in honor of the emperor Septimius Severus and his sons Caracalla and Geta. From the recently deciphered reference to the governor in this text, L. Marius Perpetuus, it is clear that the second ʿUweinid inscription belongs to the years 200–202.[39] A Roman fort northwest of Azraq at Qaṣr Asaikhin is also probably of Severan date.[40] We have, therefore, good evidence for military establishments on either side of Azraq at the very beginning of the third century.

One might naturally expect that the principal site in this area, the Azraq oasis itself, would also have been fortified under the new Severan dispensation. Hitherto the earliest epigraphic testimony for the *castellum* now standing at Azraq belongs to the time of the Tetrarchy.[41] But aerial photography of half a century ago has provided a startling and important addition to our knowledge. The unmistakable traces of a considerably larger establishment than the present *castellum* can be seen delineated on the ground in a form which suits perfectly a *castrum* of the Severan

[37] Kennedy, *ArchExplor* (1982), p. 125 (no. 20); cf. *id.*, "The Frontier Policy of Septimius Severus," *Roman Frontier Studies 1979*, BAR International Series 71 (1980), pp. 879–88, esp. p. 881.

[38] Kennedy, *ArchExplor* (1982), p. 124; *id.*, "Frontier Policy" (above, n. 37), p. 881. The inscription was first published by S. T. Parker and P. M. McDermott, *ZPE* 28 (1978), 61–66.

[39] On Perpetuus' governorship, see D. L. Kennedy, *ZPE* 49 (1982), 284–86. Also, below, p. 160.

[40] For the fort at Asaikhin and its pottery (there is no inscription as yet), see Kennedy, *ArchExplor* (1982), pp. 107–13. Sartre (above, n. 24), p. 20, n. 17, appears to have thought that Asaikhin and ʿUweinid were the same place, but he was careful to note that Parker (above, n. 38) treated them as distinct.

[41] See the important discussion of Azraq and its *castellum* in Kennedy, *ArchExplor* (1982), pp. 75–96.

period.[42] These traces are no longer visible either on the ground or from the air because of the growth of habitation in the neighborhood of the *castellum*. The aerial photographs are thus precious and persuasive proof that Severus' organization of the head of the Wādī Sirḥān did indeed include a major camp at the oasis of Azraq.

Severus' concern with the Arabian army seems also to underlie the appearance during his reign of the first contingent of Goths on the eastern frontier. An inscription at Iʿnāt in the southern Ḥawrān proclaims a monument of one Guththa, son of Erminarius, who is described as a commander of the tribal troops (*gentiles*) stationed among the Mothani.[43] The Mothani were the natives of the village of Motha, modern Imtān. The names Guththa and Erminarius have been decisively shown to be German, and as a result we can see here a commander of *Gothi gentiles*.[44] The date of the inscription, by the era of the province, is A.D. 208. It would appear that Septimius Severus had brought Gothic troops with him in his second Mesopotamian campaign against the Parthians and chose, after the successful conclusion of that campaign, to leave these soldiers as part of the garrison in the Arabian frontier. It has been rightly suggested that the importance of Goths in the Roman army during the first half of the third century has been largely underestimated in the past, as we can see from the account of Shapur I's campaign against the field army of Gordian III later in the century.[45] Severus' decision to leave the Goths on the Arabian frontier fits nicely with the Roman policy of keeping troops acquired by military victory far away from their own country.

[42] One photograph (*ca.* 1928) is published as plate 58.2 in Kennedy, "Frontier Policy" (above, n. 37), p. 882, and is republished below (plate 12). Another photograph (*ca.* 1922) appears as plate 17b in Kennedy, *ArchExplor* (1982), p. 72. A drawing of the *castrum* outline in relation to the extant remains appears as fig. 18 on p. 87 of the latter work (cf. Kennedy's comments on pp. 88–90).

[43] *PAES* III.A, no. 223.

[44] Cf. O. Fiebiger, *ZDPV* 66 (1943), 69–71, and J. and L. Robert, *Bull. épig.* 1943.76.

[45] This is the interpretation of M. Speidel, *ANRW* II.8 (1977), 712–16. For the *Res Gestae* of Shapur, see A. Maricq, *Syria* 35 (1958), 295–360. In line 7 the Greek reads Γορδιανὸς Καῖσαρ ἀπὸ πάσης τῆς Ῥωμαίων ἀρχῆς Γούθθων τε καὶ Γερμανῶν ἐθνῶν [δύναμιν συνέλεξ]εν.

Septimius Severus' interest in the Near East and his understanding of the workings of an open frontier in desert zones may be, in part, a reflection of his origins in North Africa. He came from the Tripolitanian city of Leptis Magna, and the care which he gave to the desert fortifications in the Near East can be paralleled by his operations in the deserts of Libya and Algeria. He seems to have taken particular care to extend frontier outposts far into the desert and, for this purpose, even to have imported a contingent from Syria. The Severan outposts at Bu Njem, Gheria el Gharbia, Gadamès, and at Castellum Dimmidī constitute a striking parallel with the fortifications at the head of the Wādī Sirḥān.[46] The governor, Anicius Faustus, in charge of the operations in Numidia throughout the five-year period in which forts were built was himself familiar with the problems of the desert, since he is known to have been a native of Uzappa in the vicinity of Mactar (in modern Tunisia).[47]

The policy of Septimius Severus in Arabia and the introduction of Arabs into the court at Rome naturally augured well for future recognition of the region in the early third century. The grandchildren of Julia Domna's sister, Julia Maesa, both showed favor to the province. Elagabalus gave Petra the honorific title of *colonia*, and Severus Alexander gave the same title to the newer city of Bostra.[48] Petra, however, continued to have the distinction of being the only city in Arabia with the title metropolis. It was not until the reign of Philip in the middle of the century that Bostra finally achieved parity in honorific titulature.[49] Under the same emperor Bostra introduced the Actia Dusaria,

[46] For Bu Njem and its foundation in A.D. 201: R. Rebuffat, "L'arrivée des romains à Bu Njem," *Libya Antiqua* 9–10 (1972–1973), 121–34. On the Severan date of the fort at Gheria el Gharbia: R. Goodchild in *Libyan Studies*, ed. J. Reynolds (1976), p. 55, together with the supplementary n. 26 on p. 58. Ghadamès: Goodchild, p. 56. For Dimmidī, see G. Charles Picard, *Castellum Dimmidi* (1947), p. 45 (foundation in A.D. 198). For the involvement of a vexillation of III Gallica, Picard, pp. 47–48.

[47] A. Birley, *Septimius Severus* (1971), p. 337.

[48] See Spijkerman (above, n. 1), p. 237 (Petra), p. 81 (Bostra); and *SNG* (above, n. 1), nos. 1373–77 (Petra), 1217–28 (Bostra). Cf. also S. Ben-Dor, "Petra Colonia," *Berytus* 9 (1948), 41–43. Despite Ben-Dor's speculation, no genuine coin exists showing Bostra as *colonia* under Elagabalus.

[49] Spijkerman (above, n. 1), p. 83, and *SNG* (above, n. 1), nos. 1242–45: *COL METROPOLIS BOSTRA*.

festive competitions in the Greek manner for athletes and performing artists.[50] The name for these competitions proclaimed the union of Rome and Arabia by evoking Augustus' victory at Actium and the principal god of the Nabataeans, Dushara (Dousares in Greek).

Philip was an Arab from the city Shahbā, at the edge of the Leja' near the western slopes of the Jebel Drūz.[51] His arrival on the throne of the Caesars was a momentous event in pre-Islamic Arab history. He commemorated it at home by renaming his natal city Philippopolis and by recognizing the capital of his province as metropolis. For it is clear that with the incorporation of the Leja' during the reign of Septimius Severus, this savage area had drawn increasingly close to the more developed regions of the Ḥawrān. Severus deserves the ultimate credit for making possible the emergence of a figure such as Philip. Aurelius Victor was not merely describing the situation of Shahbā in his own day when he narrated the origin of Philip the Arab. He was, as so often, exact in stating that M. Julius Philippus Arabs Trachonites came to Rome after he had founded the city of Philippopolis *apud Arabiam*.

[50] Spijkerman (above, n. 1), p. 83, and *SNG* (above, n. 1), nos. 1246–50. The coins of Philip's son as Caesar bear an agonistic wreath on the reverse with the Greek words ΑΚΤΙΑ ΔΟΥΣΑΡΙΑ added to the Latin *COL METROPOLIS BOSTRA*. The Greek words are appropriate for the Hellenic institution they denote, although the coins issued after Philip show only the Latin form *Actia Dusaria:* Spijkerman, pp. 87–89. For a victor at the Actia of Bostra, see *ILS* 5233 (Ostia): *Actia aput Bo[s]tram*.

[51] Aur. Victor 28.1.

IX

FROM PHILIP TO ZENOBIA

THE PROTRACTED WAR of Gordian III against the Sassanid Persians, who had overthrown the Parthians in Iran less than two decades before, provided M. Julius Philippus, the Arab from Shahbā, with his opportunity. Timesitheus, the praetorian prefect of the young emperor Gordian and the most powerful member of his entourage, died on campaign and was replaced in 243 by Philip. The Arab prefect had the singular advantage of close familiarity with the Near East and knowledge of one or more local languages. His rise to the prefecture of the guard cannot have been altogether fortuitous.[1] His brother, C. Julius Priscus, was a distinguished member of the equestrian order, and his wife, Otacilia Severa, shows by her name that she came from a family of Arabs that had been favored by Septimius Severus.[2] It is true that an anonymous epitomator in the fourth century described Philip's origins as exceedingly humble and Philip's father as a leader of brigands.[3] In publishing such a report, the writer was simply illustrating yet again the widespread prejudice in the Roman world against the Arabs. The much touted absence of racial prejudice in the Roman Empire is a myth of modern times, and distinguished writers from Cicero to Zosimus can be seen indulging in the most irresponsible slander

[1] *HA*, Gord. 28.5–6, asserts that Philip had Timesitheus murdered by complicitous doctors who replaced the prefect's medicine with a lethal potion. That does not have to be believed. On Philippus' succession to the prefecture, cf. Festus 22, Aur. Victor 27.8, *Epit. de Caes.* 27.2, Zosimus 1.18.2, as well as Amm. Marc. 23.5.17 and Waddington, *IGLS* 2598 (*OGIS* 640). Note that the text of the *HA*, as we have it, lacks a biography of Philip; but it is obvious that he would not have been treated favorably (cf. *HA*, Aur. 42.6).

[2] On Priscus, cf. *PIR*² I 488. He served as prefect of Mesopotamia: Waddington, *IGLS* 2077 (*IGR* 3.1201); see further Zosimus 1.19.2 and 20.2. The entry in *PIR*² opts to restore Priscus instead of Philippus at the erasure in Waddington, *IGLS* 2598 (*OGIS* 640). For Otacilia Severa, see, e.g., *ILS* 510, 513.

[3] *Epit. de Caes.* 28.4: *Is Philippus humillimo ortus loco fuit, patre nobilissimo latronum ductore.* Cf. *HA*, Gord. 29.1: *Philippus Arabs, humili genere natus.* There is no comparable statement in Aurelius Victor.

of Arab peoples.[4] The equestrian rank of Philip's family is proof enough of a superior provincial background. His father, Julius Marinus, coming from a city at the edge of the Leja', may well have been assimilated by the ignorant with the brigands for which the area was so famous.[5]

Philip was therefore no simple upstart. Whether he was privy to intrigues that led to the death of the young Gordian in the field is now beyond telling.[6] The boy was certainly incapable of conducting the war on his own. A military coup of some kind is more than plausible. In any case, the one who reaped the profit was Philip, proclaimed emperor by the troops in the East in A.D. 244. His reign lasted five years and was inaugurated by a swift and effective conclusion of hostilities with the Persians.[7] If Philip's negotiations brought some humiliation to Rome, they nevertheless terminated a wasteful and debilitating war and allowed the emperor to be again in Rome where he could attend to the central direction of the empire. The five years of Philip's reign were a time of uncommon stability and repose in a century that was notorious for turbulence. In 247–248 he presented the Romans with the spectacular secular games which commemorated the thousandth anniversary of the founding of Rome. The celebrations were an intoxicating blend of religious ceremonials and death. Exotic men and animals were imported to test their skills in sport, and many died in the process.[8]

[4] The absurd notion that the Roman Empire knew cultural but not racial prejudice has lately prevailed in certain quarters, such as A. N. Sherwin-White, *Racial Prejudice in Imperial Rome* (1967). Toward the Arabs, sometimes called Syrians or Saracens, a firm prejudice is well attested. In his forthcoming work on Byzantium and the Arabs in the fourth century, Irfan Shahîd has an excellent treatment of Ammianus' attitude: cf. the excursus in Amm. Marc. 14.4, which ends *hactenus de natione perniciosa*. See also Cicero, *de prov. cons.* 5.10: *Iudaeis et Syris, nationibus natis servituti*, and Zosimus 1.18.3: ὁρμώμενος γὰρ ἐξ Ἀραβίας, ἔθνους χειρίστου.

[5] On Marinus, *PIR*² I 407.

[6] See the allegations in sources such as *HA*, Gord. 29–30; Eutropius 9.2.3; and Zosimus 1.18.2–19.1. The account of the *Res Gestae Divi Saporis* implies that Gordian died in battle. For discussion of Philip's guilt, see F. Paschoud in his Budé edition of Zosimus, I (1971), p. 144; X. Loriot, *ANRW* II.2 (1975), 770–74; and H. A. Pohlsander, *Historia* 29 (1980), 464–65.

[7] On the treaty with Shapur, Zosimus 1.19.1 and Zonaras 12.19. Cf. Aurelius Victor 28.1: *rebus ad Orientem compositis*.

[8] Cf. Aurelius Victor 28.1: *ludis omnium generum*. *HA*, Gord. 33.1–3, provides a lurid list of creatures—*quae omnia Philippus ludis saecularibus vel dedit vel occidit*.

An Arab negotiating a Roman peace with the Persians was notable, and an Arab presiding over the millennial celebrations of the foundation of Rome was even more notable. But undoubtedly the most surprising testimony about Philip is the widespread report that he was a Christian. Most modern historians have been understandably reluctant to credit Philip's Christianity.[9] His role at the secular games seems scarcely consonant with it, and we happen to know that he saw to the deification of his father at Philippopolis.[10] Furthermore, no pagan author seems to have noticed that Philip was a Christian. Nevertheless the evidence is compelling to some degree and raises the whole question of the spread of Christianity in Arabia in the middle of the third century.

All the Christian sources for Philip's faith depend ultimately on the text of the *Ecclesiastical History* of Eusebius. There, in an account of Philip's attendance at an Easter service in the guise of a penitent, he is explicitly called a Christian.[11] Furthermore, in another passage, Eusebius states that Origen had written letters both to Philip and to his wife Severa.[12] Inasmuch as Eusebius had seen the text of these letters, it is reasonable to assume that the story of Philip's appearance at the Easter service appeared in one or the other of them.[13]

It would be rash to condemn the letters of Origen, which Eusebius had read, as some kind of later forgery. There can be no doubt that Origen had close connections with Christian Arabs, and he would naturally have taken a particular interest in the first Arab emperor. Already in the reign of Caracalla, when Origen was at Alexandria, the governor of the province of Arabia wrote formal letters both to the prefect of Egypt and to the bishop of Alexandria to request that Origen be sent to him for discussion of Christian doctrines.[14] Origen went to Arabia for this purpose.

[9] There is a comprehensive survey of modern opinions in Pohlsander (above, n. 6), 463–64. Pohlsander scrupulously lists the sources, all Christian, on Philip's faith.

[10] Waddington, *IGLS* 2075 (Μαρῖ[νον] θεόν), 2076 (θεῷ Μαρείνῳ), reproduced in *IGR* 3.1199, 1200. See also *BMC*, Arabia, Mesop., Pers., p. 42 (θεῷ Μαρίνῳ).

[11] Eusebius, *HE* 6.34: τοῦτον [i.e., Φίλιππον] κατέχει λόγος Χριστιανὸν ὄντα.

[12] Eusebius, *HE* 6.36.3. Eusebius himself collected various letters of Origen, including those to Philip and Severa. Jerome, *de viris ill.* 54, gives a confused copy of Eusebius' evidence.

[13] See H. Crouzel, "Le christianisme de l'empereur Philippe l'Arabe," *Gregorianum* 56 (1975), 545–50, and T. D. Barnes, *Constantine and Eusebius* (1981), p. 351, n. 95.

[14] Eusebius, *HE* 6.19.15. Cf. Barnes (above, n. 13), p. 83.

It may be presumed that the governor had noticed the spread of Christianity among the Arabs and desired to inform himself further about the cult.

Origen's further associations with the Arabian church are indicated in two separate reports in Eusebius. Both involve Origen's successful correction of deviant theology among the Arabs, and in one case it was the bishop of Bostra himself whose views had become heretical.[15] Because of Origen's contacts with his Arab brethren, it is perhaps not surprising that another Arab, the imperial mother Julia Mamaea, should have conceived a desire to hear what Origen had to say about his faith. When she was at Antioch during the course of the campaign which her son, Severus Alexander, was waging against the new Persian dynasty, she summoned Origen to meet with her.[16] Her intellectual curiosity was presumably not much inferior to that of her aunt, Julia Domna, and the spread of new doctrines among the peoples of her homeland would naturally have provoked a lively curiosity.

The connections Origen had with the province of Arabia, as well as with the royal house, make it plausible that he was in communication with Philip and his wife. The communication may well have taken place while Philip was still in the East and accordingly before he ascended to the throne. But whenever it took place, it seems hard to deny that Philip had shown some interest in Christianity. He may have sampled Christian theology and worship in a spirit not unlike that of Julia Mamaea. He was presumably acquainted with Christians in his own city as well as in Bostra and elsewhere. But his conduct as emperor and the universal silence of pagan sources in the matter of any Christian leanings make it highly unlikely that Philip had actually become a Christian. The silence of Zosimus is particularly impressive, inasmuch as he vigorously disliked both Arabs and Christians. His account of Philip is most unflattering in ethnic terms; and if there had been anything to say about his being a Christian, Zosimus would surely have said it. The evidence is, however,

[15] Eusebius, *HE* 6.33.1 (Beryllus, bishop of Bostra); 6.37 (Arabian heresies).

[16] Eusebius, *HE* 6.21.3–4. For the date of the meeting of Origen and Mamaea at Antioch, see Barnes (above, n. 13), p. 328, n. 32.

sufficient to state that Philip dabbled in Christianity and that his dabbling is an indication of the considerable spread of the new religion in the Arab countries.

When Philip and his son, whom he had associated in the imperial power, were eliminated in 249 in a revolt raised by one of his own generals, Trajan Decius, the repose which Philip had brought to the Roman world was soon over. The fierce persecution of Christians that Decius initiated may well have been a reaction to what he considered excessive tolerance on the part of his predecessor.[17] And, in addition, he chose not to honor all the terms of the peace agreement that Philip had made with the Persians.[18] The result was that the Decian persecution was soon followed by a renewal of hostilities with the powerful dynasty of the Sassanids, now led by Shapur I. When Decius and his persecution were swept away in more civil strife, the Persians chose the time of confusion for a major invasion of the Roman provinces in Syria. As we can see from the magniloquent inscription in three languages which Shapur left behind as a record of his military exploits, he led a campaign that reached as far as Antioch and involved the destruction of substantial numbers of Roman troops.[19] The fall of Antioch to Shapur is also recorded in a late Greek source, explaining how the city was betrayed from inside. That same source goes on to tell how the Persians were repulsed from the city of Emesa through the forceful leadership of a priest of Aphrodite by the name of Sampsigeramus.[20] Once again, just as with Philip, we can see an eminent Arab rising up to meet a crisis posed by the Persian threat. Shapur retreated with his forces across the Euphrates after his unsuccessful attempt to capture Emesa.

[17] According to Eusebius, *HE* 6.41.9, Dionysius of Alexandria, writing under Decius, looked back to a more generous policy toward Christians under Philip: *ἡ τῆς βασιλείας ἐκείνης τῆς εὐμενεστέρας ἡμῖν μεταβολή*. For Decius' persecutions, see G. W. Clarke, "Some Observations on the Persecution of Decius," *Antichthon* 3 (1969), 63–76.

[18] Cf. A. T. Olmstead, *CP* 37 (1942), 261–62.

[19] A. Maricq, *Syria* 35 (1958), 308–10.

[20] Malalas, pp. 295–96 (Bonn); 64–65 (Stauffenberg). On Mariades, who betrayed Antioch to the Persians, see G. Downey, *A History of Antioch in Syria* (1961), pp. 254–55. For an excellent discussion of Malalas' account of Sampsigeramus, see H. R. Baldus, *Uranius Antoninus* (1971), pp. 236–50.

It was at exactly this time, in 253, that Emesa issued a series of coins proclaiming a new emperor of Rome. He bore the magnificent name L. Julius Aurelius Sulpicius Uranius Antoninus.[21] With the last of his names, he clearly tried to forge a link with the ultimate Antonines, who were the Arab emperors from the family of Julia Domna.[22] Uranius must be classed as a usurper, for his claim to the purple was never recognized; and his usurpation would be totally unknown apart from the coins that commemorate it. Nevertheless, in establishing with certainty a date of 253 for the Uranius issues at Emesa, a recent scholar has been able to draw attention to the coincidence of Sampsigeramus' repulse of the Persians from Emesa and Uranius' claims to the throne in the same city at the same time.[23] Uranius must inescapably be the Hellenized name for an Arab whose native name was Sampsigeramus.[24] In turning back the Persians, this man will have seen a suitable occasion for proclaiming himself emperor and, like Philip and the grandchildren of Julia Domna, of restoring the Arab domination of the central government.

The instability in the Middle East which the Persian threat had caused provided unique opportunities for the advancement of Arab power in the region. The opportunities were all the greater because of the inability of the central government to maintain any coherent foreign policy. The succession of five Roman emperors in the five years before the Persians took Antioch was obviously not calculated to produce continuity in administration.[25] It was no accident that, since the rise of the Sasssanids in Iran, the principal actions in confronting the Persians had been carried out by knowledgeable Middle Easterners—Severus Alexander, Philip, and then Uranius. Other prominent figures in the area must have assessed the situation with interest, and the potential for rivalry

[21] For a catalogue and thorough analysis of the Uranius coins, see Baldus (above, n. 20), whose book supersedes all previous work on this coinage.

[22] Note that Elagabalus is called *ultimus Antoninorum* in *HA*, Heliogab. 1.7.

[23] Baldus (above, n. 20), pp. 236–50.

[24] Baldus (above, n. 20), p. 248, exploits *Orac. Sibyll.* 13.151, which alludes obliquely to Sampsigeramus as ἡλιόπεμπτος (a Greek paraphrase of *šmš-grm*, "the sun has decided"). The name Uranius may thus represent "heaven-sent." Another possibility is an allusion to Urania (Aphrodite), whose priest Sampsigeramus was.

[25] The emperors were Philip, Decius, Gallus, Aemilianus, and Valerian.

among Arab troops in a struggle for power was no doubt considerable. After the end of the Nabataean kingdom, the dominant independent Arab force in the area had been indisputably the mercantile state of Palmyra, located at a major oasis in the Syrian desert in the vicinity of the principal trade routes through the northern desert. Palmyra had grown prosperous and strong during the second century, with revenues from customs duties and trading activities of its own that extended as far as the Euphrates. It may have been the only desert city whose merchants had their own seagoing ships.[26]

In the second and early third centuries the power of Palmyra in the desert was widely appreciated. The city's representatives provided protection in the desert through outposts and police operations and, as loyal allies of Rome, facilitated the passage of armies across the desolate wastes. A Roman military outpost such as that at Dura Europus overlooking the Euphrates could not have existed as it did without the symbiosis with Palmyra. The importance of Palmyra can be seen in the emergence of the first senator from the city in the time of Septimius Severus[27] and perhaps more memorably in the tributes paid by the great and the small to those who protected the trade routes. A certain Palmyrene by the name of Soados was honored by merchants, the provincial governor, and the emperor himself, as "a pious man and a lover of his country, who in numerous and great emergencies nobly and generously stood by the merchants and their caravans, who was unsparing of himself and his property."[28]

By the middle of the third century the Palmyrenes might well have judged that other Arabs had laid claims to positions of prominence to which their own long history of service and loyalty had properly entitled them. There are small but significant indications that the rulers of Palmyra, now Odaenathus and his queen

[26] See the relief, discovered in 1946 and now in the museum at Palmyra, depicting a Palmyrene standing by his ship: Khaled Assʿad and O. Taha, *Welcome to Palmyra* (1966), p. 89. There is a good photograph of this relief, taken before its installation in the museum, in H. Ingholt, *Gandharan Art in Pakistan* (1957), plate VI.2.

[27] *CIS* II.4202.

[28] On the Soados dossier, R. Mouterde, *Syria* 12 (1931), 111; Chr. Dunant, *Museum Helveticum* 13 (1956), 216–25. Cf. J. and L. Robert, *Bull. épig.* 1958.506. See also, on Palmyra in the second century, G. W. Bowersock, *Chiron* 6 (1976), 349–55.

Zenobia, were not willing to sit idly by when a priest at Emesa claimed the purple only a decade after a citizen of Shahbā had done the same. It looks as if Odaenathus at this moment contemplated disavowing Rome and making common cause with the Persians, who had already demonstrated that they were a major force. But the Persian king is said to have rejected overtures from Odaenathus and to have left him to advance within the Roman system.[29]

Rome needed Palmyra. Gifted and cunning individuals could render great service and reap great reward, but Palmyra was a well organized state with far-flung outposts and good communications. It was this organization which proved indispensable during the course of the Persians' next invasion, the most devastating of them all. In 259 Shapur and his armies swept westward out of Iran once again, and this time they not only defeated Roman troops but captured the emperor himself.[30] The humiliation of Valerian was the humiliation of Rome, but it was at the same time a great opportunity for Palmyra. The Persians were finally driven back by the Palmyrenes, who were more adept at desert warfare.[31] In the decade that followed, the Roman government under Gallienus seems to have been content to leave Palmyra as the principal protector of the Roman governors and their provinces in the Near East.[32] Odaenathus became the vicegerent of Rome in the area. It became less likely that an individual, such as

[29] Petrus Patricius, *FHG* (Müller) IV.187. Cf. the remarks in Malalas, p. 269 (Bonn), 65 (Stauffenberg), concerning Ἔναθος (i.e., [Od]aenathus): ἀντιποιούμενος Ῥωμαίων. See also Baldus (above, n. 20), pp. 238–39.

[30] See the proud boast of Shapur: Maricq (above, n. 19), 313, and the relief at Naqsh-i-Rustam representing Valerian's submission. For the date see F. Paschoud, *Zosime* (Budé) I (1971), pp. 154–55. Cf. Zosimus 1.36.2 on the shame brought to the Roman name. A Safaitic inscription (*CIS* 5.4448) names a year in which the Persians ("Medes," *mdy*) fought the Romans at Bostra, and M. Rodinson has connected this with Shapur's third campaign: *Arabica* 6 (1959), 216–17.

[31] Zosimus 1.39.1–2. The remaining legionary forces in the East were added to the troops of Palmyra.

[32] Zosimus 1.39.1–2: τοῖς δὲ περὶ τὴν ἑῴαν πράγμασιν οὖσιν ἐν ἀπογνώσει βοηθεῖν Ὀδαίναθον ἔταξεν, ἄνδρα Παλμυρηνὸν καὶ ἐκ προγόνων τῆς παρὰ τῶν βασιλέων ἀξιωθέντα τιμῆς. Odaenathus called himself *mlk mlk*' ("king of kings") and *mtqnn*' *dy mdnḥ*' *klh* ("ruler of all the East"): *CIS* II.3946. Cf. *CIS* II.3971, of Odaenathus' son Vaballathus, who is called *'pnrtṭ' dy mdnḥ' klh* ("ἐπανορθωτής of all the East"). In this and the preceding inscription, *mdnḥ* had formerly been misread as *mdyt*. See the commentary in *CIS*, *ad loc.*

Philip or Uranius, would again be able to seize an opportunity for self-advancement. Even so, not all Arabs can have watched the ascendancy of Odaenathus with equanimity. The jockeying for power among the Arabs themselves in this period is perhaps the most neglected theme in accounts of the aftermath of the third Persian invasion.

A substantial group of inscriptions from Derʿā as well as from Bostra makes it plain that a need was felt for strong fortifications, not only during the time of the Persian invasion but also for many years after it.[33] It looks as if the Persians were not thought to be the only threat to the region, and the rising power of Palmyra may thus have been viewed with some apprehension. Certainly in the cities of the northern part of the Arabian province there were strong village and tribal allegiances which flourished under the Roman government but would have undoubtedly been threatened by submission to a powerful Arab state. The independence of Arab tribes was a precious heritage, whether these social units were sedentary or nomadic. Inscriptions provide substantial documentation of tribes in the Ḥawrān area,[34] as well as of nomadic groups with their own officers. We hear of a *stratēgos* of a nomad camp, as well as an *ethnarchēs* (both of these terms may designate sheikhs), and another text gives us a *syndikos*.[35] The confederation of smaller social units into a larger group with common objectives was nothing new to the pre-Islamic world. The confederation of the Thamūd is well attested in the inscription at Ruwwāfa in Saudi Arabia, and indeed the Palmyrene state itself represents a confederation of tribes. If any individual village or tribal group were to withstand imperialist pressure from a confederation, it

[33] The texts are assembled in H.-G. Pflaum, "La fortification de la ville d'Adraha d'Arabie (259–260 à 274–275) d'après des inscriptions récemment découvertes," *Syria* 29 (1952), 307–30.

[34] The material has been assembled by H. I. MacAdam in his dissertation, "Studies in the History of the Roman Province of Arabia" (Univ. of Manchester, 1979), chap. 6 ("The Provincial Tribes"). It is unfortunate that documentation on tribes is largely confined to the north of the province.

[35] *PAES* III.A, no. 752 (στρατη[γ]ὸς παρε[μ]βολῶν [ν]ομάδων); cf. Waddington, *IGLS* 2196 (*OGIS* 616), for a στρατηγὸς νομάδων. Also *IGR* 3.1247 (ἐθνάρχης) and *PAES* III.A, no. 383 (σύνδικος). The last must be the equivalent of the tribal *iudex* in the Latin text in G. L. Harding, *ADAJ* 2 (1953), 46, no. 173. For further examples and discussion, M. Sartre, *Trois études sur l'Arabie romaine et byzantine* (1982), pp. 122–28.

would obviously be necessary for them to join in some way a rival confederation that could take common action in their interest. Hence the greatest Arab threat to the Palmyrenes would have been another Arab confederation. And there was one.

With the help of three epigraphic discoveries in the present century, it is now possible to piece together the history of a confederation of tribes known as the Tanūkh in the third century and, in relation to this history, the foundation of the Lakhmid dynasty which took root at the site of Ḥīra. Information about these groups has long survived in the historical and genealogical works of the Arabs, in particular the *Universal History* of Ṭabarī; but without confirming evidence among the documents, scholars had refused to credit their testimony.[36] It must accordingly be counted a great gain that it is now possible to interpret the tensions in Syria and Arabia during the last decade of the rule of Odaenathus and Zenobia in the light of the activities of the Tanūkh and early Lakhmids. These Arab groups provide just the counterbalance to Palmyra that one was looking for. If Rome felt relieved to have its eastern flank administered by the Palmyrenes, others who dwelt there will have had feelings of concern and hostility. The Tanūkh emerge as the consolidated enemies of Palmyra; and when Zenobia decided, after her husband's death, to revolt against the Roman authorities, her action was as much an assault upon her Arab neighbors as it was a defection from the government in Italy.[37]

The Tanūkh which Ṭabarī describes as a confederation of many tribes had been settled in the area of al-Qaṭīf in the northeastern portion of the Arabian peninsula.[38] Later Arab sources are in agreement on this original homeland of the Tanūkh,[39] and according to Ṭabarī it was not until the arrival of the Sassanids in Iran that many tribes within the confederation opted to leave

[36] Cf., for example, the agnosticism of G. Rothstein, *Die Dynastie der Laḫmiden in al-Ḥīra* (1899), p. 40.

[37] Odaenathus was murdered at Emesa: Zosimus 1.39.2, probably in 267/268. See F. Millar, *JRS* 61 (1971), 8–9. A separate tradition has Odaenathus killed in Cappadocia: Syncellus 1, pp. 716–17 (Bonn).

[38] Ṭabarī, *Ta'rīkh* (Ibrāhīm) II (1961), p. 42.

[39] Ibn al-Athīr I.243; Yāqūt II.376. Cf. W. Caskel, *Mél. Univ. St. Joseph* 45 (1969), 367–79.

their homeland, in order to escape from the rule of the new Persian dynasty.[40] Ṭabarī's report has received striking confirmation in recent years from an inscription of the first half of the third century in which the area of the northeast peninsula is described as containing "provinces of Persia and the land of the Tanūkh."[41] There is therefore every reason to believe that it was the subjugation to the Persians which decided substantial segments of the Tanūkh to emigrate.

Ṭabarī reports that they headed northwards and settled in the area of Ḥīra, joining Arabs who were already established there. From Ḥīra many of them pressed farther north toward Anbār and beyond.[42] They thus became a potent force in the inner desert regions west of the Euphrates. Among the names associated with the Tanūkh in the new location is a certain Jadhīma, who was the ruling sheikh of the confederation in the time of Zenobia.[43] The presence of Jadhīma and his people in the northern part of the Arabian province is dramatically attested by an inscription from Umm al-jimāl, in both Nabataean and Greek, commemorating a teacher of this powerful sheikh, who is explicitly named and described as "king of the Tanūkh."[44] The teacher of Jadhīma was presumably a Nabataean Arab living in the province of Arabia, and his services to the king of the Tanūkh must reflect the penetration of that confederation into the desert area of Arabia and probably Syria as well.

The Arab sources bring Jadhīma directly into conflict with Zenobia and ascribe his destruction to a clever ruse of the Palmyrene queen.[45] It was left to Jadhīma's successor, ʿAmr ibn ʿAdī,

[40] Ṭabarī (above, n. 38), p. 42. This part of Ṭabarī is included in Th. Nöldeke's magisterial translation, *Die Geschichte der Perser und Araber zur Zeit der Sasaniden* (1879; repr. 1973), p. 23.

[41] J. Ryckmans, "Le texte Sharafaddin, Yemen, p. 44 bas, droite," *Le Muséon* 80 (1967), 508–12. The crucial words are [*m*]*lkty frs wʿrḍ tnḫ*.

[42] Ṭabarī (above, n. 38), p. 42, with which cf., in the same history, I (1960), p. 612, where the Tanūkh are called *ʿarab al-ḍāḥiyya*. Ṭabarī uses *al-ḍāḥiyya* to refer to the frontier zone, much as Graeco-Roman authors use *limes* or τὸ λίμιτον.

[43] For Jadhīma, see esp. Ṭabarī (above, n. 38) I (1960), pp. 618–21.

[44] *PAES* IV.A, no. 41, with commentary by E. Littmann. The text is not wholly literate either in Nabataean or in Greek, as Littmann shows. It reads *dnh nfšw fhrw br šly rbw gdymt mlk tnwḥ* and ἡ στήλη αὕτη Φερου Σολλεου τροφεὺς Γαδιμάθου βασιλεὺς Θανουηνῶν.

[45] She persuaded him to come to her and then cut his veins so that the blood would

who was the son of his sister and the first king in the line of Lakhmid rulers, to take vengeance on the Palmyrenes. It is in fact ʿAmr ibn ʿAdī who is credited in the Arabic sources with the conquest of Palmyra and the death of Zenobia.[46] The struggle waged by these newcomers from al-Qatīf against the long-established power in Palmyra must now be seen as an important cause of the military explosion in 270 which brought the Palmyrene armies swarming across the border into the province of Arabia and took them ultimately on into Egypt, where Zenobia presented herself as the new Cleopatra.[47] The authenticity of the reports about Jadhīma and ʿAmr ibn ʿAdī is further confirmed by the inscription at Namāra in the Arabic language but in Nabataean script: the text commemorates a certain Imru'l-qais, who is said to be the son of ʿAmr ibn ʿAdī.[48] This Imru'l-qais is none other than the son of the nephew of Jadhīma and is named by Ṭabarī as Imru'l-qais *al-bad'* (meaning "the first").[49] The Namāra inscription confirms the succession of rulers as reported in the literary texts, as well as the approximate date to which they are assigned, for the inscription is explicitly dated to A.D. 328, when Imru'l-qais may be presumed to have died.

---

collect in a golden basin. Not surprisingly he died: Ṭabarī (above, n. 38) I (1960), p. 621.

[46] Ṭabarī (above, n. 38) I (1960), pp. 625 and 627. In Arabic Zenobia is *al-zabbā'* (cf. her name in Palmyrene, *bt zby*, in *CIS* II.3947 and 3971). It is odd to find that J. S. Trimingham refuses to accept the identification of *al-zabbā'* as Zenobia: *Christianity among the Arabs in Pre-Islamic Times* (1979), p. 155, n. 66. The chronology fits well in the light of the inscription at Umm al-jimāl, and the form of the name, by comparison with the Palmyrene, is reasonable. Furthermore, Ṭabarī makes plain that *al-zabbā'* is a ruler at Palmyra (cf. I, p. 618, *wa-tasīru ilā tadmūr*). Littmann (above, n. 44) accepts the identification, as do most historians of the Arabs: e.g., P. Hitti, *History of the Arabs* (1970), pp. 75–76, and Ch. Pellat, *Encyclopedia of Islam* A.450.

[47] On the invasion of Egypt, see Zosimus 1.44 and 50.1, with the discussion by Millar (above, n. 37), 9. For the name Cleopatra, see *HA*, Aur. 27.3 and Prob. 9.5, with the arguments of A. Stein, "Kallinikos von Petrai," *Hermes* 58 (1923), 448–56.

[48] The Namāra text, with a good drawing of the Nabataean letters as well as a version in Arabic script, can be found in J. Cantineau, *Le nabatéen* II (1932), p. 49. The inscription was first published by J. Dussaud and F. Macler in *RA* 2 (1902), 409–21.

[49] Ṭabarī (above, n. 38) II (1961), p. 53. On the meaning of *al-bad'*, see Nöldeke (above, n. 30), p. 47, n. 1, and p. 79, n. 1. From the passage in II, p. 53, it seems that Ṭabarī thought—perhaps mistakenly, see Chap. X—that Imru'l-qais was the first of the Lakhmids to become a Christian.

All of this means that during the reign of Gallienus, in the 260s, the situation in Syria and Arabia must have been growing increasingly tense. The Palmyrenes had become menacingly powerful as a result of their success in keeping the Persians at bay. The Tanūkh, which had fled from Persian domination in the south, were now contesting the supremacy of the Palmyrenes and were thereby disturbing the fragile equilibrium which the Roman government was relying upon to guarantee peace in the area. At Palmyra Zenobia appears to have seen herself more and more in the role of a Hellenistic queen and a patron of culture. Like Julia Domna and Julia Mamaea, she interested herself in the intellectual life of the age and is reported to have gathered a distinguished group of literary figures around her.

There can be no doubt that, in the Near East, Arab Hellenism flourished in this period as it had earlier in the century. The sophist Heliodorus, whom Philostratus describes as an Arab, had already made a profound impression on Caracalla in earlier times,[50] and his trade seems to have been practiced by others in subsequent generations. In the heartland of old Nabataea Hellenic culture prospered. We can identify a certain Callinicus from Petra, a sophist who was sufficiently distinguished to practice rhetoric in Athens itself.[51] And there he was confronted with a rival, Genethlius, who was also a native of Petra.[52] Complex philosophical discussions appear to have been conducted among the educated persons in Callinicus' city, and one may suspect that all these people at one time or another paid their respects at the court of Zenobia.[53]

At any rate, when the armies of Palmyra had installed Zenobia as the queen of Egypt, Callinicus was on hand to present her with a history of the city of Alexandria with no less enthusiasm than he

[50] Philostratus, *Vit. Soph.*, pp. 625–27 (Olearius).

[51] Suda, *s.v.* Καλλίνικος. See Stein (above, n. 47): at some point Callinicus presented Virius Lupus, the governor of Arabia, with a treatise περὶ κακοζηλίας ῥητορικῆς.

[52] Suda, *s.v.* Γενέθλιος. On Genethlius as the possible author of the first treatise in the corpus of Menander Rhetor, see D. A. Russell and N. G. Wilson (eds.), *Menander Rhetor* (1981), p. 226.

[53] On others in Zenobia's entourage, notably Paul of Samosata, see Millar (above, n. 37). One may speculate about the date of the Nabataean author uncovered by J. Bernays, "Ein nabatäischer Schriftsteller," *RhM* 17 (1862), 304–6, reprinted with revisions in *Ges. Abhandl.* II (1885), pp. 291–93.

had shown to the governor of the province of Arabia who, some years previously, had been the recipient of his treatise on rhetoric.[54] It is unlikely that Jadhīma and ʿAmr ibn ʿAdī interested themselves very much in things of this kind or even fully appreciated the delicate interplay between culture and politics in the provinces of Rome. ʿAmr ibn ʿAdī would doubtless have welcomed an elegant poem on his victories, but not perhaps a well-turned treatise in prose on the history of Ḥīra.

By seizing cultural as well as military and political initiatives in the Near East, Zenobia was enhancing her prospects of success. When she finally launched the war that took her to Egypt, she crashed through the capital of the province of Arabia without regard for Arab traditions unlike her own. Her forces destroyed the temple of Zeus Hammon at Bostra, the very symbol of the city and the legion that was based there.[55] The vehemence of Zenobia's onslaught in northern Arabia, together with the extensive work on fortifications over the decade before she launched her campaign, would seem to imply that the residents in the Ḥawrān at least were expecting trouble. This may have had something to do with the arrival of the Tanūkh in the area. Although the base of the tribes was in Ḥīra to the south, it is clear, not only from the presence of Jadhīma's teacher at Umm al-jimāl but also from the location of the tomb of ʿAmr ibn ʿAdī's son at Namāra (to the northeast of the Jebel Drūz), that the Tanūkh representation in northern Arabia was highly influential. Zenobia must have observed with alarm the buildup of her Arab enemies just across the southern border of Syria inside the Roman province of Arabia.

The ultimate destruction of Zenobia and her kingdom at Palmyra is ascribed in the Roman sources to the emperor Aurelian and his troops.[56] Obviously Aurelian's intervention was decisive.

[54] Stein (above, n. 47) has demonstrated that Callinicus' work on Alexandria, listed in the Suda as *πρὸς Κλεοπάτραν περὶ τῶν κατ' 'Αλεξάνδρειαν ἱστοριῶν βιβλία ι'*, was presented to Zenobia. On the treatise for Virius Lupus, see n. 51 above.

[55] H. Seyrig, *Syria* 22 (1941), 46: *templum Iovis Hammo[nis dirutum a Pal]myrenis hostibu[s]*. See also the text published by Seyrig in *Syria* 31 (1954), 214–17, which appears to record in the Ḥawrān the deaths of persons in Egypt. This presumably reflects the return through the area of some of Zenobia's forces after the conquest of Egypt.

[56] See the long narration in Zosimus 1.50–59, as well as Festus 24, Eutropius 9.13.2, and *HA*, Aurel. 22–34. It is odd that Aurelius Victor makes no mention of Aurelian's war against Zenobia in his biography of that emperor.

But from the Arab perspective it was ʿAmr ibn ʿAdī who eliminated Zenobia, as an act of vengeance for the death of Jadhīma. In fact, it must have been a potent coalition of the Roman and Lakhmid forces that brought success to Zenobia's enemies. If the Palmyrenes had been able to turn back a Persian army that had captured a Roman emperor, theirs must have been a formidable desert force. The tribes of ʿAmr ibn ʿAdī would have known how to deal with the Palmyrenes on their own terms, and with the support and leadership of a gifted Roman emperor, such as Aurelian, the ultimate victory was assured. There even appears to have been some cooperation from within Palmyra itself, where at least one Roman senator of Palmyrene origin can be identified as an enemy of Zenobia.[57]

The coalition of Roman troops and the Arab tribes of ʿAmr ibn ʿAdī may already have taken shape within the province of Arabia during the last years of Zenobia's rule. Certainly, once she had begun to sweep down into Egypt, these two presences in the province would have been necessarily thrown together in a common cause. Aurelian's victory was also ʿAmr's victory. With the collapse of Palmyra, the province of Arabia, as well as the Syrian provinces to the north, required a new Arab force in the desert. ʿAmr ibn ʿAdī and his son were there to provide it.

[57] Septimius Addoudanes: M. Gawlikowski, *Syria* 48 (1971), 413, with *Invent. Inscr. Palmyre* IX.28. Cf. G. W. Bowersock, "Roman Senators from the Near East," *Acta* of the colloquium *Epigrafia e ordine senatorio* (forthcoming), Register no. 24.

X

KING OF ALL THE ARABS

When Imru'l-qais, the son of ʿAmr ibn ʿAdī, was buried near the Roman fort at Namāra inside the province of Arabia in A.D. 328, dramatic changes had taken place in the Roman government. In a little over a decade after the overthrow of Palmyra, a gifted general from the Balkans took over the government of Rome under the imperial name of Diocletian and transformed the whole system that Augustus had created. Diocletian's new empire was administered by two senior emperors and two junior ones, and the provinces were broken up into smaller and more manageable administrative units. After struggling among themselves, the heirs of Diocletian made possible the ultimate ascendance of Constantine, who transferred the capital from Rome in Italy to a new Rome at Byzantium, named Constantinople after himself. These profound changes in the Roman Empire brought the center of authority much closer to the Hellenized East and made possible that vibrant culture which we know today as Byzantine.

The two generations of Lakhmid kings, ʿAmr ibn ʿAdī and Imru'l-qais, span this entire period of transformation within the Roman Empire. The inscription on the tomb of Imru'l-qais, although fraught with philological difficulties, is nonetheless a precious primary source for the Arab contribution to the stability of the Near East under Diocletian and Constantine. This early Arabic text, written in Nabataean letters, is in itself an illustration of the emergence of the Arabs from their long dependence on various dialects of Aramaic, such as Nabataean and Palmyrene, for public documents.[1] The Namāra inscription begins: "This is the

[1] The inscription has been extensively discussed in recent years: W. Caskel, "Die Inschrift von En-Nemara: neu gesehen," *Mél. Univ. St. Joseph* 45 (1969), 367–69; G. W. Bowersock, "The Inscription at el-Nemāra," in an article on the Ruwwāfa inscriptions, *Le monde grec: Hommages à Claire Préaux* (1975), pp. 520–22; F. E. Peters, in an article "Romans and Bedouin in Southern Syria," *Journ. Near Eastern Studies* 37 (1978), 324–26; A. F. L. Beeston, "Nemara and Faw," *BSOAS* 42 (1979),

tomb of Imru'l-qais, the son of 'Amr, king of all the Arabs."[2] It then states that Imru'l-qais put on the diadem of rule and reigned over tribes and cities of Arabs all the way down to the southern Arabian peninsula. Toward the end of the text we read: "No king has ever achieved what he has achieved."[3] And that is probably no idle boast. Furthermore, for the Arabian province in the tumultuous times of Diocletian and Constantine, when the Persian threat remained as serious as before, a friend like Imru'l-qais would have been a great asset. It might have been supposed from the collaboration of the father of Imru'l-qais with the forces of Aurelian in the suppression of Palmyra that the king of all the Arabs would have stood on the side of Rome. In determining whether or not this was actually the case, the Namāra inscription is of supreme importance.

In the fourth line of this difficult text, there is an undisputed reference to the Romans, preceded by a preposition meaning "to" or "for." Immediately before this are the letters *fršw*, which can be read as the noun "Persians" (with a characteristically Nabataean terminal *w*) or as a word meaning "horsemen" (with the same terminal *w*).[4] In the original publication of 1902, the first editor of this inscription believed that Imru'l-qais had provided cavalry for the Romans; but by the end of his life he had changed his mind and decided that the Arab king had entered into some kind of relationship with both Persians and Romans.[5] Unfortunately the correct resolution of the letters immediately preceding the word *fršw* is still not evident. It must be stressed, however, that there is no prepositional letter meaning "for" or "to" before the word that means either "Persians" or "horsemen."[6]

1–6; I. Shahîd, "Philological Observations on the Namara Inscription," *JSS* 24 (1979), 33–42; H. I. MacAdam, "The Nemara Inscription: Some Historical Considerations," *Al-abḥāth* 28 (1980), 3–16; M. Sartre, in *Trois études sur l'Arabie romaine et byzantine* (1982), pp. 136–39.

[2] The Nabataean letters are *ty nfš mr 'lqyš br 'mrw mlk 'l 'rb klh*: R. Dussaud and F. Macler, *RA* 2 (1902), 409–21, or see, conveniently, the drawing in J. Cantineau, *Le nabatéen* II (1932), p. 49.

[3] *flm ybl' mlk mbl'h*: *bl'* represents Arabic *balagha*, thus *yablugh* and *mablaghahu*.

[4] *wwklhn fršw lrwm*.

[5] R. Dussaud, *La pénétration des arabes en Syrie avant l'Islam* (1955), p. 64.

[6] I argued (above, n. 1) in favor of "Persians" and proposed that the *nūn* before *fršw* be read as a *lām*, since the shape is virtually the same, and that the *wāw* after *frš* be

The author of the most acute philological discussion of this text is convinced that the word can only be "horsemen" here,[7] and another scholar has recently argued persuasively from the place of Imru'l-qais' burial that he can only have been an ally of Rome.[8] Namāra was the site of a Roman fort that constituted part of the defense of the Arabian province. Any Arab leader with a tomb in such a place could not have boasted of providing aid to the Persians. Accordingly, on the basis of both philological and topographical arguments, we must now accept the allegiance of Imru'l-qais to the Roman government.

From the start, the principal difficulty in crediting such a role for the king of all the Arabs has been the testimony of Ṭabarī in his *History*. As we have seen, Ṭabarī refers several times to Imru'l-qais, the son of ʿAmr ibn ʿAdī, and in one passage he says that this king was the first of a series of Lakhmid agents of the Persians to have become a Christian.[9] Such a remark is highly surprising, not only for its claim that Imru'l-qais was allied to the Persians. There is no indication on the inscription that he was ever a Christian; nor is there any symbolic indication of Christian sympathies at the tomb itself. If Ṭabarī is wrong in believing that Imru'l-qais was a vassal of the Persians, he is just as likely to be wrong about the Christian association.

In fact, it is possible to see how Ṭabarī made his error. In the second half of the fourth century there was another Lakhmid ruler by the name of Imru'l-qais, and it seems that Ṭabarī has confused the history of this king with the earlier one. When Ṭabarī introduces Imru'l-qais in the course of his narrative, he calls him Imru'l-qais *al-bad'*. This word is explained elsewhere as meaning "the first," and indeed Ṭabarī goes on immediately to say that Imru'l-qais was the first of the Persian agents to become

understood as a connective "and" before *lrwm*. But G. J. Toomer has pointed out to me that the *hā'* in *wwklhn* does not have the terminal form of the Nabataean letter, as one would expect if *wwklh lfrš wlrwm* were to be read. On *wwklhn* see the brilliant suggestions of Shahîd (above, n. 1), 37–41.

7 Shahîd (above, n. 1), 40, n. 1.

8 MacAdam (above, n. 1), 8–14.

9 The principal text mentioning Imru'l-qais' Christianity is in Ṭabarī, *Ta'rīkh* (Ibrāhīm) II (1961), p. 53: *wa-huwa awwal man tanaṣṣara min mulūk āl-naṣr-b.-rabīʿa wa-ʿummāl mulūk al-furs*. See also pp. 61–62 and 65.

a Christian.[10] So it seems clear that he understood, just as later writers did, *al-bad'* to mean "the first," but it becomes obvious that he had mistakenly attached the designation to the early fourth century king when he returns to the history of the Lakhmids in the latter years of the fourth century. He introduces the second Imru'l-qais also as *al-bad'* and at one point, in giving the genealogy of this later figure, names the homonymous ancestor as Imru'l-qais without *al-bad'*.[11] Inasmuch as an epithet meaning "the first" can be applied only to one ruler, it seems much more appropriate to accept the attachment to the second Imru'l-qais as the first Christian Lakhmid.

In the second half of the fourth century, Persian allegiance on the part of the Lakhmids at Ḥīra would cause no historical problem, nor would a conversion to Christianity. This would, after all, fall in the days of Queen Mavia, who is the most celebrated Arab convert in the reign of Valens.[12] In view of the spread of Christianity in the province of Arabia—which was so pronounced in the time of Eusebius that he called special attention to it[13]—it remains possible that the first Imru'l-qais was a Christian, and that Ṭabarī's confusion goes deeper than the simple misattribution of an epithet. In other words, it could be that one Imru'l-qais was a Christian and the other a Persian agent. But, on the evidence we now have, it would be more prudent to assume that Ṭabarī has transferred entirely the innovations of the second Imru'l-qais to the first.

The king of all the Arabs emerges therefore as an honorable and loyal successor to his father on the Roman side. With the Lakhmids based at Ḥīra near the Euphrates in the south, and the

[10] Ṭabarī (above, n. 9) II (1961), p. 53. Cf. above, p. 134, n. 49.

[11] Ṭabarī (above, n. 9) II (1961), p. 65, in the second enumeration of the ancestors of the later Imru'l-qais. MacAdam (above, n. 1), 7, raises the possibility that Ṭabarī confused two rulers of the same name but does not discuss the problem of *bad'* as *awwal* and the Christianity of Persian *'ummāl*.

[12] See G. W. Bowersock, "Mavia, Queen of the Saracens," *Studien zur antiken Sozialgeschichte: Festschrift für F. Vittinghoff* (1980), pp. 477–95. In his forthcoming book on Byzantium and the Arabs in the fourth century, Irfan Shahîd will give an important account of Mavia, from which I profited at an early stage in my work.

[13] Eusebius, *Comm. on Isaiah*, with references to 42.11, *PG* 24.392, p. 273 (Ziegler): churches at Petra and even among the Saracens in the desert (*ἐν ταῖς ἐρήμοις δὲ τῶν Σαρακηνῶν καθ' ἡμᾶς αὐτοὺς ἱδρυμένων*).

tomb of their king at Namāra in the north, together with references in his inscription to control of such far-flung realms in the Arabian peninsula as Maʿadd and Najrān, the extraordinary range of authority can be appreciated. In the peninsula it goes far beyond the limits of the old Nabataean kingdom and the Arabian province. To the east the Lakhmids controlled the desert between the road network of the Roman *limes* defenses and the Euphrates. They had not only assumed the role of the Palmyrenes: they had enlarged it.

Although Ṭabarī's dates for the reigns of the early Lakhmid kings are notoriously inexact and inconsistent with each other, it appears likely that ʿAmr ibn ʿAdī died toward the end of the third century.[14] If Imru'l-qais assumed the kingship at about that time, he will have played a crucial role in the important campaigns against the Persians which occupied both Diocletian and Galerius at various times between 295 and 299. In particular, when Galerius carried out his successful attack on the Persians in 298, he marched all the way to Ctesiphon and then returned up the Euphrates.[15] Such a route brought him very close to the Lakhmid capital at Ḥīra and was presumably possible only with the active support of the Arab forces on the western side of the river. Since the resolution of the Persian question was of capital significance for the stability of the Tetrarchy, the close rapport between Imru'l-qais and the Roman government may well have grown out of the cooperation of Romans and Arabs in the very last years of the third century.

Once the Persian wars of this period were over, it was possible for Diocletian to devote himself directly to the administrative reorganization of the eastern provinces. No later than 314, the

[14] Ṭabarī (above, n. 9) I (1960), p. 627, records ʿAmr's succession to Jadhīma and a lifespan of 120 years—which is impossible. An earlier genealogist, such as al-Kalbī, may again have confused the Imru'l-qais who succeeded ʿAmr with the later Lakhmid of that name, and hence given ʿAmr such a long life. In II (1961), p. 53, Ṭabarī gives the earlier Imru'l-qais a life of 114 years, perhaps also as a result of confusion in al-Kalbī.

[15] See T. D. Barnes, *The New Empire of Diocletian and Constantine* (1982), p. 63. David Graf has suggested to me that a neglected Latin inscription found thirty miles east of Mafraq in northern Jordan (*QDAP* 10 [1944], 62) may show renewed instability on the frontier after the death of Imru'l-qais: it records a Saracen ambush in A.D. 334.

lower part of the Trajanic province of Arabia, south of the Wādī Ḥaṣā, had been detached from the north with its capital at Bostra. This lower segment, which included Petra, the Negev, and probably the Ḥejāz, became part of Palestine and was therefore associated with the provinces that lay on the western bank of the Jordan. In works dated to 311 and 313, Eusebius declared that the governor of Palestine sentenced Christians to labor in the copper mines at Phaeno "in Palestine."[16] This place, to the south of the Dead Sea, had certainly been a part of the old Arabian province but, at least by the time of Eusebius' writing, was evidently reckoned in Palestine. The whole southern part of Arabia, on both sides of the ʿAraba, became known as Palaestina Tertia by the mid-fourth century.[17] The truncated province in the north, preserving the name Arabia, appears to have kept the northern boundaries which, as we have seen, Septimius Severus had already given it.[18]

Diocletian's transformation of the Arabian province shows an exceptional understanding of the geographical necessities of the region. Bostra and the northern cities of Gerasa, Philadelphia, and Adraa were naturally linked to the Damascus roads and the inner passageway of the Wādī Sirḥān. By contrast, the southern portion, with its principal city of Petra in the interior and Aela at the head of the Gulf of ʿAqaba, was more naturally tied to the route across the Wādī ʿAraba and through the Negev to the Mediterranean in the vicinity of Gaza or Rhinocolura. The long north-south line of the King's Highway from Damascus to ʿAqaba had, in former times, been crucial in providing communications when the western bank of the Jordan was under alien rule, as in the days of the Nabataeans or later during the period of unrest among the Jews. But now Diocletian must have recognized the geographical cohesion of the eastern and western sectors below the Dead Sea. This was a cohesion which had been evident on the eve of the provincial annexation, when the family of Babatha and her friends settled at Zoar. Diocletian took strong

[16] Eusebius, *Mart. Pal.* 7.2, in the two recensions: see Barnes (above, n. 15), p. 205.
[17] See K. C. Gutwein, *Third Palestine: A Regional Study in Byzantine Urbanization* (1981).
[18] Cf. Chap. VIII and the arguments of Sartre (above, n. 1), pp. 54–70.

action to strengthen the southern half of the former Arabian province by installing there, for the first time, a full legion, in addition to the one in the north. This southern legion was the Fourth Martia, probably based at the camp at Lejjūn in the vicinity of modern Karak.[19] From the present indications of excavation at that site, this camp was created at some point during the Tetrarchy and therefore seems the obvious candidate for the base of the Fourth Martia. Lejjūn's ancient name would accordingly have been Betthoro, the name of the legion's camp as given in the *Notitia Dignitatum*.[20]

Just as the south was reorganized and fortified, so too was the north of old Arabia. A group of new constructions at this period can be discerned at Azraq and surrounding sites that were important for the protection of the head of the Wādī Sirḥān.[21] In strengthening this area Diocletian was following the lead of Septimius Severus one hundred years before. He also enlarged the communications link between Arabia and the Syrian provinces to the north by bringing his new Syrian frontier road, the Strata Diocletiana, down to Azraq along a course that lay well to the east of the old road to Damascus. Inscriptions have shown that it passed through the town of Saʿane on the eastern slopes of the Jebel Drūz.[22] Fortification, communication, and administrative reorganization were the hallmarks of Diocletian's policy in Arabia, as elsewhere.

The partition of old Arabia into a new and small province of that name and a much enlarged Palestine to the south has often been thought to underlie a peculiar item in the so-called Verona List. In this problematic register of provinces from a date relatively early in the fourth century, there appear in succession

[19] See M. Speidel, *ANRW* II.8 (1977), 699.

[20] *Not. Dig.* 37.22. On the possibility of a general military buildup in central Arabia under the Tetrarchy, see S. T. Parker, "Towards a History of the *Limes Arabicus*," *Roman Frontier Studies 1979*, BAR International Series 71 (1980), 865–78, together with the observations above, p. 105, n. 44.

[21] Deir al-Kahf: *PAES* III.A, no. 228. Umm al-Quṭṭein: *PAES* III.A, nos. 205–206. Cf. G. W. Bowersock, *HSCP* 80 (1976), 223. For Azraq, see now Kennedy, *Arch-Explor* (1982), p. 75, and, for a revised text of the inscription I published in *JRS* 61 (1971), 241, see Kennedy, p. 90, no. 13. On Deir al-Kahf, Kennedy, p. 299.

[22] R. Mouterde, *Mél. Univ. St. Joseph* 15 (1930), 219. Cf. M. Malavolta, "Interiores Limites," *Ottava miscellanea greca e romana* (1982), 587–610. See also Sartre (above, n. 1), p. 133.

Aegyptus Iovia Aegyptus Herculea Arabia item Arabia Augusta Libanensis. The existence of Jovian and Herculean Egypt proves a date no earlier than 314. Accordingly, at a date consonant with the existence of these two Egyptian provinces, there were two Arabias (*Arabia item Arabia*).[23] For a long time it had been tempting to assume that the second Arabia was the second half of the old province before it was incorporated as a part of Palestine, but after it had been broken off from the north. Yet such an interpretation seemed to conflict with the evidence of Eusebius, from before 314, that the southern part was already considered Palestine. A solution to this hoary problem has now at last been made possible through the appearance of a new papyrus from Oxyrhynchus.[24]

The new text is a letter to the governor of Aegyptus Herculea. The governor's name, Aurelius Antonius, is a familiar one. We know that he was in office in 315/316.[25] The author of the letter, an illiterate with the Arab name of Aurelius Malchus, had been obliged to hire a scribe to write for him, and he indicated at the start that he came from the territory of Eleutheropolis in Νέα Ἀραβεία, "New Arabia." This is a new and exciting discovery. We had never before heard of a province called New Arabia or, presumably, Arabia Nova. At first glance the document seems paradoxical, since the most famous city called Eleutheropolis lies in Palestine, close to Jerusalem, and by 315 the whole area southward into the Negev would have been part of the newly enlarged Palestine. Nor would it be immediately obvious why such a person would be writing to the governor of Aegyptus Herculea. But in presenting his case Malchus refers to a defaulting debtor as Saeibas ἀπὸ Σκηνῶν τῶν ἐκτὸς Γέρρους. A third party to the case, a hard-hearted moneylender with a Greek name, is a man from Boubastis. These details leave no doubt that the location of

[23] For the text of the *laterculus Veronensis*, see now Barnes (above, n. 15), p. 202. Sartre (above, n. 1), pp. 68–69, provides a review of earlier opinion on these entries in the Verona List. In *JRS* 61 (1971), 242, I had already followed A. Alt in separating *Augusta Libanensis* from the second *Arabia* in the list: *ZDPV* 71 (1955), 173.

[24] I am deeply grateful to John Rea for showing me the text of this papyrus before publication. It is Oxyrhynchus inventory no. 29 4B.48/G(6–7)a. I had occasion to present my view of this text to T. D. Barnes in conversation, and he has incorporated it (with generous acknowledgment) in his book (above, n. 15), pp. 204–5 and 213–14.

[25] *Pap. Oxy*. 896 and 2113; *Pap. Isid*. 74; and *Pap. Mert*. 2.91 (Karanis).

the troubles must be Egypt itself: it was in the vicinity of Aegyptus Herculea that Boubastis was to be found, and not very far away, near Pelusium, were the nomadic tents outside Gerrhon.[26] It was precisely in this area that there had been an Egyptian nome called Arabia. It would therefore be reasonable to assume that this was the homeland of Malchus, who was writing to the governor of Aegyptus Herculea because the dispute involved someone in the adjacent area which happened to be under his jurisdiction. Obviously if Malchus lived in Egyptian Arabia, then there must have been an Eleutheropolis in it. One thing is certain: the Eleutheropolis near Jerusalem, even with a large territory around it, lay far outside the confines of old Arabia and its successor province. It belonged to Palaestina Prima.

It thus seems clear that the nome of Arabia was elevated to the status of a province when the two Egypts were created. Because of the existence of another province of Arabia, it was obvious that the nome as a province would have to be distinguished by the adjective *nova*. The second Arabia in the Verona List must be Arabia Nova, and the dating of this evidence is fully consistent now with the dates of Jovian and Herculean Egypt. The problem of the second Arabia may perhaps be near to a solution.

With the dissolution of the old province of Arabia and the death of Diocletian's ally Imru'l-qais, the history of Roman Arabia comes to an end. But a rich and variegated history now begins, that of Byzantine Arabia. Just three years before Imru'l-qais was laid to rest at Namāra, Constantine had transferred the capital of the Roman world. At Byzantium, now Constantinople and celebrated as the new Rome, the traditions of Hellenism were to flourish for nearly a thousand years more. Under the new dispensation the Arabs were to play an increasingly important part in the Byzantine administration of the Near East. Imru'l-qais was a harbinger of things to come, and if his descendants were to take the side of the Persians and leave a legacy that would bring confusion to Ṭabarī, there were others to fill the gap he had

[26] For Gerrhon (sometimes Gerrha), see Ptolemy, *Geog.* 4.5.11; also Strabo 1.3.4, C 50; 1.3.13, C 56; 16.2.3, C 760. Seeck, in his edition of the *Not. Dig.*, had already recognized that the place in 28.29, *Scenas extra Gerasa*, must allude to tents near Egyptian Gerrhon. The new papyrus obviously names the same tent-village.

left in relations with the central imperial government. Without the cooperation of the Arabs, the eastern provinces could not be maintained. In the past Pompey, Augustus, Trajan, Septimius Severus, and Diocletian had all operated on this assumption. Their wisdom was confirmed when it could no longer be applied. In the seventh century the Arabs rallied to the banner of Islam and created an independent and powerful nation, rich in internal struggles but monolithic in its crusading zeal. The clients of Byzantium had become its rivals.

APPENDIX I

THE NEW BILINGUAL INSCRIPTION FROM BARĀQISH

IN THE CENTER of Minean civilization, on an elevation that commands a broad view of the plain known as the Jawf of the Yemen, lie the imposing remains of an ancient settlement. The place is known today as Barāqish, but inscriptions prove that in the pre-Islamic era it was called YṮL. The name may be resolved as Yathil, although other possibilities have lately been explored by H. von Wissmann.[1] The large, strong city wall, of which substantial parts survive, as Ahmed Fakhry has well recorded,[2] shows that the site was not only well suited to serve as a fortress but actually was one. No systematic excavation has been conducted in this area; but the Department of Antiquities at Sanʿa has endeavored, since the establishment of the National Museum in 1971, to encourage clandestine diggers to sell or donate their finds to the museum. Paolo Costa has recently published a most interesting inscription sold by the tribesmen of the Banu Ashraf and said to come from a cemetery near Barāqish.[3] The text is in both Greek and Latin, and it is the first of its kind to have appeared in southwest Arabia. The highly unusual character of this find prompts one to look for an historical explanation of its presence in a region so remote from the habitation of Greeks and Romans.

The text is tantalizingly brief, but it is at least clear that the substance was identical in the two languages:

[1] H. von Wissmann, "Die Geschichte des Sabäerreichs und der Feldzug des Aelius Gallus," *ANRW* II.9.1 (1978), 705–7, on YṮL: "Yaṯill, Stadt der ʾAṯlūlān."

[2] A. Fakhry, *An Archaeological Journey to the Yemen* I–III (1951–1952).

[3] P. Costa, "A Latin-Greek Inscription from the Jawf of the Yemen," *Proc. of the Seminar for Arabian Studies* 7 (1977), 69–72. I should like to express my warm thanks to Paolo Costa for his generosity in sending me a good photograph of the new inscription as well as a copy of his article as soon as it was available. My disagreement with some of his interpretations should in no way obscure my deep appreciation of the care with which he saw to the publication of his text. This Appendix and the next were originally drafted as contributions to the Second International Conference at Riyadh on pre-Islamic Arabia in the spring of 1979.

[P ·] CORNE[LIVS -----]
EQVES · Ṇ [---------]

3 ΠΟΥΒΛΙΣ ΚΟΡΝ[ΗΛΙΟΣ---]

The restoration of the praenomen in the Latin is assured by the line of Greek. The letter after the point in the second line could be either N or M, and there is really no way of telling. Costa's suggestions, *n*[*umeri*] or *M*[*aurus*], are indefensible and improbable. *N*[*atione*] or *N*[*at.*—] is possible, followed by an indication of ethnic origin,[4] but nothing more than that. Costa correctly recognized that *eques* could not mean here a member of the equestrian order, whose rank would be shown by the offices he held, but simply means a cavalryman. Presumably the Greek text had an equivalent word, such as ἱππεύς; and it seems likely, in view of the distribution of words in the first three lines, that the Greek equivalent term was the first word in the fourth line.

Since there is so much more space between lines two and three than between lines one and two, it is evident that the text consisted of two parts, distinctly separated—one in Latin and one in Greek—and that each part consisted of two lines. It is impossible to say exactly how far the lines extended to the right; but since *eques* would naturally occur after the name, one may assume that the first line of both the Latin and the Greek parts contained nothing more than the remainder of the *gentilicium* Cornelius and a filiation or cognomen or both. The existence of the word beginning with N or M guarantees that the first line in each case went on farther than the *gentilicium*. In general we can form a fairly reliable notion of the format and size of the inscription: it was balanced in two sections of two lines each, and it commemorated the name and occupation of a certain P. Cornelius.

This was clearly a simple text, designed for a community of persons among whom Greek and Latin were, to a greater or lesser degree, current languages. Costa believes the stone to be dedicatory rather than funerary, but he offers no argument for this presumption. It is, on the contrary, far more likely to be a tombstone

[4] Cf., e.g., *ILS* 2319, 2345.

than anything else. (Of course, the fact that it was found in a cemetery, where it had undoubtedly been reused by natives at some later time, is entirely irrelevant.) Costa is right in assuming that the stone, with its back left unworked, was not a statue base; but it may well have been fitted into a small funerary monument. The brevity of the text suggests as much, and line two in the two parts could best be completed, after the enigmatic word beginning N or M in the Latin, with *h(ic) s(itus) e(st)* and ἐνθάδε κεῖται. Since the length of line can be no longer in its entirety than the name P. Cornelius with the addition of (at most) filiation and cognomen, a sepulchral formula commends itself above any other. There is room for only a few words or spaced abbreviations.

No conclusions should be drawn about the date of this stone from the shape of the letters that appear on it. Dating by letter forms is at best a risky business, even where there is a large dossier of texts for comparison. Hands and styles varied in the different parts of the Roman Empire, and in the most remote corners we have no adequate controls for letter forms. The wide range of possibilities in a single place was well illustrated several decades ago by Bradford Welles in his outstanding epigraphical contribution to the volume on Gerasa prepared by C. H. Kraeling. Welles noted that the large number of Gerasene inscriptions in Greek permitted an attempt at a rough classification of the various styles,[5] but he refrained from doing anything of this kind for the Latin texts because there were not enough of them at Gerasa alone. It is true, as Costa observes, that in the Barāqish text the letters O and Q are oval-shaped, that the letter E has short horizontal bars, and that the letter V has an unusually wide angle. He might also have noted that the Greek employs a lunate sigma and a kappa with short side strokes, of which the bottom one is close to horizontal. Costa's article included a photograph, and the reader is referred to it here (plate 13). No date can be extracted from these letter forms when there is no other inscription from the same part of the world with which to compare them.

Costa opts for a date ultimately on the basis of the Greek spelling of the name Publius. He argues as follows: "It is in fact to be

[5] C. B. Welles, in C. H. Kraeling, *Gerasa: City of the Decapolis* (1938), p. 358.

noted that the way of writing 'PUBLIS' instead of 'PUBLIUS' is not to be considered a mistake, but it is due to a peculiar way of pronouncing the popular Latin *prenomen* [*sic*] in the Greek-speaking area of the Roman Empire, which became rather common during the late third century A.D. and is never attested before. I think therefore that the bilingual inscription can be tentatively dated to the end of the third century or the beginning of the fourth century A.D."[6] Now the name Publius, which appears in Greek dress as Πούβλιος, Πόβλιος, Πόπλιος, *vel sim.*, could suffer an alteration in the termination just as many other words in Greek with the ending -ιος. The use of -ις and -ιν in place of -ιος and -ιον appears already in the Hellenistic period from the third century B.C.[7] There is accordingly no reason why this phenomenon should not show itself at any time after that in an inscription from an area where the very existence of a text in reasonably correct Latin and Greek is in itself remarkable. No date should be inferred from the Greek equivalent of Publius here. Some might even wish to restore Κορν[ήλις] in the last line.

The only way to date and understand this new inscription is by searching for an historical context within which it will plausibly fit. Barāqish, the ancient YṮL, appears on only one occasion in the annals of Graeco-Roman history. Two important Greek sources, Strabo and Cassius Dio, recounting the same story, mention a city of southwest Arabia, north of Mārib, and not too far from it. The city served as base from which the forces of Aelius Gallus moved on to their unsuccessful siege of Mārib in the early years of the reign of Augustus at Rome. Strabo calls the place Athroula and Dio Athloula. The confusion of the liquids L and R is insignificant, unless one follows von Wissmann in believing that the L in YṮL is double and therefore that the second liquid in the Greek is indeed significant. But most scholars are agreed that the name Ath(?)oula represents a Greek version of YṮL.[8] Strabo reveals that the Roman forces under Gallus installed a

[6] Costa (above, n. 3), 70.

[7] Cf. E. Schwyzer, *Griechische Grammatik* (1939), I.472. For a full discussion D. J. Georgacas, "On the Nominal Endings -ις, -ιν in Later Greek," *CP* 43 (1948), 243–60.

[8] See, for example, A. Grohmann, *Arabien* (1963), p. 164.

garrison at the site: εἰς Ἄθρουλα πόλιν ἧκε, καὶ κρατήσας αὐτῆς ἀκονιτί, φρουρὰν ἐμβαλών... ("he went to the city Athroula, and having conquered it without a struggle, he placed a garrison in it...").[9] After this the army went on to what Strabo calls Marsiaba, clearly Mārib. Dio, writing in the third century A.D., notes that this expedition was the first and, as far as he was aware, the only time that Roman forces had penetrated so deep into the Arabian peninsula: πρῶτοι μὲν δὴ Ῥωμαίων οὗτοι, νομίζω δ' ὅτι καὶ μόνοι, τοσοῦτον ἐπὶ πολέμῳ τῆς Ἀραβίας ταύτης ἐπῆλθον· μέχρι γὰρ τῶν Ἀθλούλων καλουμένων χωρίου τινὸς ἐπιφανοῦς ἐχώρησαν ("these were the first of the Romans, and I think the only ones, to invade so far into this part of Arabia in the course of war; for they advanced as far as so-called Athloula, a famous place").[10] The uniqueness of this episode, at least as far as the second or third decade of the third century A.D., is thus attested. The suitability of Barāqish for a garrison is underscored by Ahmed Fakhry's eyewitness account of its situation. "The traveller," he wrote, "can see Barāqish from a great distance, as it is built over a high ridge commanding the whole neighborhood."[11] Photographs of the site fully substantiate Fakhry's description.[12]

The seizure of the city by the troops of Aelius Gallus and the imposition of a garrison there provide the only reasonable historical context for the new inscription. The presence of his army in about 26 B.C. is the only known occasion on which a community of Greek and Latin speakers was settled, however momentarily, in the Jawf of the Yemen. The cavalryman Cornelius can be seen as one of the occupying troops. If he died during the short life of the garrison at Barāqish, it may well have been while the garrison army was securing the rear of the besiegers at Mārib.

In any case, this unique presence of a Graeco-Roman army in the Yemen serves to explain the equally unique bilingual inscription from the area of Barāqish. It sheds new light on a famous

[9] 16.4.24, C 782.

[10] 53.29.8. W. Müller, *ZDMG* Suppl. III.1 (1977), 734, acutely perceived the relevance of the Barāqish stone to the expedition of Gallus, but he was unfortunately deterred from pursuing the matter by consideration of letter forms.

[11] Fakhry (above, n. 2) I, p. 141.

[12] Fakhry (above, n. 2), plates 52–54, and Grohmann (above, n. 8), plates 5–6.

Roman failure, which has already been thoroughly investigated by other scholars in recent decades. It would be fitting to mention in particular the treatment of Gallus' expedition by Jacqueline Pirenne,[13] Albrecht Dihle's remarks on the campaign (with speculations about Athroula which the new text will perhaps lay to rest),[14] Shelagh Jameson's argument for a date of 26 B.C.,[15] Naphtali Lewis' reinterpretation of *Pap. Oxy.* 2820,[16] and the important paper, already mentioned, by von Wissmann.[17]

[13] J. Pirenne, *Le royaume sud-arabe de Qatabān et sa datation* (1961).

[14] A. Dihle, "Der Zug des Aelius Gallus," *Umstrittene Daten* (1965), pp. 80–84.

[15] S. Jameson, "Chronology of the Campaigns of Aelius Gallus and C. Petronius," *JRS* 58 (1968), 71–84.

[16] N. Lewis, "*P. Oxy.* 2820: Whose Preparations?," *GRBS* 16 (1975), 295–303.

[17] See n. 1 above.

APPENDIX II

NABATAEANS AND ROMANS IN THE WĀDĪ SIRḤĀN

THE EXPERIENCE of the Nabataeans in building up an influential kingdom from nomadic beginnings gave them exceptional skill in dealing with the nomads inside and outside their borders. Or, to be more precise, they knew that in the desert there were no real borders at all; to safeguard their cities and crops as well as to maintain inland trade they had to control the movement of tribes far out in the desert itself. Recent epigraphical discoveries in places that foreigners have rarely visited show the Nabataean presence and domination. Of these the deep inland depression of the Wādī Sirḥān, with its scattered oases, constituting the principal desert route from the Arabian peninsula into Syria, is as prominent in Nabataean administration as the gloomy basalt country of northern Jordan and southern Syria and the bleak northwest corner of Saudi Arabia.

Graffiti allude mysteriously but unmistakably to wars of Nabataeans with nomadic tribes. A well known Safaitic text, first published by Littmann, records *snt ḥrb nbṭ* ("the year of the Nabataean war").[1] F. V. Winnett and G. Lankester Harding have published another Safaitic text with the same words.[2] Both are best understood in terms of local conflicts with Safaitic tribes (not, certainly, wars with Rome).[3] One Nabataean inscription from the oasis of Jawf, far out in the desert at the southern end of the Wādī Sirḥān, testifies to the presence of a *rb mšryt'*—the head of the camp, whose title is evidently a Semitic version of the Greek *stratēgos* or, as it appears in Semiticized dress, *'srtg'*.[4] Forts and fortified cities were built by the Nabataeans in the desert to monitor tribal movements and to intimidate the nomads far from the

[1] E. Littmann, *PAES* IV (1904), p. 143, no. 45.

[2] F. V. Winnett and G. L. Harding, *Inscriptions from Fifty Safaitic Cairns* (1978), no. 2113.

[3] Winnett and Harding (above, n. 2), no. 1734 = 2815 may possibly be relevant.

[4] R. Savignac and J. Starcky, "Une inscription nabatéenne provenant du Djôf," *RB* 64 (1957), 215.

settled land. The Nabataeans were adept in the use of camels, like their fellow Arabs, the Palmyrenes, to the north.

The Nabataeans' desert patrol was in their own interest in the first century, when their kingdom flourished. But it was equally in the Romans' interest because incursions of nomads into Nabataea would automatically take them to the gates of Syria and Palestine. In the Syrian desert above the Nabataean sphere of influence, the Palmyrenes were exercising much the same kind of vigilance as the Nabataeans. It was they who kept the line of trade and communication open to the Euphrates from the great cities of Damascus, Emesa, and Antioch. The Palmyrenes functioned as Roman clients like the Nabataeans. Both Arab peoples had commercial interests of their own, the protection of which was advantageous to the Romans as well.

As Glueck and Stein both surmised, the Nabataeans made good use of the Wādī Sirḥān as an inner passage for commerce with the north.[5] The wadi communicated directly with the environs of Bostra, and this explains in part the growing preeminence of that city—from which links with Damascus were well established. At the southern end of the Wādī Sirḥān lay the significant stations of Jawf and Sakāka. In the former the Nabataean presence has been attested for some time, notably by the military inscription found there;[6] and the investigations of Winnett and Reed have confirmed it.[7] At Sakāka too Winnett and Reed discovered, just as was to be expected, evidence of Nabataean occupation.[8] At the north of the Wādī Sirḥān, the story is the same. Nabataeans are now documented in the salt villages, at Ithrā.[9] From there tribes and traders could pass directly to Azraq and on to major Nabataean settlements on the way to Bostra, especially Umm al-jimal.

Although precise details of Nabataean activity within the Wādī Sirḥān are not yet available, it is clear in general that nomads

[5] Cf. G. W. Bowersock, "A Report on Provincia Arabia," *JRS* 61 (1971), 221 and n. 13.

[6] Cf. Savignac and Starcky (above, n. 4).

[7] F. V. Winnett and W. L. Reed, *Ancient Records from North Arabia* (1970), pp. 15 and 144.

[8] Ibid., pp. 7 and 144.

[9] Ibid., pp. 60 and 160.

posed problems right down to the Roman annexation of Transjordan as provincia Arabia in A.D. 106. It is not only the graffiti that evoke the struggles between the Nabataeans and the raiding desert people, but also the signs of destruction at excavated Nabataean settlements where the archaeological record is punctuated by periodic fresh starts. One dossier of graffiti examined by Winnett points to a major tribal rebellion by a certain Damasī in A.D. 71 at the time of the accession of the last Nabataean king, Rabbel II.[10] The implication is that the leaders of certain desert tribes had formerly been coopted by the Nabataean administration and were disappointed, at a time of changing authority, not to be preferred for positions of trust in the control of the desert. The traditional titulature of the new king, as seen on inscriptions, *dy ʾḥyy wšyzb ʿmh* ("he who brought life and deliverance to his people"), may well refer to this crisis of his accession. Certainly no better explanation has been produced, and this one suggests a reasonable, if occasionally risky policy of using nomadic groups as allies of the government of the sedentary nation at the edge of the desert.

The disturbances that shook the last decades of Nabataean rule have important implications for the historian of the Wādī Sirḥān. For it was during this period at the end of the first century A.D. that the center of gravity in the kingdom was shifting from Petra to Bostra, where it was to remain under Roman rule. The diminished role of Petra seems to have been due, in large measure, to the enfeeblement of the old overland trade route after the discovery of the commercial utility of the monsoons. Trade that formerly passed northward through Petra to Gaza was going more and more to the Egyptian coast and thence north to the Mediterranean. Inland traffic became concentrated on the Wādī Sirḥān, which provided an efficient route for conveying goods from the ports on the east coast of the Arabian peninsula as well as from the south.

From the moment of the annexation of Arabia, the Romans inherited the desert patrol of the Near East to the south of the

[10] "The Revolt of Damasī: Safaitic and Nabataean Evidence," *BASOR* 211 (1973), 54–57. For another possible reflection of this crisis see above, p. 72, n. 48.

region that was policed by the Palmyrenes. The extent of the Roman province was almost certainly identical to that of the Nabataean kingdom. Recent discoveries at Ruwwāfa in the Ḥejāz have revealed the direct intervention of the provincial governor of Arabia in temple construction there;[11] and inscriptions showing *beneficiarii* between Madā'in Ṣāliḥ and al-ʿUlā imply, as M. Speidel has observed, the existence of a border station in that area.[12] Furthermore, Abdullah al-Wohaibi has demonstrated that the expression *Qurā ʿArabiyya* for a region in the Ḥejāz mentioned by Arab geographers preserves the ancient designation of the province of Arabia.[13] *Qurā*, which is the same here as *kūra*, represents the Greek χώρα rather than (as al-Wohaibi has suggested) the Latin *curia*.

With the evidence that has accumulated it becomes clear that the Romans undertook from the start to continue and to strengthen the patrol system they took over; and they did this, as much as they could, with Nabataean personnel. Trajan, who authorized the annexation of the new province, was responsible for installing a legion there (I am now persuaded by Speidel that this was the Third Cyrenaica) and for raising troops from the former Nabataean army both to serve in the legion and to supplement it with auxiliaries. The natives were particularly valuable to Rome for their expertise in mounted archery and in camel riding. Some indeed, like the new cohorts *Ulpiae Petraeorum* (Trajanic units from Petra), were used elsewhere in the Near East to reinforce defenses. But there is explicit epigraphical testimony for the use of Nabataean cavalry in the Third Cyrenaica and for camel riders in the Arabian *auxilia*. A group of rock inscriptions in the Ḥejāz in northwest Saudi Arabia records the presence of *dromedarii* in the southernmost part of the Nabataean kingdom.[14] Some of the inscriptions are in Greek, some in Nabataean. One mentions, as we have already noted, a *beneficiarius*.

[11] Cf. G. W. Bowersock, "The Greek-Nabataean Bilingual Inscription at Ruwwafa, Saudi Arabia," *Le monde grec: Hommages à Claire Préaux* (1975), pp. 513–22.

[12] M. Speidel, "The Roman Army in Arabia," *ANRW* II.8 (1977), 703–4.

[13] A. al-Wohaibi, *The Northern Hijaz in the Writings of the Arab Geographers, 800–1150* (1973), p. 214.

[14] Speidel (above, n. 12). See above, pp. 107–8.

The presence of detachments of the Third Cyrenaica at key points deep in the desert is now at last beyond doubt, thanks to the new discoveries, and proves that the Roman administration undertook a general patrol of the desert, just as the Nabataeans did, far away from the settled areas. The pattern discernible in the Ḥejāz could be expected to recur in the Wādī Sirḥān. And it does. A centurion is strikingly attested at the main oasis of the central desert, Jawf, whence traders took the inner route of the Wādī Sirḥān into Syria. The inscription recording this centurion was courteously made public by Mahmud Ghul in 1972 at a conference on pre-Islamic Arabia at Harvard University.[15] At the head of the Wādī Sirḥān is a cluster of military installations (forts or watchtowers) set up by the Third Cyrenaica, some at Nabataean sites like the desert city of Umm al-jimāl, others of a simple design on elevations or at oases. The system of forts and watchtowers provided for early warning as well as for the prompt intimidation and dispersal of nomadic raiders.[16] The exact chronology of this Roman move into the desert, with the aid of experienced native recruits, is elusive; but the name Ulpia attached to various cohorts and cavalry units suggests that the strategy was adopted in principle by Trajan soon after he annexed Arabia and was carried forward by others.

Of subsequent emperors before the tetrarchy, Septimius Severus was particularly concerned to strengthen the desert defenses. This may have been due to his annexation of Mesopotamia, which required that the intervening tracts of desert be even more secure than before. In any case, his reign witnessed notable activity in the Arabian frontier zones, especially at the head of the Wādī Sirḥān in the vicinity of Azraq. In a recent article S. Thomas Parker and P. M. McDermott have documented construction in the area of Qaṣr al-ʿUweinid under Severus,[17] and the well known inscription of 213 at Qaṣr al-Ḥallabāt presupposes attention to the site in the foregoing years.[18] The evidence

[15] Cf. *JRS* 63 (1973), 139, n. 58. For a text of this inscription, see Kennedy, *ArchExplor* (1982), p. 190, no. 39.

[16] Cf. G. W. Bowersock, "Limes Arabicus," *HSCP* 80 (1976), 219–29.

[17] S. T. Parker and P. M. McDermott, "A Military Building Inscription from Roman Arabia," *ZPE* 28 (1978), 61–66. See now Kennedy, *ArchExplor* (1982), pp. 124–25.

[18] Kennedy, *ArchExplor* (1982), pp. 39–40, no. 3.

of the fort at Qaṣr Asaikhin suggests a Severan garrison there too.[19] Severus' extension of the provincial boundaries of Arabia in the north seems, in the light of present evidence, to reflect a recognition of the central role of the Wādī Sirḥān in the administration of the area. That passage through the desert, from south to north (in the direction of Bostra and Damascus), was at least as crucial for trade and for control as the old King's Highway to the west.

It is gratifying to observe that the Nabataeans fully understood the importance of the Wādī Sirḥān in the geography of their realm. With their ancient desert traditions, that was to be expected of them. More remarkable perhaps was the Roman arrogation of the Nabataean organization of the region, with the help of the Nabataeans themselves. The Wādī Sirḥān played a vital role in the prosperity and the defenses of Roman Arabia.

[19] See above, p. 119.

APPENDIX III

THE GOVERNORS OF ARABIA

MAURICE SARTRE has recently provided a valuable new listing of the evidence for the governors of the Arabian province into late antiquity: *Trois études sur l'Arabie romaine et byzantine* (1982), pp. 77–120. Since his work is so thorough, it will suffice to give here, for convenience in reference, a summary list of the governors for the period covered by the present work. Such revisions as need to be made in Sartre's study are discussed below and presumed in the ensuing summary list. Anonymi are omitted.

Tiberius Claudius Alpinus: This governor, identified in 1968 by J. Starcky and C. Bennett on a Latin inscription from Petra, has been placed immediately after the province's first governor, Claudius Severus. But H. Halfmann, in *Die Senatoren aus dem östlichen Teil des Imperium Romanum bis zum Ende des 2. Jh. n. Chr.* (1979), p. 135, has accurately pointed out that the name on the stone is not Alpinus but Severus. Hence the text becomes yet another testimony to Severus' presence in Arabia, and the governor Alpinus must be banished from the fasti of the province.

L. Aninius Sextius Florentinus: The praenomen of this governor, as given in the Naḥal Ḥever papyri, is Titus, not Lucius (*IEJ* 12 [1962], 259; *Ex Oriente Lux* 17 [1963; publ. 1964], 238). The inscription on the tomb of this person at Petra shows a praenomen that is not clearly legible. According to Brünnow and Domaszewski, *Die Provincia Arabia* I, p. 382, the name appears as L ANINIO L FIL PAP SEXTIO FLORENTINO, but it is stated that the first letter could also be read as a P. If the papyrus has been read correctly (and Polotsky's eye is certainly reliable), we should prefer Titus as the praenomen.

L. Marius Perpetuus: Sartre wrote without knowledge of the ʿUweinid inscription, published by S. T. Parker and P. McDermott, *ZPE* 28 (1978), 61–65, and reedited by Kennedy, *ArchExplor* (1982), pp. 124–25, no. 19. Kennedy argues persuasively there for a date between 200 and 202. Likewise Kennedy, *ZPE* 49 (1982), 284–86.

Q. Scribonius Tenax: Sartre was unable to take account of D. L. Kennedy, *ZPE* 37 (1980), 24–26, on the date of the governorship of Scribonius Tenax. Kennedy made a good case for 194–196.

Sex. Furnius Iulianus: The Ḥallabāt inscription mentioning this governor has been discussed anew by Kennedy, *ArchExplor* (1982), pp. 39–40, no. 3.

Pomponius Iulianus: This person, attested as a governor in 236 at Kafr al-Laḥā, was omitted from Pflaum's list of Arabian governors. Sartre has rightly restored him on the grounds that the site must have belonged to Arabia in 236. E. Kettenhofen, *ZDPV* 97 (1981), 62–73, came independently to the same conclusion.

M. Bassaeus Astur: Sartre proposes possible dates of 238–244 or 249–250. But E. Birley, *ZPE* 37 (1980), 19–21, has made a powerful case, by comparison with M. Bassaeus Rufus (*ILS* 1326, a procurator of Asturia), for an Arabian governorship late in the reign of Commodus or early under Severus.

Amius Flaccus: Although Sartre enters this name in his list, he accepts in the final paragraph H. I. MacAdam's demonstration, seen by Sartre before publication, that the inscription giving this name should be read as showing part of the name of the known governor, C. Allius Fuscianus: *ZPE* 38 (1980), 72–74.

SENATORIAL *LEGATI* OF ARABIA

C. Claudius Severus, in the province between 107 and 115 at least
Q. Coredius Gallus Gargilius Antiquus
Ti. Iulius Iulianus Alexander, attested in 125
T. Aninius Sextius Florentinus, attested in 127
T. Haterius Nepos, attested in 130: his name erased on inscriptions of Gerasa in that year (Welles, in Kraeling, *Gerasa* (1938), nos. 58 and 143–44)
L. Aemilius Carus, attested in 141–142
L. Attidius Cornelianus, attested in 150–151
C. Allius Fuscianus, as *cos. desig.*, *cos.*, and *consularis* (*cos.*? 162)
P. Iulius Geminius Marcianus, attested in 162–163
Q. Antistius Adventus, attested in 166–167

L. Claudius Modestus, attested between 167 and 169
. . . **Severus**, probably between 177 and 180
Flavius Iulius Fronto
M. Bassaeus Astur, late Commodus to early Severus
P. Aelius Severianus Maximus, attested in 193–194
Q. Scribonius Tenax, between 194 and 196
M. Caecilius Fuscianus Crepereianus Floranus, before 198
L. Marius Perpetuus, between 200 and 202
Q. Aiacius Modestus Crescentianus, between 204 and 211
L. Alfenus Avitianus, attested soon after 212
Sex. Furnius Iulianus, attested in 213–214
Q. Flavius Balbus, between 213 and 220
Pica Caerianus, attested in 218
Flavius Iulianus, succeeded the foregoing
[**C. Furius Sabinus Aquila Timesitheus**, equestrian who twice replaced the legate of Arabia]
Caecilius Felix, between 223 and 226
Claudius Sollemnius Pacatianus, between 223 and 235
L. Egnatius Victor Marinianus, perhaps not long before 230
Pomponius Iulianus, attested in 236
D. Simonius Proculus Iulianus, attested in 237 (or 238)
M. Domitius Valerianus, between 238 and 239
Claudius Capitolinus, attested in 245–246
Aelius Aurelius Theo, between 253 and 259
Virius Lupus
. . .**ius Gallonianus**, attested in 259–260
Coc[– –] **Rufinus**, perhaps in 261–262

UNDATABLE SENATORIAL *LEGATI* OF ARABIA

Erucius Clarus
P. Pomponius Secundinus
Plotius Romanus
Aelius
Aurelius Aurelianus

EQUESTRIAN *PRAESIDES* OF ARABIA

(Note that the term *praeses* can also be used of senatorial *legati*, as for M. Bassaeus Astur [*IGLS* 13.9082] and Virius Lupus [*ILS* 1210].)

Iunius Olympus, attested in 262–263
Statilius Ammianus, attested in 253–264
Iulius Heraclitus
Aurelius Antiochus
Flavius Aelianus, attested in 274–275
Aurelius Petrus, attested in 278–279
Aemillius Aemillianus, attested in 282–283
Domitius Antonius
M. Aurelius Aelianus, between 293 and 305
Aurelius Asclepiades, between 293 and 305
Aurelius Felicianus, between 293 and 305
Aurelius Gorgonius, between 293 and 305

UNDATABLE AND EITHER SENATORIAL OR EQUESTRIAN

Aelius Flavianus

APPENDIX IV

ANCIENT MAPS OF ROMAN ARABIA

THE INTELLIGENT FORMULATION of imperial policy demands many sources of information, but in the area of communication and military strategy perhaps none is so important as geographical information. For the Roman Empire Strabo, in the age of Augustus, stated that his concern with geography presupposed its utility in affairs of state. It is clear, he wrote, that all geography is oriented to the practice of government (*πράξεις ἡγεμονικαί*).[1] Descriptive treatises, such as his own, evidently served this end; but so too, in a more compact and immediately comprehensible way, did maps. In a famous passage in the second book of his *Geography*, in which Strabo discusses the preparation of good maps, he refers to the relationship of sea and land masses as it appears in *ὁ χωρογραφικὸς πίναξ*.[2] This *πίναξ* has been generally taken to refer to the first, and perhaps most important, map created under the Roman principate—the *Orbis Terrarum* of M. Agrippa.[3] Of course this celebrated construction no longer survives, but it provides the starting point for any treatment of cartography in the Roman Empire.

Some remarks on Agrippa's map will serve, therefore, as an introduction to a detailed consideration of the maps available in the Roman Empire for the territories of provincial Arabia. A comparative study of the cartographic evidence can provide substantial help in understanding the organization of the area. A few years ago Israel Finkelstein addressed this problem in an article entitled "The Holy Land in the *Tabula Peutingeriana*: An Historical-Geographical Approach."[4] That was exactly the subject that needed to be treated, and much still remains to be done. Finkelstein took no account of the most important work on the

[1] Strabo 1.1.16, C 9: *δῆλον οὖν ὅτι ἡ γεωγραφικὴ πᾶσα ἐπὶ τὰς πράξεις ἀνάγεται τὰς ἡγεμονικάς*. The substance of this Appendix was presented to Fergus Millar's seminar in London on 11 May 1981. I am grateful for the discussion that ensued.

[2] Strabo 2.5.17, C 120.

[3] See, for example, J. J. Tierney, "The Map of Agrippa," *Proc. Royal Irish Acad.* 63, sect. 6, no. 4 (1963), 152, and W. Kubitschek, "Karten (Agrippa)," *RE* 10.2.2102.

[4] *PEQ* 111 (1979), 27–34.

Peutinger Table in modern times, that of Detlefsen and Kubitschek; and he also neglected the only comparative evidence we have for the Peutinger Table's depiction of Palestine, the mosaic map on the floor of a Christian church in Mādabā.

If we make the reasonable assumption that Strabo was referring to Agrippa's map in his reference to the chorographic pinax, it is to the elder Pliny that we must turn for such explicit details as we have about that famous map. In the third book of his *Natural History*, in connection with distances along the coast in southern Spain, Pliny wrote:

> *Agrippam quidem in tanta viri diligentia praeterque in hoc opere cura, cum orbem terrarum urbi spectandum propositurus esset, errasse quis credat et cum eo divum Augustum? is namque conplexam eum porticum ex destinatione et commentariis M. Agrippae a sorore eius incohatam peregit.*
>
> ("Agrippa was a very painstaking man, and also a very careful geographer. Who, therefore, could believe that when intending to set before the eyes of Rome a survey of the world, he made a mistake and with him the deified Augustus? For it was Augustus who completed the porticus containing his map that had been begun by his sister, in accordance with the intention and the *commentarii* of Marcus Agrippa.")[5]

As often happens with the elder Pliny, just when one wants exact and clear testimony, his language is opaque. But it appears from this text that Agrippa had sketched a map and that its display in the porticus, obviously the Porticus Vipsania, was undertaken by his sister after his death, as Cassius Dio confirms.[6] Augustus carried the project to completion after *her* death. There was still ample time for Strabo to have seen it before his own death sometime after A.D. 23.

As Cuntz, Detlefsen, and Kubitschek argued at the turn of the century,[7] Pliny evidently made repeated use of Agrippa's map in

[5] Pliny, *NH* 3.2.17. *Urbi* is a generally accepted emendation of the transmitted word *orbi*.

[6] 55.8.4.

[7] O. Cuntz, "Agrippa und Augustus als Quellenschriftsteller des Plinius in den

providing geographic details within his *Natural History*. It never seemed altogether likely that Pliny would have gone to visit the Porticus Vipsania every time he wanted a measurement. Nor was it likely that he ever lingered in front of the map in the Porticus Vipsania for the purpose of making detailed notes for his own use, although this is of course not beyond the bounds of credibility. It was the merit of Detlefsen to have established from late antique and mediaeval geographic works that Pliny's formulation of details of longitude and latitude, and indeed the language by which these details were expressed, reflected a common source that contained some sort of written commentary.[8] Kubitschek believed that Agrippa's map was circulated in copies, together with a descriptive text, presumably not unlike the combination of map and text which we know to have made up the *Geography* of Claudius Ptolemaeus in the second century A.D. In fact, it is a fair guess that the *commentarii* mentioned by Pliny in his second book are precisely the annotations for the map and not, as some have thought, instructions for setting up the map in the porticus. In any case, it can be taken as probable, if not certain, that there were copies of the map that were circulating together with an accompanying text in the first century A.D. and later.

The map itself will presumably have taken its form from the space in which it had to be displayed, that is, within the porticus. Pliny's words suggest that it was a spectacle which everyone in Rome who cared to go there could enjoy: *cum orbem terrarum urbi spectandum propositurus esset*. Accordingly, copies of this

---

geographischen Büchern der *Naturalis Historia*," *Neue Jahrb. f. Phil. u. Pädag.*, *Jahrb. f. Klass. Phil.* 17 (1890), 475–527; D. Detlefsen, *Ursprung, Einrichtung and Bedeutung der Erdkarte Agrippas* (1906); W. Kubitschek, "Karten (Agrippa)," *RE* 10.2.2100–9. These scholars are by no means in agreement on points of detail, but all concur in Pliny's use of the map. Recently, B. D. Shaw, following L. Teutsch, has questioned their consensus in the case of Pliny's African geography: "The Elder Pliny's African Geography," *Historia* 30 (1981), 424–71, esp. 427 (with n. 5)–430. Shaw prefers a Caesarian source, but he observes on p. 429: "It is hardly necessary. . .that the information in Agrippa was an accurate reflection of the contemporary situation in Africa between 7 B.C. and A.D. 14." In other words, a Caesarian source for Agrippa's treatment of Africa would not preclude Pliny's use of the map, for which the evidence in Pliny's text is overwhelming.

[8] Detlefsen (above, n. 7). There is room for debate as to whether explanations were actually written on the map or, as assumed here, in an accompanying text.

map could reasonably be expected to take the form of a longish roll that would represent the horizontal panorama within the porticus. It is evident from the excerpts in Pliny and later geographers that Agrippa's work was not mathematically scientific. Strabo's reference to πράξεις ἡγεμονικαί implies that the primary considerations were communications and topographic features, such as mountains, rivers, deserts, and the like. "Above all," wrote Strabo, "it is the sea which determines geography and marks out the shape of the land, fashioning the gulfs, oceans, straits, and likewise isthmuses, peninsulas, and promontories. One must add rivers and mountains. These are the ingredients which allow one to distinguish continents, peoples, and sites that are appropriate for cities. And it is all of these characteristics that one finds in ὁ χωρογραφικὸς πίναξ."[9]

From the time in which Konrad Peutinger of Augsburg acquired the mediaeval map which now bears his name, the *Tabula Peutingeriana* (that is to say, from the early sixteenth century), it has occurred to most knowledgeable people that there might well be some kind of connection between this document and the map of Agrippa. The Peutinger Table consists of eleven segments of parchment, designed to fit together side by side so as to make one extended roll, depicting the entire inhabited world. This document, which reached Peutinger in an assembled state, has now been separated again and reposes in its eleven segments in the National Library of Vienna.[10] The present copy of the map lacks its westernmost part. It has therefore been apparent to everyone concerned with the copy that the original sequence contained twelve segments, and for that reason the Peutinger Table may be reasonably identified with the map mentioned in the Annals of

[9] 2.5.17, C 120.

[10] The *TP* can now be studied in the superb facsimile edition published by the Akademische Druck u. Verlagsanstalt, Graz: *Tabula Peutingeriana, Codex Vindobonensis 324, Vollständige Faksimile-Ausgabe im Originalformat* (1976). There can be no excuse for continued use of the unsatisfactory publications by Konrad Miller, *Itineraria Romana* (1916) and *Die Peutingersche Tafel, oder Weltkarte des Castorius* (1916; 2nd unchanged ed., 1929), on both of which see the important review by Kubitschek in *GGA* 179 (1917), 1–117. Those who can afford it may wish to use A. and M. Levi's facsimile edition, *La Tabula Peutingeriana* (1978), on which see L. Casson, *Archaeology* 34.1 (1981), 66–67.

Colmar: *anno 1265 mappa[m] mundi descripsi in pellis duodecim pergamenae*, "in the year 1265, I drew a world map on twelve pieces of parchment." Authoritative palaeographers confirm that the Peutinger Table looks as if it were done in the twelfth century or a century on either side of it.[11] There has never been any real doubt that this map was a copy of an ancient map, but naturally there has been considerable discussion as to the date and character of the ancient archetype.

The Peutinger map is constructed on the basis of the road system of the Roman Empire. These roads are clearly marked out in red lines, and the principal cities are, in one way or another, attached to the road systems. There is nothing scientific about the layout. Ptolemy would have been horrified at the bizarre compression accorded to the land masses of the Roman Empire to accommodate them all within the rather squashed but very extended horizontal frame. The orientation of the map is from the south; that is to say, the viewer must envisage himself as somehow standing in the Sahara and looking northwards, where he will see the emperor beckoning to him, opposite, from Antioch, or see another emperor beckoning from Constantinople, and a third from Rome. The names of cities are arranged so as to be read from the position in North Africa, and the distortion of the land masses is such as to flatten them all out along the line of the North African coast.

The map, as we have it, contains a number of Christian legends, such as the annotation in the Sinai, *hic legem acceperunt in monte Syna*, or again the note of *Mons Oliveti* by Jerusalem, or the desert, *ubi quadraginta annis erraverunt filii Israelis ducente Moyse*. Constantinople is called by that name, although the people in the region are designated *Byzantini*. The elaboration of the vignette for Antioch also implies a date in late antiquity. Obviously there has been Christian annotation, but overall the map does not serve as a particularly edifying or self-consciously instructive document in Christian mythology.

Furthermore, the names of several cities on the map are those of an era well before the time of Constantinople and suggest that

[11] Cf. A. and M. Levi, *Itineraria Picta* (1967), p. 22.

the original form did not include the late and Christian elements.[12] For example, the town of Eleutheropolis in Palestine acquired that name in the Severan age. Previously it had been called by the local name Betogabri, which is the name it has in the *Geography* of Ptolemy and on the Peutinger Table. It still has the same name today (Bet Guvrin). Lydda (modern Lud) also received a new name in the Severan age; it had been known previously as Diospolis, and that is its name in the Peutinger Table. Another striking instance is that of Paneas, known in the days of the Herods as Caesarea or Caesarea Philippi. But its name was changed afterward to Paneas; and in the transitional period, which included the second century, as we can tell from Ptolemy's *Geography*, it was called Caesarea Paneas. This is the form that appears on the Peutinger map.

In fact, the correspondences between the names in Ptolemy's *Geography* and the names on the Peutinger Table have led scholars to assume that the map, although overlaid with Christian legends and copied in mediaeval times, was originally created no later than the late second century, possibly on the basis of the material in Ptolemy. That is the view of Cuntz and Kubitschek, and it is fair to say that it is the regnant opinion at this time.[13] Finkelstein has reverted to the theory of Konrad Miller that the original map was composed in the fourth century by the Roman cosmographer Castorius. This is to miss the vital distinction between an immediate model for the Peutinger artist and the archetype. There is no need to dilate on Miller's improbable view, except to observe that a fourth-century date presupposes that the Christian legends were part of the original map. This is impossible. We shall see that there are far more indications than simply the early place names to establish that the map represents conditions that obtained well before the fourth century.

The collocation of toponyms in the Peutinger Table and the *Geography* of Ptolemy need not, however, necessarily mean that

[12] Note Kubitschek, *GGA* 179 (1917), 21: "Es ist doch sicherlich an der TP im Lauf der Überlieferung geändert worden; die wenigen christlichen Zusätze sind unverkennbar, und auch für die mittelgrossen Vignetten der Städte Ancyra, Aquileia, Nicaea, Nicomedia, Ravenna und Thessalonice ist behauptet worden, ich glaube mit vollem Recht, dass sie erst nachträglich eingefügt worden sind."

[13] See the brief survey in Levi, *Itineraria* (above, n. 11), p. 22.

the Peutinger Table was designed on the basis of the evidence of Ptolemy. Ptolemy's work was scientific, with measurements to determine the location of places and due attention to the mathematics of surveying. His *Geography* was accompanied by a set of πίνακες which provided maps in accordance with his measurements. Although the originals of these undoubtedly splendid productions are now lost to us, his work, with the maps, was reproduced so frequently in the Middle Ages that it is reasonable to assume that the many maps surviving in the codices of Ptolemy in Greek, Latin, and Arabic give a relatively clear indication of what his maps looked like for the areas concerned.[14]

From the maps of Arabia and Palestine, which display a distinctive treatment wholly different from that of the Peutinger Table, it is clear that the Ptolemaic and Peutinger archetypes can have nothing to do with each other.[15] The disfiguration in the Peutinger map could not possibly have been made by a person working directly from Ptolemy's materials. Parallels between Ptolemy and the Peutinger evidence can only be due to a common tradition of place names in the time of the early Roman Empire.

If one grants that the Peutinger Table does not have to follow the work of Ptolemy (and close inspection of the Ptolemaic cartographic tradition makes this imperative), then there is no alternative to connecting the original of the Peutinger Table with the maps that were available to Pliny as copies of the great map of Agrippa displayed in the Porticus Vipsania. The nature of the

[14] The similarities of most of the maps in the various codices point to a common archetype. A good sample may be found in J. Fischer, *Claudii Ptolemaei Geographiae Codex Urbinas 82: Pars altera, tabulae geographicae LXXXIII Graecae-Arabicae-Latinae e codicibus LIII selectae* (1932). A gigantic supplementary volume of the *pars altera* contains more facsimiles under the general title plus *accedunt tabulae XXVII codicis Vaticani Latini 5698 III Urbinatis Graeci 82*.

[15] Cf. for Arabia and Palestine the Latin map from the *Codex Vaticanus Latinus* 5698 (plate 4 below) with the Greek map from the *Codex Urbinas Graecus* 82 (plate 3 below). On the date of these maps and their archetypes in Ptolemy's original work, see Fischer (above, n. 14), pp. 108, 130, 221, and 290. Both maps show the same configurations of land depressions as well as the same regional boundaries. Philadelphia and Gerasa are interestingly dislocated so as to appear in Coele Syria rather than Arabia Petraea. This of course follows Ptolemy's assignment of those cities. The coins of Philadelphia proclaim the city a part of Coele Syria: cf. A. Spijkerman, *The Coins of the Decapolis and Provincia Arabia* (1978), pp. 242–57. We see here regional divisions quite different from the Roman provincial organization.

geographic distortions on Peutinger's map is thus easily explained. Even scholars who opt for a date in the fourth century have to admit that the distortions would be best explained by reference to the Porticus Vipsania. A close inspection of the treatment of the road system and of the cities in the area of provincia Arabia on the Peutinger Table provides a useful test of this suggestion for an early date of the Peutinger archetype.

In the meantime, it is necessary to invoke the one other piece of cartographic evidence for Roman Palestine which we have. That is the spectacular mosaic from Mādabā, which can provide a basis of comparison and a control for discussion of the Peutinger map.[16] Mādabā is still an important town in northern Jordan, and the map known by the town name was executed in mosaic on the floor of an antique Christian church there. It was discovered in the late nineteenth century, when a new church was being built on the site; but it was unfortunately ignored for a considerable time during the course of construction, so that substantial parts of this priceless document were lost. It took nearly a decade for scholars in the West to learn that an ancient map had been uncovered at Mādabā.[17] When they did, they then launched appropriate efforts to conserve what remained.

It is a map full of lively illustrations, not only of the land and its cities but also of water, especially the Dead Sea, with two charming boats afloat on it, and the Jordan River with some personable fish swimming away from the Dead Sea. The orientation is totally different from that of the Peutinger Table. It is from the west, looking east—that is, as if one were standing in the Mediterranean, off the coast of Palestine, and looking toward Jerusalem. Jerusalem is clearly the centerpiece of the mosaic, and it is depicted in considerable topographic detail. But other cities are shown as well, and the map is replete with Christian legends to

[16] See M. Avi-Yonah, *The Madaba Mosaic Map* (1954). Of the new edition by H. Donner and H. Cüppers, only the *Tafelband* has appeared so far: *Die Mosaikkarte von Madaba*, Abhandl. des Deutschen Palästinavereins (1977).

[17] The patriarch of Jerusalem was informed of the existence of the map in 1884, but no notice was taken of the discovery until 1896 when the librarian of the patriarchate went to Mādabā to inspect the new church that was being built over the ancient one with its mosaic map. He was the first to publish a notice of the remains of the map: K. Κοικυλίδης, Ὁ ἐν Μαδηβᾷ μωσαϊκὸς. . .χάρτης (1897). Other scholarly publications soon followed, notably J. Germer-Durand, *La carte mosaïque de Madaba* (1897).

edify the pious. These legends are so numerous and so ample that it seems reasonable to assume that instruction and inspiration were the principal purpose in the creation of the mosaic.

Ever since scholars began seriously to study the document, it has been clear from the names of cities that are presented and from their Christian associations that the basis for the map was the *Onomastikon* of Eusebius. The thorough study by Michael Avi-Yonah quite rightly accepts this source and goes on to argue with considerable plausibility that the *Onomastikon* itself had been accompanied by a map, to which the creator of the Mādabā map had access.[18] This map would be the document referred to somewhat ambiguously by Eusebius in Greek as a *καταγραφή*: *καταγραφὴ τῆς ᾿Ιουδαΐας ἀπὸ πάσης βιβλίου*, "a map [or, according to dissident scholars, a list] of ancient Judaea, according to the entire Bible."[19] The presentation of the cities illustrated on the map and the way in which they are oriented in respect to each other make it plain, as Avi-Yonah also emphasized, that the map's framework was a road system, just as had been the case in the archetype of the Peutinger Table. But it is important to recognize that, if this is so, the roads as such are sufficiently unimportant to the compositor of the mosaic as to be themselves omitted. The map is a Christian document, then, unquestionably of late antiquity. It was designed to illustrate exclusively the Holy Land from the perspective of west to east.

We may now consider first the Peutinger Table and then the Mādabā map for the evidence each provides about the settlements and roads of Roman Arabia. We shall move, station by station, along the Peutinger Table from the head of the Gulf of ʿAqaba northward within the territory of the Roman provincia Arabia. The head of the gulf, where the twin cities of Elath and ʿAqaba are now to be found, is clearly marked on the map by the designation Haila (more commonly in classical texts, Aela), the ancient city at the head of the gulf. As often in inquiries of this kind, a modern place name provides a precious confirmation of the location of an ancient site. Since there is no doubt about the location of ancient Aela, we can be certain that this name has survived in

[18] Avi-Yonah (above, n. 16), pp. 30–31.

[19] Ibid.

the modern form Elath. Moving northwards, we have next a choice on the Peutinger map of proceeding into the Negev by a northwesterly route, or up into Transjordan by a more direct northerly one, headed toward, ultimately, Damascus.

If we take first the Transjordan road, the next station after Aela is indicated as Praesidio (Praesidium), coming at a distance of twenty miles from Aela. It is worth remarking that the intervals in Roman miles as indicated in the Peutinger table are, where they can be controlled, often of a remarkably high degree of accuracy. What is curious is that the intervals of space on the map by no means regularly reflect the intervals given in the numbers, so that a shorter distance can be attached to a somewhat longer stretch of line. This is evidently due to the peculiar distortion caused by the map's horizontal design. Twenty miles from the head of the Gulf of ʿAqaba, up into the Jordanian Ḥismā, along the Wādī Yutm, brings us with remarkable precision to an ancient ruin, Khirbet al-Khālde, which has been reasonably identified in recent times with the site of Praesidium. The next station is that of Hauarra, at a distance of twenty-four miles; and here the coincidence of the Peutinger place Hauarra with the substantial remains of the modern site called Ḥumaima, still in the Ḥismā, calls for special emphasis. Hauarra appears in Ptolemy's lists as Αὔαρα, both words clearly reflecting the Arabic term *ḥawwāra*, meaning "white."

Travelers who are familiar with the Levant will know how frequently local sites have color names. Some of this is familiar from the Muslim West as well: Dār al-baiḍā' ("the white house") in Morocco, better known as Casablanca, or the Alhambra, which is simply "the red (sc. castle)," Al-ḥamrā'. As Musil, the great Czech explorer at the beginning of this century, once observed, the use of "white" for a place in this part of southern Jordan undoubtedly reflects the color of stone and buildings in the region.[20] The remains of Ḥumaima, with which Hauarra must certainly be identified, bear a name, Ḥumaima, which also means "white" in Arabic. It seems quite clear that the sense of the original toponym has been preserved in the present name, although the actual word has been altered. David Graf of the University of

[20] A. Musil, *The Northern Heǧaz* (1926), p. 59, n. 20.

Michigan has undertaken several explorations of Ḥumaima and environs in recent years. He has conclusively established the importance of this as a Roman site, and he has given authoritative confirmation of the traces of the Via Nova Traiana after its descent from the plateau of the Sharā' on the way down to the Gulf of ʿAqaba.[21] This is just north of Ḥumaima at a site called Baiḍā', which also means "white." Graf's observations mean that the Trajanic road in southern Jordan definitely did not follow the older modern road in ascending the escarpment.

From Hauarra the road marked on the Peutinger Table proceeds northward up onto the plateau for a distance of twenty miles to the site marked as Zadagatta. This is clearly identical with the Zanaatha of Ptolemy's *Geography*[22] and with the Zodacatha of the *Notitia Dignitatum*.[23] The name has survived to the present day in its current form, Ṣadaqa. From Zadagatta the road on the map continues to the most famous city in southern Jordan, Petra, marked with one of the characteristic vignettes of the Peutinger Table, a two-towered edifice that has been interpreted by the Levis, in their important study of the Peutinger Table, as a sign for a station in the *cursus publicus*.[24] It is not clear that they have proved their point. It certainly remains a possibility, although a detachment of troops would seem to provide a somewhat more plausible explanation of the vignettes. In any case, Petra is marked as a notable site along the route.

From here the road proceeds by twenty-two miles to the site of Negla, which must be the same as Nekla in Ptolemy's list.[25] This site can be fixed from the survival of the place name in the modern ʿAin (for "spring") Nejl, *j* and *g* being interchangeable in the transmission of Arabic names. ʿAin Nejl is just below the great promontory of Shōbak, with its mediaeval fortress, and one may suspect that Negla on the map represents the whole area, including the acropolis, as well as the spring itself.

[21] David F. Graf, "A Preliminary Report on a Survey of Nabataean-Roman Military Sites in Southern Jordan," *ADAJ* 23 (1979), 121–27, esp. 125 with plates 45 and 46. Cf. Musil (above, n. 20), p. 58, and the report by Aurel Stein, published in Kennedy, *ArchExplor* (1982), pp. 271–87. See above, p. 94, n. 9.

[22] 5.15.5.

[23] *Or.* 34.24.

[24] Levi, *Itineraria* (above, n. 11), pp. 169–76.

[25] 5.17.5.

The map omits the distance from Negla to the next post, Thornia, but this can be fairly reasonably ascertained by calculating the distance on either side of these two sites, as against the total known distance between Petra and Philadelphia, the modern ʿAmmān. As Brünnow and Domaszewski realized, Thornia ought to be the site along the Roman road known today as Thawāna. The modern name would be a corruption from the ancient one. Thornia seems to be identical with Thana in the *Geography* of Ptolemy.[26] The forms Thana and Thawāna point to Arabic *thawā* as the root, implying overnight lodging. The difference in the form of these names may be noted particularly as an indication that, rather than being dependent upon Ptolemy, the archetype of the Peutinger Table must depend upon a common source with Ptolemy.[27]

There are forty-eight miles from Thornia to Rababatora, or Rabba, Rabbatmoab, a well known site in central Jordan. The long form of the name for Rabba or Rabbatmoab may contain the element Betoro, or Betora, which became, according to reasonable conjecture, the name for the legionary camp established in the fourth century near Karak, at Lejjūn.[28] But it is notable that no such camp and no independent place, Betoro or Betora, is marked in the Peutinger map in its present form. The road proceeds directly to Philadelphia, or ʿAmmān, while a separate road verges to the west from Rabba, to cross the deep and hot depression of the Wādī ʿAraba, south of the Dead Sea. We shall return to that crossing in a moment, in connection with an examination of the cities of the Negev.

Above Philadelphia the road proceeds to a place called Gadda, at a distance of thirteen miles, and on to another site called Hatita after an interval of eleven miles. Although scholars have been tempted to identify the modern Ḥadīd with Hatita,[29] the mileage

[26] Ibid.

[27] There is no warrant to identify Thornia-Thana-Thawāna with Thamana in *Not. Dig.*, *Or.* 34.46. Thamana looks like Θαιμάν in Eusebius. In his edition of the *Not. Dig.*, Seeck unfortunately lumps all these together.

[28] On the current excavation of Lejjūn, see S. Thomas Parker, *AASOR News* 8 (June 1981), 8–20.

[29] R. Brünnow and A. von Domaszewski, *Die Provincia Arabia* II (1905), p. 222; H. C. Butler, "Trajan's Road from Boṣra to the Sea," *PAES* III.A.2, appendix p. xv. I also mentioned the possibility of identifying Ḥadīd with Hatita (Aditha in *Not. Dig.*, *Or.* 37.30–31) in *JRS* 61 (1971), 238, with n. 124.

from ʿAmmān is too great to allow this. Moreover, the replacement of *d* by *t* is more of a problem than might appear. The distance to Gadda means that Ḥadīd is, in fact, Gadda, with *g* representing the aspirated *h* and the doubled consonant separated in the modern name. Hatita will then be at the site of Khirbet Samrāʾ. At this point the road on the Peutinger Table divides into two, one passing to Thantia and points west to Tiberias, the other passing by way of Canatha (Qanawāt) to Damascus.

The bifurcation to Thantia clearly crosses a wadi and passes directly to the great city which served as the legionary center of the province of Arabia, Bostra, marked by a vignette. The wadi which the road crosses looks on the map almost parallel to the Jordan River, because of the compression of features into the horizontal plan, but it is identified as the Hieromax, which is the present Wādī Yarmūk together with its extensions into the Wādī Butm and other depressions moving into the Syrian desert north of the Wādī Sirḥān. Thantia, lying between Hatita and Bostra, has been identified with a great Nabataean and later Roman-Byzantine city, built entirely of basalt in the steppe region and known as Umm al-jimāl, "mother of camels."[30] A Roman road clearly discernible near but not alongside the site of Umm al-jimāl leads directly to the provincial capital of Bostra. There can be no doubt that this is the route depicted on the Peutinger Table (even if the present paving is of a later date). But since Umm al-jimāl is not actually on this route, it may perhaps be wise to look for other identifications of Thantia.[31]

What is particularly striking about the westward extension of the road after Gadda, quite apart from the puzzles of identifying sites, is that it does not proceed from Bostra north to Damascus, as most historians and students of the Roman Levant would assume. Instead, it heads due west to Adraha, the modern Derʿā, to the Decapolis city of Capitolias, on to Gadara (modern Umm Qeis), crossing the Jordan over into the western Palestinian city of Tiberias, whence there is a connection southward to

[30] Cf. Butler (above, n. 29), pp. xv–xvi.

[31] D. L. Kennedy makes a case for Thughrat al-jubb in an exceptionally valuable study of roads in northern Arabia according to the *TP: ArchExplor* (1982), pp. 152–54.

Scythopolis, and from there on to Jerusalem and also out farther west to the Mediterranean coast.

The connection to Damascus on the Peutinger map is not, therefore, through Bostra, as one would certainly have expected. Bostra serves rather to make a link with the west, all the way to the coast. For the northern trajectory the road passes from Hatita over a longish stretch without designated stations, finally to Chanata, which is undoubtedly Canata (Canatha), the modern Qanawāt.[32] After Qanawāt comes a place called Aenos.[33] From there the road passes direct to Damascus, designated by still another vignette.

The course of this route between Philadelphia and Damascus warrants thoughtful attention. Qanawāt is the key. It proves that a considerably more eastern passage than one would have expected was the standard route at the time of the archetype of the Peutinger Table. This great Nabataean city in the Ḥawrān did not lie on the road which the Romans eventually built to link Damascus with Ṣalkhad by way of the Leja'. To go to Damascus via Qanawāt meant precisely passing along the western slopes of the Jebel Drūz on the traveler's right, and then northwest along the edge of the desolate lava plateau of the Leja', ancient Trachonitis. From the south the route passed from Suweidā' to Qanawāt. It circled round the Leja' instead of crossing it. Of considerable importance is the fact that the great Roman road across the Leja' does not appear on the Peutinger Table.[34] We may infer that it had not been built at the time of the archetype.

[32] On Qanawāt see H. C. Butler, *AAES* II: *Architecture and Other Arts* (1903), pp. 351–65; Brünnow and Domaszewski (above, n. 29) III (1909), pp. 107–44. See also *PAES* III.A.5, pp. 351–53, and M. Dunand, "Kanata et Kanatha," *Syria* 11 (1930), 272–79. Waddington's remarks are still worth consulting: *IGLS*, pp. 533–35. In the view of M. Sartre, the territorium of Canatha extended far to the west to include the village of Karak: "Le territoire de Canatha," *Syria*, forthcoming.

[33] Aenos has been located at Mismīye: Waddington, *IGLS*, p. 574, arguing that Aenos is a corruption of the name Phaenos; R. Dussaud, *Topographie historique de la Syrie antique et médiévale* (1927), p. 377. But Kennedy, *ArchExplor* (1982), pp. 152–57, argues cogently against this identification.

[34] On the road the Romans built across the Leja', see M. Dunand, "La voie romaine du Ledja," *Mém. Acad. Inscr. et Belles-Lettres* 13.2 (1930), 521–57. On the Qanawāt-Damascus route around the Leja' by way of Shahbā, see Kennedy, *ArchExplor* (1982), pp. 157–58.

Even if travelers had wished to pass from Bostra by the Qanawāt route to Damascus, they would have had to make their way over to Suweidā' first. They could have joined the road marked on the Peutinger map (the Suweidā'-Qanawāt road) south of Suweidā' at its intersection with the road between Bostra and Ṣalkhad.[35] The implication of this bifurcation of the main via, coming up from the south, is that there was considerable traffic deep in the interior. This conclusion seems to be confirmed by the traffic we know was present in the Wādī Sirḥān in Nabataean times, as well as later, and the presence of Roman settlements from a relatively early date at Umm al-Quṭṭein and Deir al-Kahf in the region between the oasis at Azraq and the Jebel Drūz.

Overall, this more northerly segment of the Peutinger map suggests that Bostra served at the time of its creation not as a link to the north but rather as a link to the west, and that the desert regions to the east of Bostra were considerably more subject to interior traffic than one might have expected. This, together with the fact that Petra is illustrated so as to give it equal prominence with Philadelphia, Bostra, and Damascus, suggests that the situation recorded by the map is of a relatively early imperial date. After the first century A.D., Petra's importance diminished substantially, both as a result of the reduction in overland trade through the interior and out to Gaza (after the discovery of the monsoons) and as a result of the increasing prominence accorded to Bostra after the Third Cyrenaica legion was established there.[36] Needless to say, the Strata Diocletiana, which we know to have gone southeast of Damascus to Azraq by way of Saʿane, is

[35] Kennedy, *ArchExplor* (1982), pp. 152–58, makes the brilliant suggestion that the mysterious Rhose on the *TP* represents the point at which the Suweidā'-Qanawāt road intersected the Bostra-Salkhad road. Distances are just right.

[36] On the road to Gaza, see A. Negev, "The Date of the Petra-Gaza Road," *PEQ* 98 (1966), 89–98. Rudolph Cohen has suggested recently that Negev's argument for the abrupt and total abandonment of the road in the first century is incorrect: "Negev Caravanserai and Fortresses during the Nabataean and Roman Period," paper 11 in *Eighth Archaeological Conference in Israel* (Israel Dept. of Antiq., Israel Explor. Soc., 1981). In his important paper, "New Light on the Petra-Gaza Road," *BiblArch* 45 (1982), 240–47, Cohen demonstrates from excavations at ʿAwad, Qaṣr al-ʿAbd, Qaṣr al-Sīq, and Qaṣr al-Maḥalle—all along the road from Petra to ʿAvdat—that the structures at those sites served as caravansarays. Cohen shows that the road remained in use throughout the Roman imperial period, and that ʿAvdat itself was continuously occupied until the Byzantine revival.

totally absent in the Peutinger Table.[37] This absence would have to be explained away by any proponents of a fourth-century date for the Peutinger archetype.

It is worth remarking as well, for future reference in analyzing this document, that the road between Bostra and Tiberias, while, in fact, going almost due west, *appears* in the Peutinger map to be parallel with the road from Hatita to Damascus, which headed almost due north. Such distortion can be very misleading, unless one controls it with external evidence.

Returning to the bifurcations of the Roman road in the south, we can see that there are two principal crossings of the great ʿAraba depression that extends from the south of the Dead Sea down to the head of the Gulf of ʿAqaba. One of these crossings is near the southernmost point and seems to take place to the west of Praesidium, and the other is in the north from Rabba over to a place marked as Thamaro, on to Elusa, which is the modern Khalaṣa (preserving the ancient name), a site with important ancient remains and the place at which the earliest Nabataean inscription was discovered.[38] Despite the extensive efforts of Albrecht Alt in earlier days and of Mordechai Gichon in the present time to establish that there was a string of *castella* in the Wādī ʿAraba as part of the Roman *limes* system, it is obvious, at least from the Peutinger map, that there was no significant road through the ʿAraba at the time of the archetype.[39] For in the extensive stretch marked with the names of Addianam, Rasa, Gypsaria, Lusa, Oboda, and Elusa, all the sites are well to the west of the ʿAraba. This is another case that can be controlled from the known location of several of these sites. The road appears to be going north to south, by reference to another north-to-south road; but it is, in fact, moving westward. Addianam can be identified

[37] D. van Berchem, *L'armée de Dioclétien et la réforme constantinienne* (1952), p. 15. Cf. R. Dussaud, *La pénétration des Arabes en Syrie avant l'Islam* (1955), p. 81.

[38] On the site, see A. Negev, "The Nabataeans and the Provincia Arabia," *ANRW* II.8 (1977), 634. For the inscription, ibid., 546, and F. M. Cross, *JBL* 74 (1955), 160, n. 25.

[39] A. Alt, "Aus der ʿAraba II: Römische Kastelle und Strassen," *ZDPV* 58 (1935), 1–59; M. Gichon, "The *Limes* in the Negev from its Foundation to Diocletian's Times," in Hebrew (diss., Jerusalem, 1967), with related articles in *Bonn. Jahrb.*, Beiheft 19 (1967), 175–93, and *Provincialia: Festschrift Laur-Belart* (1968), pp. 317–34.

by the modern toponym Ghadyān,[40] a site with important Roman remains, on the western side of the ʿAraba. And Oboda (ʿAvdat) has been excavated in the Negev, well to the northwest of Ghadyān.[41]

So the road must already rise above the ʿAraba at Ghadyān and then move consistently westward, presumably skirting the Makhtesh Ramon, to make its own way to Oboda and then on farther, to the northwest, to Elusa (Khalaṣa). The implication of the map concerning the absence of forts along the length of the ʿAraba has recently been confirmed for all periods of Roman history by the investigations conducted by David Graf on the spot.[42] He finds that such forts as can be seen and identified—they are not numerous—are associated with springs or wadis on either side of the ʿAraba. There is no evidence for *castella* throughout its length.

The southernmost connection therefore passed across from Praesidium to Ghadyān and then ascended through the wilderness, in a northwesterly direction, to Oboda and Elusa. The other crossing, interestingly, was not through Petra but through Rabba. The route from Rabba to Thamaro and on to Elusa can be fixed by reference not only to the Thamaro of Ptolemy's *Geography*[43] and the Thamara Kōmē of Eusebius' *Onomastikon*, which Seeck has identified with Tarba in the *Notitia Dignitatum*,[44] but also by reference to ancient remains at a point which conforms to the distance in miles given on the Peutinger Table. This means that Thamaro should be identified with the site, again outside of the Wādī ʿAraba and to the west above it, Qaṣr al-Juheinīya, now known locally as Meẓad Tamar.[45] The

[40] Alt (above, n. 39), 24; and G. W. Bowersock, *JRS* 61 (1971), 240, n. 148.

[41] For a concise survey of the Oboda excavation see the report of the excavator: Negev (above, n. 38), 621–31.

[42] See David F. Graf, "A Report on the Ḥismā Survey," *Damaszener Mitteilungen*, forthcoming. Qaṣr Saʿidiyin may conceivably be an exception: both Nabataean and Roman pottery have been reported there. See also B. Rothenberg, "The ʿArabah in Roman and Byzantine Times in the Light of New Research," *Rom. Frontier Studies, VII Int. Congress* (1971), pp. 211–33.

[43] 5.16.8.

[44] *Or.* 24.40.

[45] Avi-Yonah (above, n. 16), p. 21. Avi-Yonah's notice is erroneous, however, in citing "*Not. Dig.* 74 (*sic*), 42" as naming "*Cohors I Palaestinorum*" at Thamara. That

evidence of Eusebius and the *Notitia* alone would have sufficed to confirm that this northern crossing of the ʿAraba persisted well into late antiquity and was fortified. The southern crossing, however, seems to have disappeared; at least, there is no trace of it in the later sources. The station at Ghadyān, or Addianam, appears to vanish, and in its place there is a military installation, registered in the *Notitia* at Aridela,[46] clearly the same as the modern Gharāndal, well to the north of Ghadyān, though again on the eastern side of the ʿAraba. Aridela evidently served as an observation point and garrison for the region but not as a crossing point.

As for the absence of any crossing, even in the Peutinger Table, from Petra over to the Negev, archaeological investigation in the last decade has made it plain that the route to Gaza from Petra ceased to be a major road from the first century A.D. We have, therefore, in the Peutinger Table a reflection of a situation in which there is no longer a principal line of communication west from Petra, but in which there is still a crossing of the ʿAraba in the south, as there was not to be in later centuries. This evidence, like the evidence for the north, again points unequivocally to a date for the archetype of the Peutinger map in the early period of the principate.[47]

Turning to the Mādabā map, we can have no doubt that we are dealing with a product of late antiquity. Based on Eusebius' *Onomastikon* and the maps which accompanied it (if there were such), it managed to accommodate constructions of considerably later date, such as the so-called Nea in Jerusalem, which would give a date of composition after November of 542.[48] Regrettably, not enough of the map survives to make a complete comparison with the Peutinger Table's treatment of the territory of Roman Arabia, but, in the area in which the two maps do overlap—that is, the ʿAraba and the Negev—there are striking and important differences. An attentive viewer cannot fail to be impressed by the

cohort is not mentioned in the *Notitia*. At 34.46 the fourth cohort of Palestinians is assigned to Thamana, on which see n. 27 above. Thamara and Thamana (Θαιμάν in Eusebius) are unlikely to be the same.

[46] *Or. 34.44.*

[47] Cf. n. 36 above.

[48] Avi-Yonah (above, n. 16), p. 17.

proliferation of cities in the northern Negev in this late age. Excavations over the last two decades have begun to reveal something of the prosperity of the Byzantine Negev, which had been intimated by earlier work at Nessana and also at Shivta (the latter still scandalously unpublished).[49] The blooming of the Negev in this period remained unparalleled until the agricultural miracles of modern times. Elusa appears in the Mādabā map as still an important city; and it is possible that Oboda figures in a missing portion, since we know that the city flourished in this period. The map provides the names of several places, such as Sobela and Seana, which are otherwise completely unknown.

The most conspicuous place in this surviving fragment of the Negev is the city of Mampsis, identified reasonably with modern Kurnub, where Avraham Negev has excavated with singular success.[50] The importance of Mampsis is apparent not only from its prominence on the Mādabā map but from the many buildings which have now been uncovered there. Though the city existed in the Nabataean and early Roman periods, it was obviously of much less consequence. Its absence from the Peutinger map is yet another indication of the early date of the archetype and a sign of the changing configuration in the road systems. From what survives of the Mādabā map, it seems clear that there was nothing but desolation in the southern Negev and most of the ʿAraba below the northern segment. One of the legends refers explicitly to the wilderness of Zin, where the manna was sent down. There is no hint at all of any route or of any city in the southern ʿAraba or, indeed, of any settlement coming up through the southern Negev from the ʿAraba.

There are three stations indicated just south of the Dead Sea, to the east of Mampsis. They appear to be ranged from north to south, apparently in the ʿAraba itself, below some engaging palm trees and an indication of desolation in the word ἐρημ. But, in fact, one of these sites is Thamara, already familiar from the Peutinger Table and Ptolemy's *Geography*. This, as we have seen, is not in the ʿAraba itself but sits on the elevation above it at

[49] See A. Negev, *The Cities of the Desert* (1966).

[50] For a survey, A. Negev, *Bible et Terre Sainte* 90 (March 1967), 6–17, with excellent photographs.

Qaṣr al-Juheinīya. We must therefore assume that the map is showing Thamara upon the elevation which is depicted by the variegated colors of the mountainous segment above Mampsis. Praesidium, which appears in the Greek contracted form Πρα-σίδιν, is obviously not the same as the Praesidium in the south, familiar from the road system of the Peutinger map. This garrison must almost certainly correspond with the extant remains at Qaṣr al-Feifa on the other side of the ʿAraba.[51] In other words, we have a northern crossing which is not unlike the northern crossing of the ʿAraba in the Peutinger Table, but this time not only with Thamara mentioned on the western slope above the ʿAraba but also with an eastern station, Praesidium.

A third station appears on the Mādabā map, and this has given a good deal of trouble. It is Moa, which one presumes from its relation to Praesidium and Thamara must represent a point somewhere to the west of Thamara, on the way to Mampsis. Its exact location has still to be determined, but it is tempting to make some connection between this toponym and the name in the *Notitia Dignitatum*: *equites sagittarii indigenae Moahilae*.[52] Since the Syriac-Aramaic word meaning "the military force" or "the detachment" is precisely *ḥailā*, it may be suggested that Moahila represents an attempt in Latin to say "the fort at Moa," Moahila or Moahaila. In fact, there are variants in the manuscript tradition of the *Notitia* which would tend to support this interpretation of the formation of that puzzling name.[53] So it may well be that Moahilae in the *Notitia* and Moa on the Mādabā map are one and the same place, though that, of course, does not help us to determine where that place actually was in terms of modern geography. This uncertainty does not, however, affect the inference from the Mādabā map that there was only one major crossing of the ʿAraba by road with attendant settlements. That was in the north.

[51] Avi-Yonah (above, n. 16), p. 21.

[52] *Or.* 34.29.

[53] Mohaile and Mohaila (with the vignette at *Or.* 34.14). Note that the Edict of Beersheba also registers Moa. For the possibility that Moa is to be located at the site of Moye ʿAwad, see Cohen (above, n. 36), 242. This would appear to be too far south for Moa.

The topographical indications in the vicinity of Mampsis may possibly represent the Makhtesh ha-Qatan and the Makhtesh ha-Gadol, depressions in the earth, as opposed to the elevations that are represented above Mampsis in the long stretch signaling the Judaean desert. These colors seem to be used both for great depths and for great heights. The Mount of Sinai appears very conspicuously with deep blacks and yellows and blues, to the southwest of the wilderness of Zin.

In Transjordan, where the Mādabā map unfortunately breaks off, there is still enough of the mosaic to see that Characmoba, modern Karak, was given a splendid representation, second only to that of Jerusalem itself, and perhaps equal originally to that accorded Ascalon and Pelusium. Characmoba became a major Byzantine city, although it had also existed in the earlier period under Roman domination. But despite its commanding location and its role as a local administrative center, it had not been one of the principal cities at that time. The absence of Characmoba on the Peutinger Table, by comparison with its prominent appearance on the Mādabā map, is another very strong indication of the date of the information provided in these two documents. In short, with the Mādabā map we have a picture of late antiquity that, where comparison can be made, is utterly at variance with that of the Peutinger Table.

The flourishing of the Negev and the minimal communication with the area of Palestine on the eastern side of the ʿAraba, that is to say, with the territory of Petra and the Ḥismā, reflects accurately the situation of this region in late antiquity. The Negev belonged to Palaestina Tertia and was part of the Byzantine Empire. But the territory below the Wādī Ḥaṣā—that is, the region of Edom, south of Moab—had long been relinquished to the care of native phylarchs, or sheikhs of the seminomadic tribes. It was no longer a part of the Byzantine administration. Moab, on the other hand, with Characmoba and Rabba among its principal cities, continued to flourish in this time. Of course, when Eusebius wrote his *Onomastikon* and for a century or more after that, the territory of Edom and the Ḥismā in southern Jordan had continued to be subject to the administration of the Byzantine state. It had been included within the enlarged province of Palestine to become eventually a portion of Palaestina Tertia. Accordingly, it is just conceivable that the compositor of the Mādabā map included such places as Auara and Zadagatta, which are familiar from the Peutinger Table and the *Notitia Dignitatum*. They were stations on a road that continued to be important until the abandonment of southern Transjordan. In fact, the appearance of two places named Praesidium in the *Notitia* for Palestine simply confirms an inference from the combined testimony of the Peutinger Table and the Mādabā map: there was one Praesidium in the south, within the Jordanian Ḥismā, to the east of the ʿAraba, and later another Praesidium in the north, just below the southern end of the Dead Sea as the road came over the eastern slopes of Edom to make the crossing to Thamara.

It is evident that the two maps were themselves not designed to supply information for military or communications purposes. But they did take their origin from maps that were. That is what is most important. It seems clear that the Peutinger map must be traced back to a map of the very early days of the Roman Empire and, if this is so, the source can scarcely be anything but the map of Agrippa in the Porticus Vipsania. The Mādabā map, with its origins in Eusebius' *Onomastikon*, is obviously associated in the first instance with Christian instruction, but the citation and location of cities seems evidently to depend upon a network of roads linking those cities. For the Mādabā map as a whole, almost all the known cities can be shown to stand in some evident relation to a Roman road, and Avi-Yonah has conveniently listed all of them as road stations in his edition of the Mādabā map. Clearly the cities in the Negev, such as Thamara, Elusa, and Mampsis, fit the pattern.

It should come as no surprise that maps, once created to indicate lines of communication, roads, topography, and the like, should have been put to other uses in the course of time. It was not only a Pliny or a Ptolemy who would attempt to make scientific use of this information in the most rigorous and scholarly way. It was also more ordinary people who wished to see where the Kenokephali were born, or pious people who might like to know where the Children of Israel wandered in the desert. Copies of Agrippa's map circulating in the Roman Empire provided the basis for new maps that contained mythological information, quotations from Virgil, and ultimately Christian legends, all of which we can see in the full flowering of the map from which the Peutinger Table was copied.

Furthermore, one should not lose sight of the purely artistic or aesthetic quality of these documents. Someone took considerable pleasure in drawing the many vignettes in the map that became the Peutinger Table, not to mention the charming representations of emperors at Antioch or Constantinople or Rome. The compositor of the Mādabā mosaic shows a most beguiling talent for representing scenery, plants, and animals, so that the whole of his work is suffused with a kind of good humor. Ancient maps were an evolving thing. Their original purpose continued to be important, no doubt; but, as they were redone, they took on in some quarters new and perhaps more personal objectives.

In studying the maps of the Roman Near East from the particular perspective of provincia Arabia, one has the satisfaction of achieving results on a broad front. There is profit not only in understanding the region itself at various moments and its metamorphoses under Roman and Byzantine rule, but there is also the history of the maps themselves and their place within the culture of the Roman Empire. The Peutinger Table is not merely a document of the twelfth or thirteenth century, or of the fourth century, or of the first century, because it is all of these. The Mādabā map is not merely an artistic creation of the sixth century; it is also a document of the fourth.

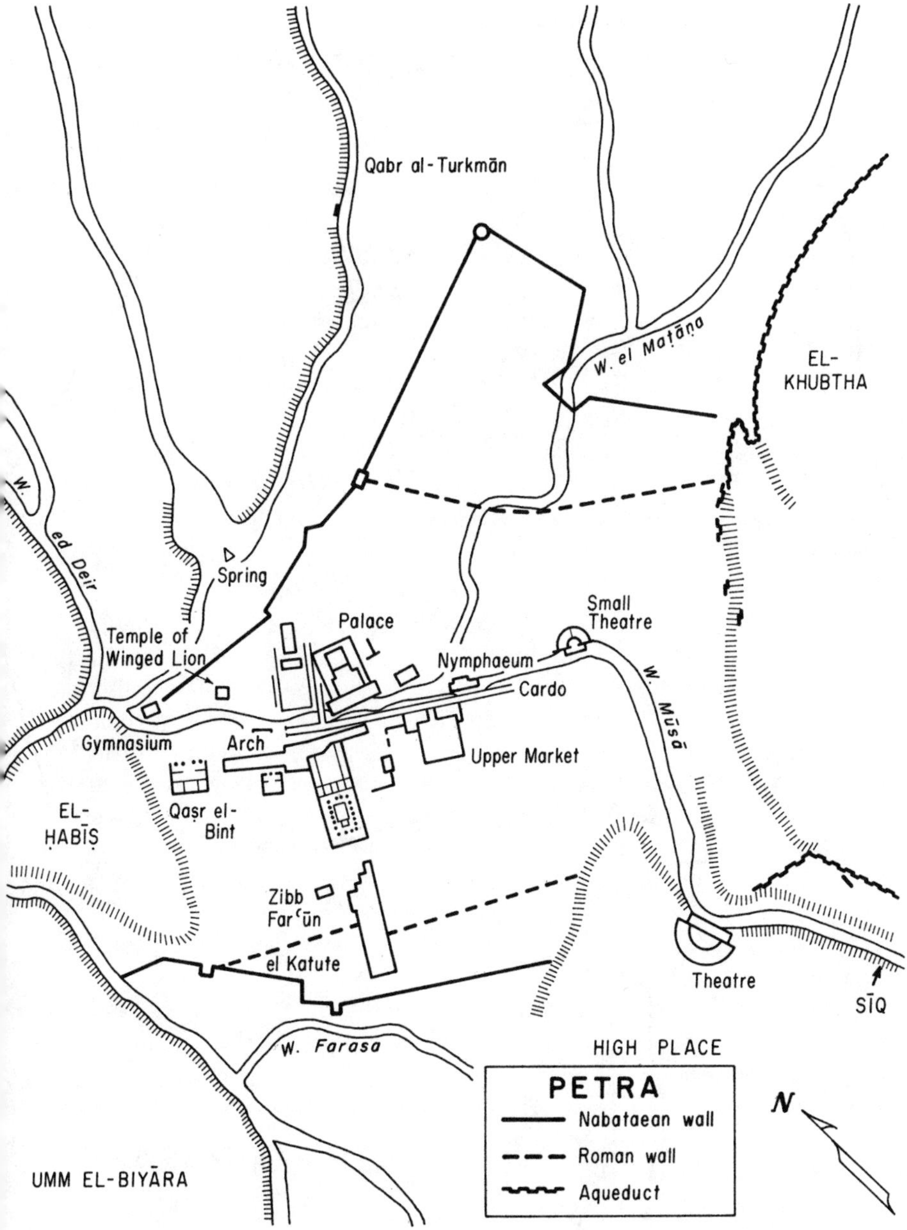
Qabr al-Turkmān
W. el Maṭāṇa
EL-
KHUBTHA
W.
ed Deir
Spring
Temple of
Winged Lion
Palace
Small
Theatre
Nymphaeum
Cardo
W. Mūsā
Gymnasium
Arch
Upper Market
EL-
ḤABĪṢ
Qaṣr el-
Bint
Zibb
Farᶜūn
el Katute
Theatre
SĪQ
W. Farasa
HIGH PLACE
PETRA
Nabataean wall
Roman wall
Aqueduct
N
UMM EL-BIYĀRA

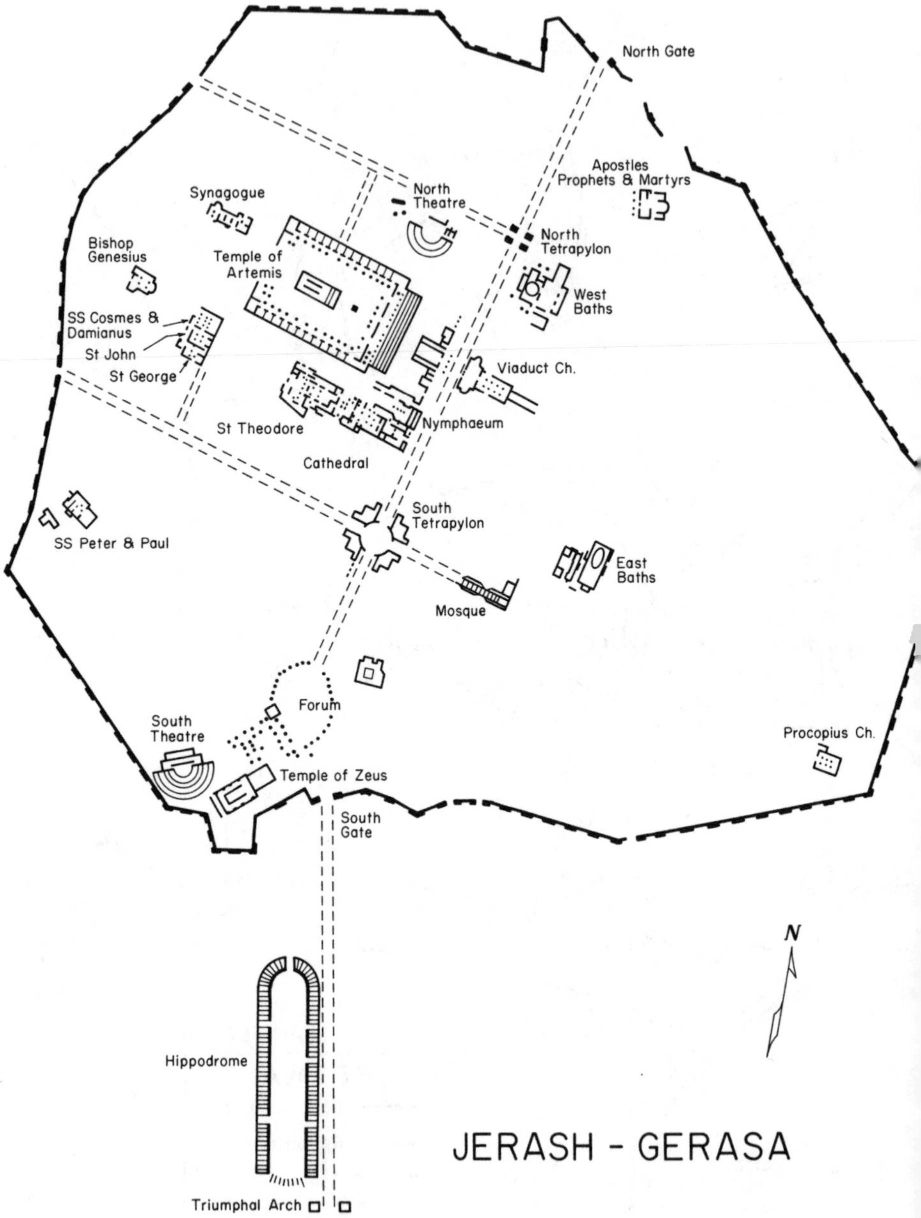
North Gate
Apostles Prophets & Martyrs
Synagogue
North Theatre
North Tetrapylon
Bishop Genesius
Temple of Artemis
West Baths
SS Cosmes & Damianus
St John
St George
Viaduct Ch.
St Theodore
Nymphaeum
Cathedral
South Tetrapylon
SS Peter & Paul
East Baths
Mosque
Forum
South Theatre
Procopius Ch.
Temple of Zeus
South Gate
N
Hippodrome
Triumphal Arch

JERASH - GERASA

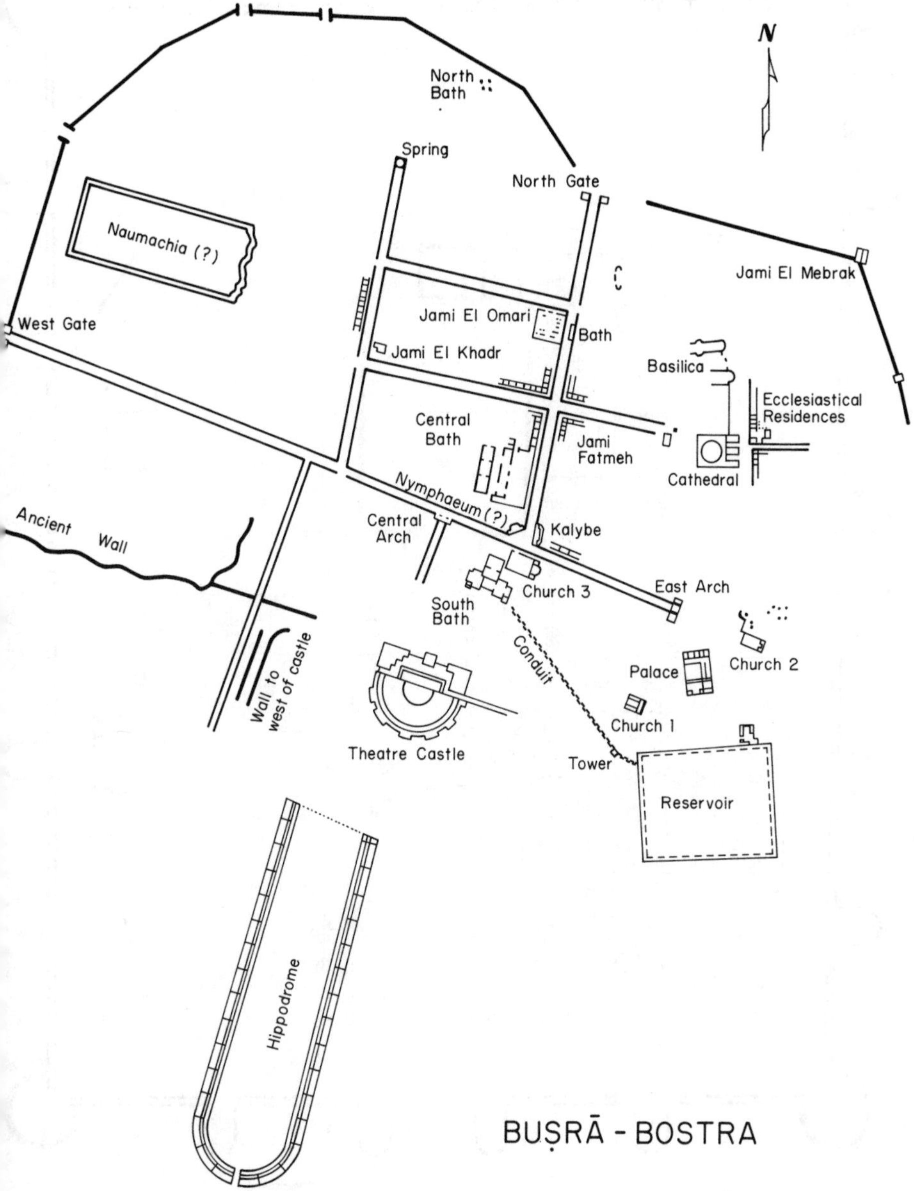

BUṢRĀ - BOSTRA

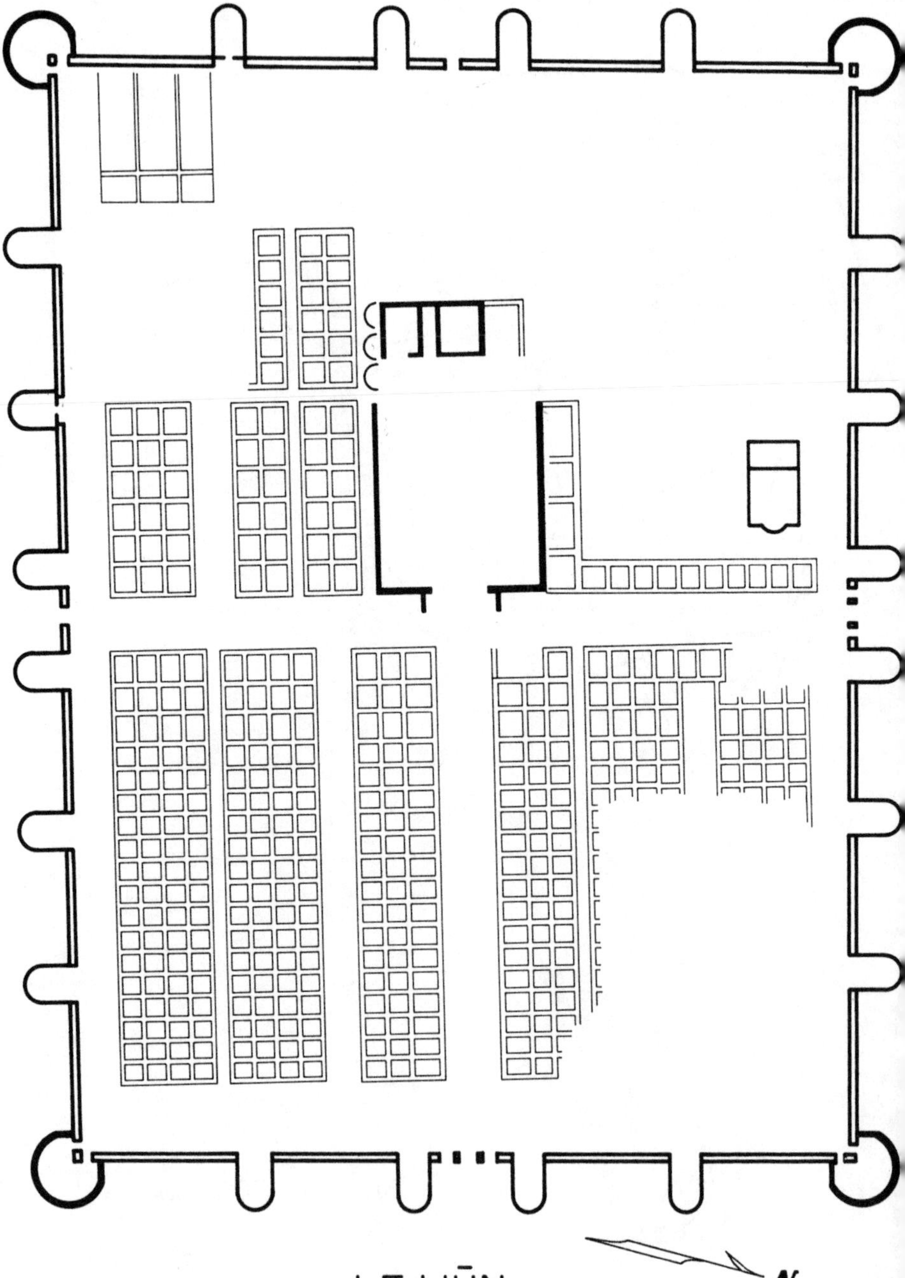

LEJJŪN

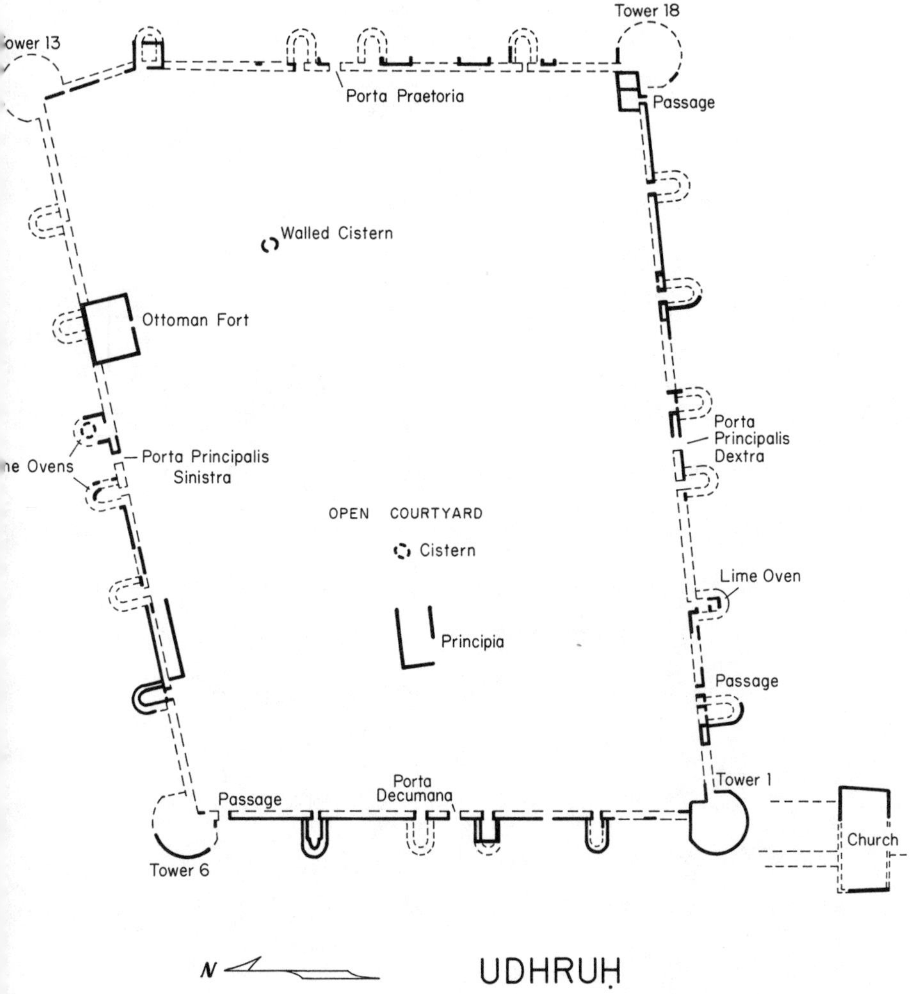
Tower 13
Tower 18
Porta Praetoria
Passage
Walled Cistern
Ottoman Fort
Porta
Principalis
Dextra
Ovens
Porta Principalis
Sinistra
OPEN COURTYARD
Cistern
Lime Oven
Principia
Passage
Porta
Decumana
Tower 1
Passage
Church
Tower 6
N

UDHRUḤ

PLATE I

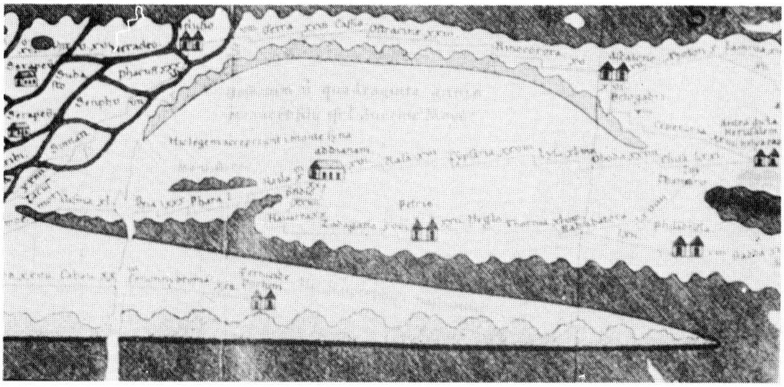

Peutinger Table: from segment 8

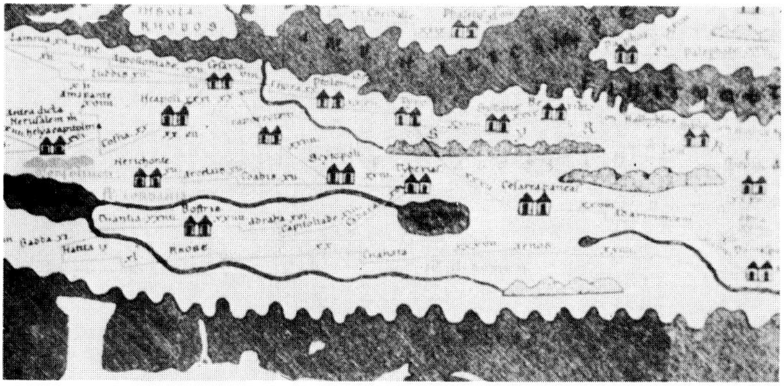

Peutinger Table: from segment 9

PLATE 2

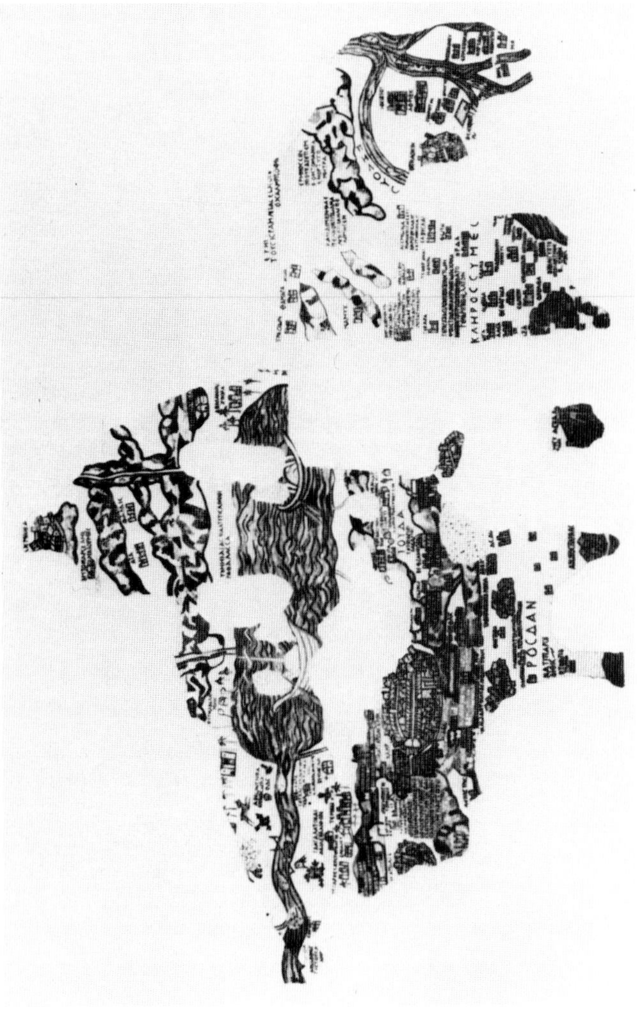

Mādabā map

PLATE 3

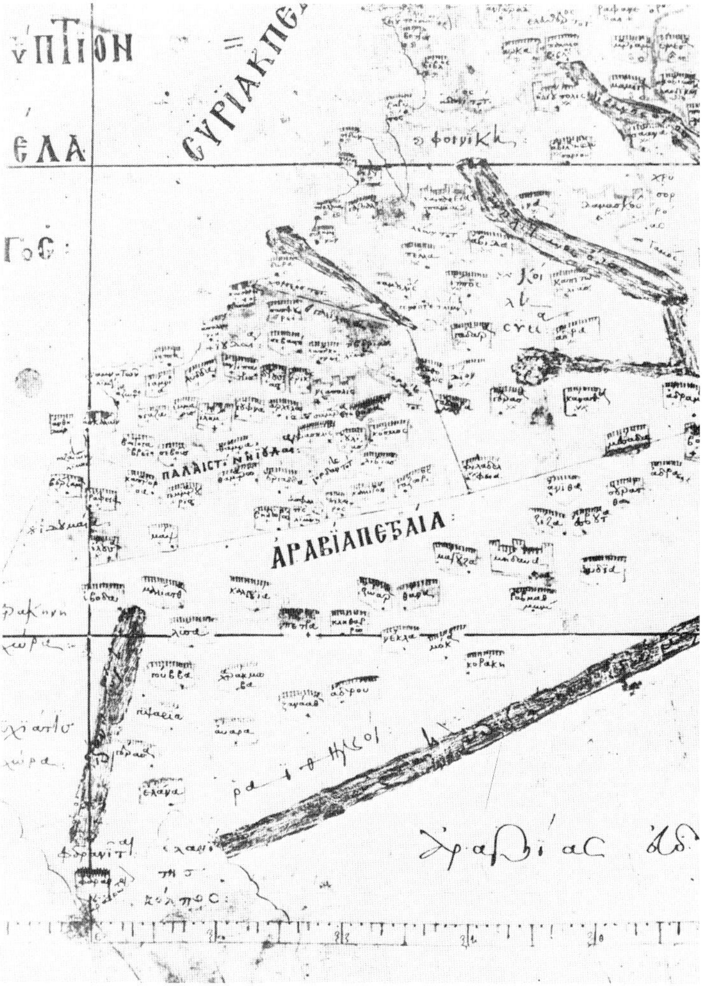

Codex Urbinas Graecus 82:
Map of Arabia in 12th c. manuscript of Ptolemy's *Geography*
(Photograph by Alison Frantz)

PLATE 4

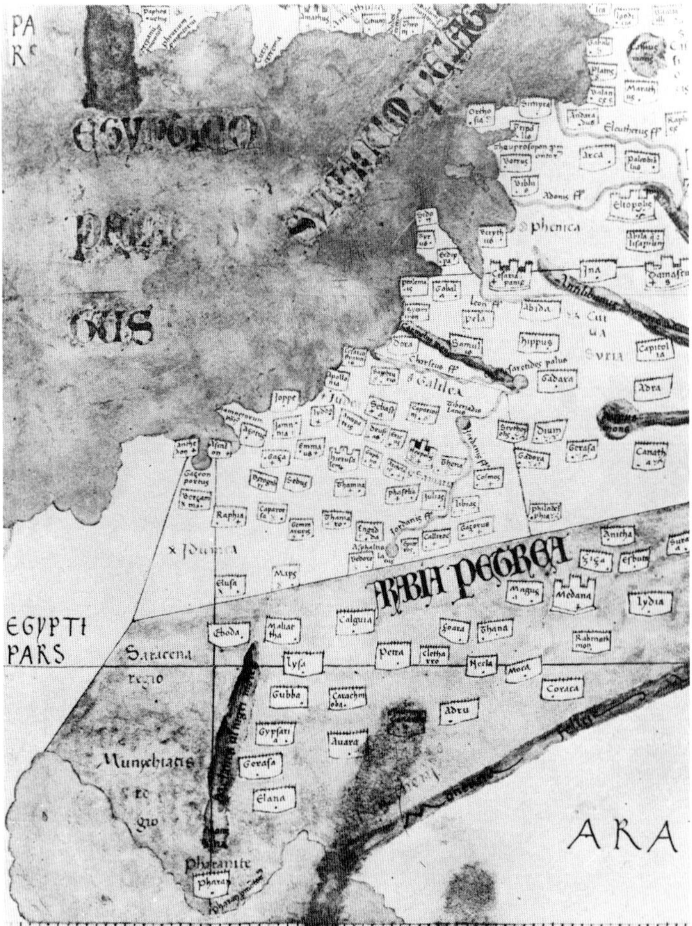

Codex Vaticanus Latinus 5698:
Map of Arabia in 15th c. manuscript of Ptolemy's *Geography*
(Photograph by Alison Frantz)

PLATE 5

The theater at Petra, *ca.* 1860
(Photograph by Francis Frith, published by permission of George Rinhart and the Metropolitan Museum of Art)

PLATE 6

Madā'in Ṣāliḥ:
Tomb no. B1 (Jaussen-Savignac), dated A.D. 31
(Photograph by Robert Reinhold)

PLATE 7

Madā'in Ṣāliḥ:
Tomb no. B7 (Jaussen-Savignac) at left, dated A.D. 35/36
(Photograph by Robert Reinhold)

PLATE 8

Milestone near the Roman road,
vicinity of Baiḍā' in southern Jordan
(Photograph by David Graf)

PLATE 9

Remains of the aqueduct from Wādī Qalkha,
vicinity of Ḥumaima
(Photograph by David Graf)

Roman road near Ḥumaima
(Photograph by David Graf)

PLATE 10

The legionary camp at Lejjūn in Jordan
(Photograph by James Sauer)

Bostra: The triple arch in the center of the city,
bearing the Latin inscription *ILS* 2771
(Photograph by David Graf)

PLATE II

Qaṣr al-Azraq
(Photograph by James Sauer)

PLATE 12

Aerial view of Qaṣr al-Azraq, *ca.* 1928, showing earlier fort (Crawford Collection, Ashmolean Museum)

PLATE 13

The bilingual inscription from Barāqish
(Photograph by Paolo Costa)

PLATE 14

The Latin inscription from Jawf
(Photograph by Mahmud Ghul)

PLATE 15

Azraq: *IGR* 3.1339
(Photograph by Fawzi el-Fakharani)

PLATE 16

Obverse and reverse, *SNG* Amer. Num. Soc.,
Part 6, no. 1153, Bostra (probably A.D. 111)
(Photograph from the American Numismatic Society)

Obverse and reverse, *SNG* Amer. Num. Soc.,
Part 6, no. 1158, Bostra (A.D. 114–116)
(Photograph from the American Numismatic Society)

BIBLIOGRAPHY

Abel, F.-M. *Géographie de la Palestine* I (Paris, 1933), II (Paris, 1938).

________ *Histoire de la Palestine*, 2 vols. (Paris, 1952).

Aharoni, Y. "Tamar and the Roads to Elath," *IEJ* 13 (1963), 30–42.

al-Ansary, A. R. *Qaryat al-Fau: A Portrait of Pre-Islamic Civilisation in Saudi Arabia* (London, 1981).

Alt, A. *Die griechischen Inschriften der Palaestina Tertia westlich der Araba* (Berlin and Leipzig, 1921).

________ "Aus der ʿAraba," *ZDPV* 58 (1935), 1–78.

________ "Die letzte Grenzverschiebung zwischen den römischen Provinzen Arabia und Palaestina," *ZDPV* 65 (1942), 68–76.

________ "Das Territorium von Bostra," *ZDPV* 68 (1951), 235–45.

________ "Augusta Libanensis," *ZDPV* 71 (1955), 173–86.

Altheim, F. (with R. Stiehl) *Die Araber in der alten Welt* I (1964), II (1965), III (1966), IV (1967), V.1 (1968), V.2 (1969).

al-Wohaibi, Abdullah *The Northern Hijaz in the Writings of the Arab Geographers, 800-1150* (Beirut, 1973).

Antiquités de l'Euphrate: Exposition des Découvertes de la Campagne Internationale de Sauvegarde des Antiquités de l'Euphrate (Aleppo, 1974).

Arte Nabateo: el primer reino árabe de la Historia: Catalogue of Exposition, Museo Arqueologico Nacional, Madrid, Sept. 1979–Jan. 1980.

Avi-Yonah, M. "The Development of the Roman Road System in Palestine," *IEJ* 1 (1951), 54–60.

________ *The Madaba Mosaic Map* (Jerusalem, 1954).

________ *The Holy Land: A Historical Geography* (Jerusalem, 1966).

________ "When Did Judea Become a Consular Province?," *IEJ* 23 (1973), 209–13.

Barger, Thomas "Greek Inscriptions Deciphered," *Archaeology* 22 (1969), 139–40.

Bardaisan: François Nau, ed., *Bardesane, Le Livre des Lois des Pays* (2nd printing, Paris, 1931).

———— H. J. W. Drijvers, trans. *The Book of the Laws of Countries* (Assen, 1965).

Barnes, T. D. "The Unity of the Verona List," *ZPE* 16 (1975), 275–78.

Bartlett, J. B. "From Edomites to Nabataeans: A Study in Continuity," *PEQ* 111 (1979), 52–66.

Beaucamp, Joëlle "Rawwafa et les Thamoudéens," *SDB* 9 (1979), 1467–75.

———— and Christian Robin "Le christianisme dans la péninsule arabique d'après l'épigraphie et l'archéologie," *Hommage à Paul Lemerle: Travaux et Mémoires 8*, Centre de Recherche d'Histoire et Civilisation de Byzance (1981), pp. 45–61.

Beeston, A. F. L. "Nemara and Faw," *BSOAS* 42 (1979), 1–6.

———— "Some Observations on Greek and Latin Data Relating to South Arabia," *BSOAS* 42 (1979), 7–12.

———— "The Authorship of the Adulis Throne Text," *BSOAS* 43 (1980), 453–58.

Ben-Dor, S. "Petra Colonia," *Berytus* 9 (1948), 41–43.

Bennett, C. M. "The Nabataeans in Petra," *Archaeology* 15 (1962), 233–43.

Bernays, J. "Ein nabatäischer Schriftsteller," *RhM* 17 (1862), 304–5; also (with supplementary material) in *Gesammelte Abhandlungen* II (1885), 291–93.

Bietenhard, H. "Die Dekapolis von Pompeius bis Traian," *ZDPV* 79 (1963), 24–58.

———— "Die syrische Dekapolis von Pompeius bis Traian," *ANRW* II.8 (1977), 221–61.

Birley, E. "M. Bassaeus Astur: A Note," *ZPE* 37 (1980), 19–21.

Bowersock, G. W. "The Annexation and Initial Garrison of Arabia," *ZPE* 5 (1970), 37–47.

———— "A Report on Arabia Provincia," *JRS* 61 (1971), 219–42.

———— "Syria under Vespasian," *JRS* 63 (1973), 133–40.

———— "The Greek-Nabataean Bilingual Inscription at Ruwwafa, Saudi Arabia," *Le monde grec: Hommages à Claire Préaux* (Brussels, 1975), 513–22.

——— "Old and New in the History of Judaea," *JRS* 65 (1975), 180–85.

——— "A New Antonine Inscription from the Syrian Desert," *Chiron* 6 (1976), 349–55.

——— "Limes Arabicus," *HSCP* 80 (1976), 219–29.

——— "A Roman Perspective on the Bar Kochba War," *Approaches to Ancient Judaism* II, ed. W. S. Green, Brown Judaic Studies 9 (1980), pp. 131–41.

——— "Mavia, Queen of the Saracens," *Studien zur antiken Sozialgeschichte: Festschrift F. Vittinghoff* (Cologne, 1980), pp. 477–95.

——— Review of A. Spijkerman, *The Coins of the Decapolis and Provincia Arabia*, *JRS* 72 (1982), 197–98.

——— "Roman Senators from the Near East," *Acta* of the colloquium *Epigrafia e ordine senatorio*, Rome, forthcoming.

——— "Hadrian and Metropolis," *Bonner Historia-Augusta-Colloquium 1982*, forthcoming.

Broome, E. C. "Nabaiati, Nebaioth and the Nabataeans: The Linguistic Problem," *JSS* 18 (1973), 1–16.

Browning, I. *Petra* (London, 1973).

Brünnow, R. E. "Die Kastelle des arabischen Limes," *Florilegium de Vogüé* (Paris, 1909), 65–77.

——— and A. von Domaszewski, *Die Provincia Arabia* I (Strassburg, 1904), II (Strassburg, 1905), III (Strassburg, 1909).

Butler, H. C. "Trajan's Road from Bosra to the Red Sea," *PAES* III.A.2 (1911), vii–xvi.

Cantineau, J. *Le nabatéen* I (Paris, 1930), II (Paris, 1932).

Caskel, W. "Die Inschrift von en-Nemāra: neu gesehen," *Mél. Univ. St. Joseph* 45 (1969), 367–79.

Casson, L. "*Periplus Maris Erythraei*: Three Notes on the Text," *CQ* 30 (1980), 495–97.

——— "Rome's Trade with the East: The Sea Voyage to Africa and India," *TAPA* 110 (1980), 21–36.

——— "*Periplus Maris Erythraei* 36: Teak, Not Sandalwood," *CQ* 32 (1982), 181–83.

Champdor, A. *Les ruines de Pétra* (Paris, 1972).

Christides, V. "Arabs as 'Barbaroi' before the Rise of Islam," *Balkan Studies* 10 (1969), 315–24.

_______ "The Names ΑΡΑΒΕΣ, ΣΑΡΑΚΗΝΟΙ, etc., and their False Byzantine Etymologies," *BZ* 65 (1972), 329–33.

Cohen, Rudolph "Negev Caravanserai and Fortresses during the Nabatean and Roman Period," *Eighth Archaeological Conference in Israel* (Israel Dept. of Antiquities, 1981).

_______ "New Light on the Petra-Gaza Road," *BiblArch* 45 (1982), 240–47.

Costa, Paolo M. "A Latin-Greek Inscription from the Jawf of the Yemen," *Proc. Seminar for Arabian Studies* 7 (1977), 69–72.

Cross, F. M. "The Oldest Manuscripts from Qumran," *JBL* 74 (1955), 147–72.

Crouzel, H. "Le christianisme de l'empereur Philippe l'Arabe," *Gregorianum* 56 (1975), 545–50.

Dayton, J. E. "A Roman/Byzantine Site in the Hejaz," *Proc. Seminar for Arabian Studies* 1–3 (1972), 21–25.

Dentzer, Jean-Marie and Jacqueline "Les fouilles de Siʿ et la phase hellénistique en Syrie du Sud," *CRAI* 1981, 78–102.

Desanges, Jehan *Recherches sur l'activité des méditerranéens aux confins de l'Afrique*, École Française de Rome 38 (Rome, 1978).

Dihle, A. "Das Datum des Periplus des Roten Meeres," in *Umstrittene Daten* (Cologne, 1965), pp. 9–35.

_______ "Der Zug des Aelius Gallus," in *Umstrittene Daten* (Cologne, 1965), pp. 80–84.

_______ "Die entdeckungsgeschichtlichen Voraussetzungen des Indienhandels der römischen Kaiserzeit," *ANRW* II.9.2 (1978), 546–80.

Domaszewski, A. von "Die Zeit des Schriftstellers Uranius," *Arch. f. Rel.* 11 (1908), 239–42.

Donner, H. and H. Cüppers *Die Mosaikkarte von Madeba*, Abhandl. des Deutschen Palästinavereins, II Tafelband (Wiesbaden, 1977).

Doughty, Charles *Travels in Arabia Deserta*, 2 vols. (Cambridge, 1888).

Drijvers, H. J. W. "Das Heiligtum der arabischen Göttin Allât im westlichen Stadtteil von Palmyra," *Antike Welt* 7.3 (1976), 28–38.

——— "Hatra, Palmyra und Edessa," *ANRW* II.8 (1977), 799–906.

——— "A Tomb for the Life of a King: A Recently Discovered Edessene Mosaic with a Portrait of King Abgar the Great," *Le Muséon* 95 (1982), 167–89.

Dunand, M. "Rapport sur une mission archéologique au Djebel Druze," *Syria* 7 (1926), 326–35.

——— "La voie romaine du Ledja," *Mém. Acad. Inscr. et Belles-Lettres* 13.2 (1930), 521–57.

——— "Nouvelles inscriptions du Djebel Druze et du Hauran," *RB* 41 (1932), 397–416, 561–80; 42 (1933), 235–54.

——— *Le musée de Soueida* (Paris, 1934).

——— "Nouvelles inscriptions du Djebel Druze et du Hauran," *Mélanges syriens offerts à René Dussaud* (Paris, 1939), pp. 559–76.

——— "Nouvelles inscriptions du Djebel Druze et du Hauran," *Archiv Orientalni* 18 (1950) I, 144–64.

Dussaud, René *Topographie Historique de la Syrie Antique et Médiévale* (Paris, 1927).

——— *La Pénétration des Arabes en Syrie avant l'Islam* (Paris, 1955).

——— and F. Macler, "Rapport sur une mission scientifique dans les régions désertiques de la Syrie moyenne," *Nouvelles Archives des Missions scientifiques et littéraires* 10 (1902), 411–744.

Evenari, M., et al. *The Negev: The Challenge of a Desert* (Cambridge, Mass., 1971; rev. ed. 1982).

Fakhry, A. *An Archaeological Journey to the Yemen* I-III (Cairo, 1951–1952).

Fellmann, Rudolph *Le Sanctuaire de Baalshamin à Palmyre* VI (Neuchâtel, 1975).

Fiebiger, O. "Herminarius," *ZDPV* 66 (1943), 69–71.

Field, Henry *North Arabian Desert Archaeological Survey, 1925–50*, Papers of the Peabody Museum 45.2 (1960).

Finkelstein, I. "The Holy Land in the Tabula Peutingeriana: a Historical-Geographical Approach," *PEQ* 111 (1979), 27–34.

Finsen, H. *Le levé du théâtre romain à Bosra, Syrie*, Analecta Romana Instituti Danici 6, Suppl. (1972).

Frank, F. von "Aus der ʿAraba I," *ZDPV* 57 (1934), 191–280.

Gaube, H. "An Examination of the Ruins of Qasr Burquʿ," *ADAJ* 19 (1974), 93–100.

Gawlikowski, M. "Le temple d'Allat à Palmyre," *RA* 2 (1977), 253–74.

Ghadban, Chaker "Un site safaïtique dans l'Antiliban," *ADAJ* 16 (1971), 77–82.

Gichon, M. "Idumea and the Herodian Limes," *IEJ* 17 (1967), 27–42.

________ "The Origin of the Limes Palestinae and the Major Phases in its Development," *Studien zu den Militärgrenzen Roms*, Beiheft 19 d. *Bonner Jahrb.* (1967), pp. 175–93.

________ "Das Verteidigungssystem und die Verteidiger des flavischen Limes in Judäa," *Provincialia: Festschrift Laur-Belart* (1968), pp. 317–34.

________ "Research on the Limes Palestinae: A Stocktaking," *Roman Frontier Studies 1979*, BAR International Series 71 (1980), pp. 843–64.

Glueck, Nelson *Explorations in Eastern Palestine* I, *AASOR* 14 (1934); II, *AASOR* 15 (1935); III, *AASOR* 18–19 (1939); IV, *AASOR* 25–28 (1951).

________ *The Other Side of the Jordan* (New Haven, 1940; rev. ed. Cambridge, 1970).

________ "Wādī Sirḥān in North Arabia," *BASOR* 96 (1944), 7–17.

________ *Rivers in the Desert* (New York, 1959).

________ *Deities and Dolphins* (London, 1965).

Grabar, Oleg, et al. *City in the Desert: Qasr al-Hayr East*, Harvard Middle Eastern Monographs 23–24 (1978), 2 vols.

Graf, David F. "The Saracens and the Defense of the Arabian Frontier," *BASOR* 229 (1978), 1–26.

________ "A Preliminary Report on a Survey of Nabataean-Roman Military Sites in Southern Jordan," *ADAJ* 23 (1979), 121–27.

——— "The Nabataeans and the Hismā: In the Steps of Glueck and Beyond," in *The Word of the Lord Shall Go Forth: Essays in Celebration of the Sixtieth Birthday of David Noel Freedman*, ASOR, forthcoming.

——— "A Report on the Hismā Survey," *Damaszener Mitteilungen* forthcoming.

——— and M. O'Connor, "The Origin of the Term Saracen and the Rawwāfa Inscriptions," *Byz. Stud./Étud. Byz.* 4.1 (1977), 52–66.

Gray, E. W. "The Roman Eastern *Limes* from Constantine to Justinian—Perspectives and Problems," *Proc. African Class. Assoc.* 12 (1973), 24–40.

Grohmann, A. *Arabien* (Munich, 1963).

Groom, Nigel *Frankincense and Myrrh* (London and New York, 1981).

Gutwein, K. C. *Third Palestine: A Regional Study in Byzantine Urbanization* (Washington, 1981).

Hadidi, Adnan "Nabatäische Architektur in Petra," *Bonner Jahrb.* 180 (1980), 231–36.

Halfmann, Helmut "Iulius Alexander und Iulius Iulianus," *Arheoloski Vestnik* 28 (1977), 153–62.

——— *Die Senatoren aus dem östlichen Teil des Imperium Romanum bis zum Ende des 2. Jh. n. Chr.*, Hypomnemata 58 (Göttingen, 1979).

Hammond, Philip "The Nabataean Bitumen Industry at the Dead Sea," *BiblArch* 22 (1959), 40–48.

——— "The Excavation of the Main Theater at Petra," *ADAJ* 8–9 (1964), 81–85.

——— *The Excavation of the Main Theater at Petra, 1961–1962* (London, 1965).

——— *The Nabataeans—Their History, Culture and Archaeology*, Studies in Mediterranean Archaeology 37 (Gothenburg, 1973).

——— "Ein nabatäisches Weiherelief aus Petra," *Bonner Jahrb.* 180 (1980), 265–69.

——— "New Evidence for the Fourth-Century A.D. Destruction of Petra," *BASOR* 238 (1980), 65–67.

Harding, G. Lankester *The Antiquities of Jordan* (2nd ed., New York, 1967).

_______ "Safaitic Inscriptions from Lebanon," *ADAJ* 16 (1971), 83–84.

Horsfield, George and Agnes, "Sela-Petra, The Rock of Edom and Nabatene," *QDAP* 7 (1938), 1–42; 8 (1938), 87–115; 9 (1942), 105–204.

Husselman, E. M. *Papyri from Karanis: Third Series* (Cleveland, 1971).

Iliffe, J. H. "A Building Inscription from the Syrian Limes, A.D. 334," *QDAP* 10 (1944), 62–64.

Ingholt, H. "Deux inscriptions bilingues de Palmyre," *Syria* 13 (1932), 278–92.

Isaac, Benjamin "Milestones in Judaea, from Vespasian to Constantine," *PEQ* 110 (1978), 47–60.

_______ "Legio II Traiana in Judaea," *ZPE* 33 (1979), 149–56.

_______ and Israël Roll "Judaea in the Early Years of Hadrian's Reign," *Latomus* 38 (1979), 54–66.

_______ "Trade Routes to Arabia and the Roman Army," *Roman Frontier Studies, 1979*, BAR International Series 71 (1980), pp. 889–901.

_______ "The Decapolis in Syria, A Neglected Inscription," *ZPE* 44 (1981), 67–74.

_______ "Bandits in Judaea and Arabia," *HSCP*, forthcoming.

Jameson, S. "Chronology of the Campaigns of Aelius Gallus and C. Petronius," *JRS* 58 (1968), 71–84.

Jaussen, A. and R. Savignac *Mission archéologique en Arabie* I (Paris, 1909), II (Paris, 1914).

Jones, C. P. "A Syrian in Lyon," *AJP* 99 (1978), 336–53.

Kammerer, A. *Pétra et la Nabatène* I (Paris, 1929), II (Paris, 1930).

Kennedy, D. L. "The Frontier Policy of Septimius Severus: New Evidence from Arabia," *Roman Frontier Studies, 1979*, BAR International Series 71 (1980), pp. 879–87.

_______ "The Date of the Arabian Governorship of Q. Scribonius Tenax," *ZPE* 37 (1980), 24–26.

——— "*Legio VI Ferrata*: The Annexation and Early Garrison of Arabia," *HSCP* 84 (1980), 283–309.

——— *Archaeological Explorations on the Roman Frontier in North-East Jordan*, BAR International Series 134 (1982).

——— "The Date of the Arabian Governorship of L. Marius Perpetuus," *ZPE* 49 (1982), 284–86.

——— and C. M. Bennett "A New Roman Military Inscription from Petra," *Levant* 10 (1978), 163–65.

Keppie, L. J. F. "The Legionary Garrison of Judaea under Hadrian," *Latomus* 32 (1973), 859–64.

Kettenhofen, Erich "Zur Nordgrenze der *provincia Arabiae* im 3. Jahrhundert n. Chr.," *ZDPV* 97 (1981), 62–73.

Khairy, Nabil "Die unbemalte nabatäische Gebrauchskeramik," *Bonner Jahrb.* 180 (1980), 270–72.

——— "A New Dedicatory Nabataean Inscription from Wadi Musa," *PEQ* 113 (1981), 19–26.

Kindler, A. "Two Coins of the Third Legion Cyrenaica Struck under Antoninus Pius," *IEJ* 25 (1975), 144–47.

Kirkbride, D. "A Short Account of the Excavation at Petra in 1955–1956," *ADAJ* 4–5 (1960), 117–22.

Kirwan, L. "Where to Search for the Ancient Port of Leuke Kome," *Second International Symposium on the History of Arabia, Pre-Islamic Arabia*, mimeographed (Riyadh, 1979).

Kollmann, E. D. "A Soldier's Joke or an Epitaph?," *IEJ* 22 (1972), 145–47.

Kraeling, C. H. *Gerasa: City of the Decapolis* (New Haven, 1938).

Lemosse, M. "Le procès de Babatha," *The Irish Jurist* 3 (1968), 363–76.

Levi della Vida, G. "Una bilingue greco-nabatea a Coo," *Clara Rhodos* 9 (1938), 139–48.

Lewis, Naphtali "Two Greek Documents from Provincia Arabia," *Illinois Classical Studies* 3 (1978), 100–14.

——— "P. Oxy. 2820: Whose Preparations?," *GRBS* 16 (1975), 295–303.

Liebeschuetz, W. "The Defences of Syria in the Sixth Century," *Studien zu den Militärgrenzen Roms II* (1977), pp. 487–99.

———— "Epigraphical Evidence on the Christianization of Syria," *Akten des XI. Internationalen Limeskongresses* (1978), pp. 485–508.

Lindner, M. *Petra und das Königreich der Nabatäer* (4th ed., Nuremberg, 1983).

———— "Deutsche Ausgrabungen in Petra," *Bonner Jahrb.* 180 (1980), 253–64.

Littmann, E. *Thamūd und Ṣafā* (Leipzig, 1940).

———— and D. Meredith "Nabataean Inscriptions from Egypt," *BSOAS* 15 (1953), 1–28; 16 (1954), 24–46.

Lyon (Musée de), *Un royaume aux confins du désert: Pêtra et la Nabatène* (1978–1979), Catalogue of Exhibition.

MacAdam, Henry I. "Studies in the History of the Roman Province of Arabia," diss. Univ. of Manchester, 1979.

———— "The Identity of Ammius Flaccus, Governor of Arabia," *ZPE* 38 (1980), 72–74.

———— "The Nemara Inscription: Some Historical Considerations," *Al-abḥāth* 28 (1980), 3–16.

———— and Nicholas J. Munday "Cicero's Reference to Bostra," *CP* 78 (1983), forthcoming.

Malavolta, M. "*Interiores limites* (nota ad Amm. Marc. XXIII.5,1-2)," *Ottava miscellanea greca e romana*, Istituto Italiano per la Storia Antica (1982), 587–610.

Mayerson, Philip "The Ancient Agricultural Regime of Nessana and the Central Negeb," in H. D. Colt, *Excavations at Nessana* I (Princeton, 1962), pp. 261–69.

———— "The Desert of Southern Palestine According to Byzantine Sources," *ProcPhilSoc* 107.2 (1963), 160–72.

———— "The Clysma-Phara-Haila Road on the Peutinger Table," *Coins, Culture, and History in the Ancient World: Studies in Honor of Bluma Trell* (Detroit, 1981), pp. 167–76.

Meshel, Ze'ev and Yoran Tsafrir "The Nabataean Road from ʿAvdat to Shaʿar Ramon" I, *PEQ* 106 (1974),103–18; II, *PEQ* 107 (1975), 3–21.

Meshorer, Y. *Nabataean Coins*, Qedem 3 (Jerusalem, 1975).

———— "Was There a Mint at Eboda?," *Schweizer Münzblätter* 27 (1977), 33–36.

——— *Sylloge Nummorum Graecorum, Coll. Amer. Numis. Soc. Part 6: Palestine-South Arabia* (New York, 1981).

Metcalf, William E. "The Tell Kalak Hoard and Trajan's Arabian Mint," *Amer. Num. Soc. Museum Notes* 20 (1975), 39–108.

Milik, J. T. "Nouvelles inscriptions nabatéennes," *Syria* 35 (1958), 227–51.

——— "Inscriptions grecques et nabatéennes de Rawwafah," *Bull. Inst. Arch. Univ. London* 10 (1972), 54–59.

——— *Dédicaces faites par des dieux* (Paris, 1972).

——— "La tribu des Bani ʿAmrat en Jordanie de l'époque grecque et romaine," *ADAJ* 24 (1980), 41–48.

——— and J. Starcky "Inscriptions récemment découvertes à Pétra," *ADAJ* 20 (1975), 112–15.

——— and J. Starcky "Nabataean, Palmyrene, and Hebrew Inscriptions," in F. V. Winnett and W. L. Reed, *Ancient Records from North Arabia* (Toronto, 1970), pp. 139–63.

Miller, J. Innes *The Spice Trade of the Roman Empire* (Oxford, 1969).

Mittmann, Siegfried "Die römische Strasse von Gerasa nach Adraa," *ZDPV* 80 (1964), 113–36; also, in English, in *ADAJ* 11 (1966), 65–87.

Mougdad, Sulaiman A. *Bosra: Historical and Archaeological Guide*, trans. by H. I. MacAdam (Damascus, 1978).

Müller, Walter W. "Ergebnisse neuer epigraphischer Forschungen im Jemen," *ZDMG*, Suppl. 3.1 (1977), 731–35.

——— "Survey of the History of the Arabian Peninsula from the First Century A.D. to the Rise of Islam," *Second International* of Arabia, Pre-Islamic Arabia, mimeographed (Riyadh, 1979).

München (Stadtmuseum): *Die Nabatäer: Ein vergessenes Volk am Toten Meer*, Catalogue (1970).

Musil, Aloïs *Arabia Petraea*, 3 vols. (Vienna, 1907).

——— *The Northern Ḥeǧâz: A Topographical Itinerary* (New York, 1926).

——— *Arabia Deserta* (New York, 1927).

Negev, Avraham "Avdat, a Caravan Halt in the Negev," *Archaeology* 14 (1961), 122–30.

——— "Nabataean Inscriptions from Avdat (Oboda)," *IEJ* 13 (1963), 113–24.

——— "The Date of the Petra-Gaza Road," *PEQ* 98 (1966), 89–98.

——— "New Dated Nabataean Graffiti from the Sinai," *IEJ* 17 (1967), 251–55.

——— "Oboda, Mampsis, and Provincia Arabia," *IEJ* 17 (1967), 46–55.

——— "Seal Impressions from Tomb 107 at Kurnub (Mampsis)," *IEJ* 19 (1969), 89–106.

——— "The Chronology of the Middle Nabataean Period," *PEQ* 101 (1969), 5–14.

——— "Notes on some Trajanic Drachms from the Mampsis Hoard," *Jahrb. f. Numismatik u. Geldgeschichte* 21 (1971), 115–20; reprinted in A. Spijkerman, *The Coins of the Decapolis and Provincia Arabia* (Jerusalem, 1978), pp. 32–34.

——— "The Staircase-Tower in Nabataean Architecture," *RB* 80 (1973), 364–83.

——— "Nabataean Capitals in the Towns of the Negev," *IEJ* 24 (1974), 153–59.

——— "The Nabataean Necropolis at Egra," *RB* 83 (1976), 203–36.

——— "Permanence et Disparition d'anciens toponymes du Negev central," *RB* 83 (1976), 545–57.

——— "The Early Beginnings of the Nabataean Realm," *PEQ* 108 (1976), 125–33.

——— "Die Nabatäer," Sondernummer, *Antike Welt* (1976).

——— "The Nabataeans and the Provincia Arabia," *ANRW* II.8 (1977), 520–686.

——— "Nabataean Inscriptions in Southern Sinai," *BiblArch* 45 (1982), 21–25.

——— "Christen und Christentum in der Wüste Negev," *Antike Welt* 13 (1982), 2–33.

——— "Numismatics and Nabataean Chronology," *PEQ* 114 (1982), 119–28.

Nöldeke, Th. "Die römischen Provinzen Palaestina Salutaris und Arabia," *Hermes* 10 (1876), 163–70.

———— *Geschichte der Perser und Araber zur Zeit der Sasaniden aus der arabischen Chronik des Tabari* (Leiden, 1879).

Parker, S. Thomas "Archaeological Survey of the *Limes Arabicus*: a Preliminary Report," *ADAJ* 21 (1976), 19–31.

———— and P. M. McDermott "A Military Building Inscription from Roman Arabia," *ZPE* 28 (1978), 61–66.

———— "The Historical Development of the Limes Arabicus," diss. Univ. of California, Los Angeles, 1979.

———— "Towards a History of the Limes Arabicus," *Roman Frontier Studies, 1979*, BAR International Series 71 (1980), pp. 865–78.

———— "The Central Limes Arabicus Project: the 1980 Campaign," *ASOR Newsletter* 8 (June 1981), 8–20.

———— "The Central Limes Arabicus Project: The 1980 Campaign," *ADAJ* 25 (1981), 171–78.

———— "The Central Limes Arabicus Project: The 1982 Campaign," *ADAJ*, forthcoming.

Parr, P. J. "Recent Discoveries at Petra," *PEQ* 89 (1957), 5–16.

———— "A Nabataean Sanctuary near Petra," *ADAJ* 6–7 (1962), 21–23.

———— "The Beginnings of Hellenisation at Petra," *VIIIe Congrès International d'Archéologie Classique* (Paris, 1965), pp. 527–33.

———— "The Date of the Qasr Bint Farʿun at Petra," *Ex Oriente Lux* 19 (1965–1966), 550–57.

———— "La date du barrage du Sîq à Pétra," *RB* 74 (1967), 45–49.

———— "Découvertes récentes au sanctuaire du Qasr à Pétra," *Syria* 45 (1968), 1–24; also, in English, in *ADAJ* 11–12 (1967–1968), 5–19.

———— "Exploration archéologique de Hedjaz et de Madian," *RB* 76 (1969), 390–93.

———— K. B. Atkinson, and E. H. Wickens "Photogrammetric Work at Petra, 1965–1968: An Interim Report," *ADAJ* 20 (1975), 31–45.

———— G. L. Harding, and J. E. Dayton "Preliminary Survey in N.W. Arabia, 1968," *Bull. Inst. Arch. Univ. London* 8–9 (1969), 193–242; 10 (1971), 23–61.

________ and J. Starcky "Three Altars from Petra," *ADAJ* 6–7 (1962), 13–20.

Peters, F. E. "The Nabataeans in the Hawran," *Journ. Amer. Oriental Soc.* 97 (1977), 263–77.

________ "Romans and Bedouin in Southern Syria," *Journ. Near Eastern Stud.* 37 (1978), 315–26.

________ "Regional Development in the Roman Empire: The Lava Lands of Syria," *Thought* 55 (1980), 110–21.

________ "City Planning in Greco-Roman Syria: Some New Considerations," forthcoming.

Peterson, L. "Iulius Iulianus, Statthalter von Arabien," *Klio* 48 (1967), 159–67.

Pflaum, Hans-Georg "La fortification de la ville d'Adraha d'Arabie (259–60 à 274–5) d'après des inscriptions récemment découvertes," *Syria* 29 (1952), 307–30.

Philby, H. St. J. *The Land of Midian* (London, 1957).

Pirenne, J. "L'expédition d'Aelius Gallus en Arabie du sud," in *Le royaume sud-arabe de Qatabān et sa datation* (London, 1961).

Pohlsander, H. A. "Philip the Arab and Christianity," *Historia* 29 (1980), 463–73.

Poidebard, A. "Reconnaissance aérienne au Ledja et au Safa," *Syria* 9 (1928), 114–23.

________ *La trace de Rome dans le désert de Syrie*, 2 vols. (Paris, 1934).

Polotsky, H. J. "The Greek Papyri from the Cave of the Letters," *IEJ* 12 (1962), 258–62.

________ "The Archive of Babatha" (in Hebrew), *Eretz Israel* 8 (1967), 46–50.

Préaux, C. "Une source nouvelle sur l'annexion de l'Arabie par Trajan," *Phoibos* 5 (1950–1951), 123–39.

Raschke, M. "New Studies in Roman Commerce with the East," *ANRW* II.9.2 (1978), 604–1361.

Rees, L. W. B. "Ancient Remains near Kasr Azrak," *Antiquity* 3 (1929), 89–92.

Reinhold, Robert "Uncovering Arabia's Past," *The New York Times Magazine* (Aug. 23, 1981), 16 ff.

Rey-Coquais, J.-P. "Nouvelles inscriptions grecques et latines de Bostra," *Ann. Arch. Syrie* 15 (1965), 65–86.

——— *Arados et sa Pérée aux époques grecque, romaine et byzantine* (Paris, 1974).

——— "Syrie romaine de Pompée à Dioclétien," *JRS* 68 (1978), 44–73.

Robert, Louis "L'épitaphe d'un arabe à Thasos," *Hellenica* 2 (1946), 43–50.

Romer, F. E. "Gaius Caesar's Military Diplomacy in the East," *TAPA* 109 (1979), 199–214.

Roschinski, Hans P. "Geschichte der Nabatäer," *Bonner Jahrb.* 180 (1980), 129–54.

——— "Sprachen, Schriften und Inschriften in Nordwestarabien," *Bonner Jahrb.* 180 (1980), 155–88.

Rosenthal, Franz, "Nabataean and Related Inscriptions," in Colt, *Excavations at Nessana* I (Princeton, 1962), pp. 198–210.

Rothenberg, B. "An Archaeological Survey of South Sinai," *PEQ* 102 (1970), 4–29.

——— "The ʿArabah in Roman and Byzantine Times in the Light of New Research," *Roman Frontier Studies, 1967* (1971), pp. 211–23.

Rothstein, G. *Die Dynastie der Laḫmiden in al-Ḥîra* (Berlin, 1899).

Sartre, Maurice "Nouvelles inscriptions grecques et latines de Bosra," *Ann. Arch. Syrie* (1972), 167–91.

——— "Inscriptions inédites de l'Arabie romaine," *Syria* 50 (1973), 223–33.

——— "Note sur la première legion stationnée en Arabie romaine," *ZPE* 13 (1974), 85–89.

——— "Ti. Iulius Iulianus Alexander, Gouverneur d'Arabie," *ADAJ* 21 (1976), 105–8.

——— "Le tropheus de Gadhimat, roi de Tanukh: Une survivance en Arabie d'une institution hellénistique," *Liber Annuus* 29 (1979), 253–58.

——— "Rome et les Nabatéens à la fin de la république (65–30 av. J. C.)," *REA* 81 (1979), 37–53.

——— "La frontière méridionale de l'Arabie romaine," *Géographie administrative et politique d'Alexandre à Mahomet,*

Actes du Colloque de Strasbourg, 14–16 juin 1979 (1982), pp. 77–92.

_______ *Trois études sur l'Arabie romaine et byzantine*, Collection Latomus 178 (Brussels, 1982).

_______ *Bostra, des origines à l'Islam*, forthcoming.

_______ "Le territoire de Canatha," *Syria*, forthcoming.

Sauvaget, J. "Remarques sur les monuments omeyyades," *Journal Asiatique* 231 (1939), 1–59.

Savignac, R. "Notes de voyage: Le sanctuaire d'Allat à Iram," *RB* 41 (1932), 581–97.

_______ "Le sanctuaire d'Allat à Iram," *RB* 43 (1934), 572–89.

_______ "Sur les pistes de Transjordanie méridionale," *RB* 45 (1936), 235–62.

_______ and G. Horsfield "Le temple de Ramm," *RB* 44 (1935), 245–78.

_______ and J. Starcky "Une inscription nabatéenne provenant du Djôf," *RB* 64 (1957), 196–217.

Schlumberger, Daniel *La Palmyrène du Nord-ouest* (Paris, 1951).

Schmidt-Colinet, Andreas "Nabatäische Felsarchitektur: Bemerkungen zum gegenwärtigen Forschungsstand," *Bonner Jahrb.* 180 (1980), 189–230.

Schmitt-Korte, Karl *Die Nabatäer: Spuren einer arabischen Kultur der Antike* (Hannover, 1976).

Seeden, Helga and M. Kadour "Busra 1980: Reports from a South Syrian Village," *Damaszener Mitteilungen*, forthcoming.

Segal, A. "The Planning of Cities along the Via Nova Traiana in the Roman Period" (in Hebrew), diss. Hebrew Univ., Jerusalem (1975).

Segal, J. B. *Edessa, "The Blessed City"* (Oxford, 1970).

Seyrig, Henri "Postes romains sur la route de Médine," *Syria* 22 (1941), 218–23.

_______ "Les Inscriptions de Bostra," *Syria* 22 (1941), 44–48.

_______ "Épigramme funéraire du Hauran (?)," *Syria* 31 (1954), 214–17.

——— "Sur trois inscriptions du Hedjaz," *Syria* 34 (1957), 259–61.

Shahîd, Irfan "Philological Observations on the Nemāra Inscription," *JSS* 24 (1979), 33–42.

——— Review of J. S. Trimingham, *Christianity among the Arabs in Pre-Islamic Times*, *JSS* 26 (1981), 150–53.

——— *Byzantium and the Arabs in the Fourth Century*, Dumbarton Oaks Monographs, forthcoming.

Smith, R. H. *Pella of the Decapolis* (Wooster, Ohio, 1973).

Sourdel, D. *Les cultes du Hauran à l'époque romaine* (Paris, 1952).

Speidel, M. "Arabia's First Garrison," *ADAJ* 16 (1971), 111–12.

——— "Exercitus Arabicus," *Latomus* 33 (1974), 934–39.

——— "The Roman Army in Arabia," *ANRW* II.8 (1977), 687–730.

Spijkerman, A. *The Coins of the Decapolis and Provincia Arabia*, Studii Biblici Franciscani Collectio Maior 25 (Jerusalem, 1978).

Starcky, J. "Un contrat nabatéen sur papyrus," *RB* 61 (1954), 161–81.

——— "The Nabataeans: a Historical Sketch," *BiblArch* 18 (1955), 84–106.

——— "Nouvelles stèles funéraires à Pétra," *ADAJ* 10 (1965), 43–49.

——— "Nouvelle épitaphe nabatéenne donnant le nom sémitique de Pétra," *RB* 72 (1965), 95–97.

——— and J. Strugnell "Deux nouvelles inscriptions nabatéennes," *RB* 73 (1966), 236–47.

——— "Pétra et la Nabatène," *SDB* 7 (1966), 886–1017.

——— and C. M. Bennett "Les inscriptions du téménos (Pétra)," *Syria* 45 (1968), 41–65; also, in English, in *ADAJ* 12–13 (1967–1968), 30–50.

——— "Le temple nabatéen de Khirbet Tannur: à propos d'un livre récent," *RB* 75 (1968), 206–35.

——— "La civilisation nabatéenne: État des questions," *IXe Congrès International d'Archéologie Classique: Rapports et Communications* (Damascus, 1969), pp. 22–29.

_______ "Une inscription nabatéenne de l'an 18 d'Arétas IV," *Hommages à André Dupont-Sommer* (Paris, 1971), pp. 151–59.

_______ "Allath, Athène et la déesse syrienne," *Mythologie gréco-romaine, Mythologies périphériques*, colloque du CNRS (Paris, 1981), pp. 119–30.

Stark, Jürgen Kurt *Personal Names in Palmyrene Inscriptions* (Oxford, 1971).

Stein, Arthur "Kallinikos von Petrai," *Hermes* 58 (1923), 448–56.

Stein, Aurel "Surveys on the Roman Frontier in Iraq and Transjordan," *Geographical Journal* 95 (1940), 428–37.

Stiehl, Ruth "A New Nabataean Inscription," *Beiträge zur alten Geschichte: Festschrift für Franz Altheim* II (Berlin, 1970), pp. 87–90; also in R. Stiehl and F. Altheim, *Die Araber in der Alten Welt* V.1 (1968), pp. 305–9.

Teixidor, Javier *The Pagan God* (Princeton, 1977).

Thomsen, P. "Die römischen Meilensteine der Provinzen Syria, Arabia, und Palestina," *ZDPV* 40 (1917), 1–103.

Tran Tam Tinh, V. *Le culte des divinités orientales en Campanie* (1972).

Trimingham, J. Spencer *Christianity Among the Arabs in Pre-Islamic Times* (London and New York, 1979).

van den Branden, A. *Histoire de Thamud* (Beirut, 1966).

Weder, Marcus "Zu den Arabia-Drachmen Traians," *Schweizer Münzblätter* 27 (1977), 57–61.

Weippert, Manfred "Nabatäisch-römische Keramik aus Ḫirbet-Dōr im südlichen Jordanien," *ZDPV* 95 (1979), 87–110.

Wellesley, Kenneth "The Fable of the Roman Attack on Aden," *ParPass* 9 (1954), 401–5.

West, J. M. I. "Uranius," summary of Harvard diss., *HSCP* 78 (1974), 282–84.

Winnett, F. V., and W. L. Reed *Ancient Records from North Arabia* (Toronto, 1970).

_______ "The Revolt of Damasī: Safaitic and Nabataean Evidence," *BASOR* 211 (1973), 54–57.

_______ and G. L. Harding *Inscriptions from Fifty Safaitic Cairns* (Toronto, 1978).

Wissmann, H. von "Die Geschichte des Sabäerreichs und der Feldzug des Aelius Gallus," *ANRW* II.9.1 (1976), 308–544.

Wolff, Hans Julius "Römisches Provinzialrecht in der Provinz Arabia," *ANRW* II preprint (1972), 1–44 (in II.13 [1980], 763–806). Cf. "Le droit provincial dans la province romaine d'Arabie," *RIDA* 23 (1976), 271–90.

Wright, G. R. H. "Structure of the Qasr Bint Far'un: A Preliminary Review," *PEQ* 93 (1961), 8–37.

———— "The Khazneh at Petra: A Review," *ADAJ* 6–7 (1962), 24–54.

———— "Structure et date de l'arc monumental de Pétra," *RB* 73 (1966), 404–19.

———— "Strabo on Funerary Customs at Petra," *PEQ* 101 (1969), 112–16.

———— "The Date of the Khaznet Fir'aun at Petra in the Light of an Iconographic Detail," *PEQ* 105 (1973), 83–90.

Yadin, Y. "Expedition D—The Cave of the Letters," *IEJ* 12 (1962), 227–57.

———— "The Nabataean Kingdom, Provincia Arabia, Petra and En-Geddi in the Documents from Nahal Hever," *Ex Oriente Lux* 17 (1963), 227–41.

———— "The Life and Trials of Babata," in *Bar Kokhba* (New York, 1971), 222–53.

Yehya, Lutfi A.-W. *al-ʿarab fi al-ʿuṣūr al-qadīma* (Beirut, 1978).

Zayadine, Fawzi "Deux inscriptions grecques de Rabbat Moab (Areopolis)," *ADAJ* 16 (1971), 71–76.

———— "Photogrammetrische Arbeiten in Petra," *Bonner Jahrb.* 180 (1980), 237–52.

Zetzel, J. E. G. "New Light on Gaius Caesar's Eastern Campaign," *GRBS* 11 (1970), 259–66.

INDEX